Accession no.
01088183

D1333357

 University of
Chester
Warrington Campus

LIBRARY

Telephone: 01925 534284

This book is to be returned on or before the last date stamped below.
Overdue charges will be incurred by the late return of books.

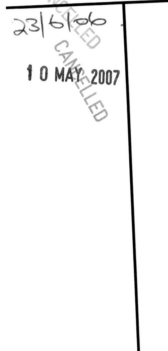

23/6/06

1 0 MAY 2007

CANCELLED
CANCELLED

WITHDRAWN

Social Influences on Ethical Behavior in Organizations

LEA's Organization and Management Series
Arthur Brief and James P. Walsh, Series Editors

Ashforth • *Role Transitions in Organizational Life:
An Identity-Based Perspective*

Beach • *Image Theory: Theoretical and Empirical Foundations*

Darley/Messick/Tyler • *Social Influences on Ethical Behavior in
Organizations*

Garud/Karnøe • *Path Dependence and Creation*

Lant/Shapira • *Organizational Cognition: Computation
and Interpretation*

Pearce • *Organization and Management in the Embrace
of Government*

Thompson/Levine/Messick • *Shared Cognition in Organizations:
The Management of Knowledge*

Social Influences on Ethical Behavior in Organizations

Edited by

John M. Darley
Princeton University

David M. Messick
Northwestern University

Tom R. Tyler
New York University

2001

LAWRENCE ERLBAUM ASSOCIATES, PUBLISHERS
Mahwah, New Jersey   London

Copyright © 2001 by Lawrence Erlbaum Associates, Inc.
All rights reserved. No part of the book may be
reproduced in any form, by photostat, microform,
retrieval system, or any other means, without prior written
permission of the publisher.

Lawrence Erlbaum Associates, Inc., Publishers
10 Industrial Avenue
Mahwah, NJ 07430

Cover design by Kathryn Houghtaling Lacey

Library of Congress Cataloging-in-Publication Data
Social influences on ethical behavior in organizations /
edited by John M. Darley, David M. Messick,
Tom R. Tyler.
     p.   cm.– (LEA's organization and management
     series)
Includes bibliographical references and index.
ISBN 0-8058-3330-7
1. Organizational behavior–Moral and ethical aspects.
2. Social influences. I. Darley, John M. II. Messick, David
M. III. Tyler, Tom R. IV. Series.
HD58.7 .S637   2001
174'.4—dc21

                                00-057682
                                CIP

Books published by Lawrence Erlbaum Associates are printed on acid-free paper,
and their bindings are chosen for strength and durability.

Printed in the United States of America
10 9 8 7 6 5 4 3 2 1

Contents

Series Editors' Foreword

Arthur P. Brief
Tulane University

James P. Walsh
University of Michigan

For too, too long, organizational scientists have not attended adequately to the problems of unethical behavior in and of organizations. Of course, the literature is punctuated with an occasional article, chapter, or book on the topic, but the subject matter is worthy of much more than this. It should be a central concern of the field, because of the human consequences attached to organizations and their representatives engaging, for instance, in fraud and deception, bribery and corruption, marketplace manipulations, and an array of civil liberty violations ranging from racial discrimination and sexual harassment to political repression and marketing of unsafe products. We in the organizational sciences have an ethical obligation to place such unethical behaviors at or very near the top of our research agenda.

Darley, Messick, and Tyler's collection of essays provides the stimulus needed to help move the study of unethical behavior to center stage in the organizational sciences. The book does so by posing one provocative question after another that not only entails a concern for understanding unethical behavior, but also strikes at the very core of how and why organizations function as they do. The book, for example, addresses the asymmetries in power and influence created by hierarchies that give rise to ethical problems; the tactics that might reduce the effectiveness of improper influence attempts; and how the inappropriate use of influence diffuses, for example, through a market. The curious organizational scientist not now interested in ethics surely will be after sampling from Darley et al.'s enticing book.

Social Influences on Ethical Behavior in Organizations fits the mold of LEA's Organization and Management Series perfectly. This potentially significant book is capable of changing the course of research in the organizational sciences. It even might change what organizational scientists deem to be important subject matter. Again, if it does, then Darley et al. have moved all of us closer to fulfilling our obligation as social scientists to seek ways of enhancing the human condition.

1 Introduction: Social Influence and Ethics in Organizations

John M. Darley
Princeton University

David M. Messick
Northwestern University

Tom R. Tyler
New York University

How do executives shape the behavior and beliefs of employees in their organizations? What are the ethical constraints on this form of influence? What obligations do employees have to their employers, and what types of conflicts, moral and otherwise, are employees confronted with when they feel that the orders they have received are unethical? How do ethical norms emerge from and govern markets, groups, and networks?

These were some of the questions about the ethical dimensions of social influence in organizations that were discussed at a conference entitled "Ethics and Social Influence" held at the Kellogg Graduate School of Management of Northwestern University. Participants included social psychologists, sociologists, organizational theorists, communication specialists, business ethicists, and lawyers. The central issue addressed by this interdisciplinary group of scholars was the analysis of appropriate and inappropriate forms of social influence in organizations and groups. This issue was considered key in understanding such organizational phenomena as trust, cooperation, deference to authority, and moral courage to oppose wrongdoing. This volume presents chapters based on the conference presentations and written by the conference participants. The chapters continue the themes of the conference report, drafted to include input from the conference discussions and from editorial reviews.

The chapters of this book fall into three categories. Part I deals with influence in hierarchical relationships in places such as organizations. These hierarchies create asymmetries in power and influence that raise many psychological and ethical problems. Some types of influence (e.g., coercion) require differential power, whereas other types (e.g., persuasion) can occur among organizational equals. Communications from superiors to subordinates may differ systematically from communications among equals. People who create the procedures by means of which others will be evaluated may be suspected of manipulating the procedures for their own benefit. In other words, hierarchies create the context in which ethical, unethical, and morally ambiguous influence strategies are found.

The targets of influence attempts may be less skillful, powerful, or sophisticated in the use of influence than those who wield it. Nonetheless, these targets of influence may sometimes become suspicious of the morality of efforts to shape their beliefs and behavior. In Part II of this book, several authors explicitly address tactics that can be employed to reduce the effectiveness of improper influence attempts. These efforts can be either organizational, as in whistle-blowing, or individual, as in personally resisting influence.

Not all influence occurs in hierarchical organizations. People are influenced by reference groups, by market processes, by competitors, and by friends and neighbors. How appropriate and inappropriate influence spreads through these systems is a topic of great interest and complexity. In negotiations, is it wrong for a party with more power to use this power when negotiating with a less powerful party? When might this be unethical? How will ethical strategies fare in a competition with unethical ones? Is there a "market" for moral ideas? The chapters in Part III discuss some of these issues.

SOCIAL INFLUENCE IN HIERARCHIES

Chapter 2. Ethical Limits on the Use of Influence in Hierarchical Relationships

Herbert C. Kelman

By definition, in a hierarchical relationship, the superior is entitled to exert influence on the subordinate, and the subordinate is obligated to accept the superior's influence. Ethical use of influence, however, presupposes certain intraorganizational and extraorganizational limits on the demands and requests that the superior is entitled to make and the subordinate is expected (or, at times, in fact permitted) to carry out. Intraorganizational limits to be discussed include (a) the definition of the domain within which the superiors can exert influence, (b) norms about the influence tactics that are deemed appropriate in the superior–subordinate relationship, and (c) the availability of mechanisms for recourse in cases of disagreement about expectations and abuses of power. Extraorganizational limits refer to the applicability of general principles of ethical conduct, whatever the particular organizational context may be. Thus, this chapter argues that (a) forms of influence that violate the norms of ethical conduct in the society at large are unacceptable in any given organization, and (b) the positive duty to promote the welfare of those with whom we interact applies to the hierarchical relationships within organizations as much as it does to other human relationships.

Chapter 3. Toward a More Deontological Approach to the Ethical Use of Social Influence

Randall S. Peterson

Scholars have long been concerned about the ethical implications of the use of social influence by leaders of groups, organizations, and nations. The concern has focused almost entirely on the direct social influence of leaders trying to sway followers. A 50-year stream of research implicates directive leadership as the cause of defective group interaction, poor information processing, and disastrous (often unethical) group decisions. This chapter argues that those results are actually the cause of process directiveness (i.e., the methods a leader uses to regulate the process by which the group makes a decision) rather than outcome directiveness (i.e., the degree to which a leader advocates a favored solution).

Following from this argument, it is suggested that leaders have strong ethical influence on their organizations via the decision-making processes that they employ (a deontological perspective). This chapter reviews social influence research through that process-oriented lens and suggests an agenda for future research.

Chapter 4. The Dynamics of Authority in Organizations and the Unintended Action Consequences

John M. Darley

There are two kinds of actions that an honest corporation wishes not to produce in its members: actions that are not in the best interests of the organization, and actions that are immoral, such as lying, cheating, claiming credit for others' work, and so on. But often, taking those actions might benefit the individual, at least in the short term. How can the organization prevent individuals from taking those actions, and what does the organization inadvertently do to make those actions more likely? In organizations, authority is legitimate, often expert, and empowered to fulfill a coordinating function in which the authority figure coordinates the actions of the organizational subordinates. As a result, authority possesses great power.

Furthermore, organizations create "incentive systems" to reward workers for achieving actions that bring about organizationally desired outcomes. But, of course, some actions that have a short-term benefit (e.g., achieving high sales during a quarterly reporting period and thus earning the sales force a bonus) may be taken in ways that eventually damage the organization. The organization expects that employees' moral standards coupled perhaps with corporate codes of conduct will be sufficient to keep employees from "taking advantage" of the system in these ways. However, in practice, the employees may not realize that these sorts of actions are not in the best interests of the corporation. That these actions carry incentives may communicate to the employees that the organization regards the actions as legitimate. Even when employees realize that certain incentivized actions produce morally bad outcomes, the fact that they see other employees taking these actions and receiving rewards for doing so creates a climate in which it is difficult for the disadvantaged employees to behave morally.

In this way, a corporate code of conflict that is not integrated with the incentive system of the organization may gradually lose its force, causing the corporate subordinates to behave in ways which, although the hierarchy may be unaware of these behaviors, are destructive to the organization's reputation and eventually its survival.

Chapter 5. Confronting Organizational Transgressions

Michael E. Roloff and Gaylen D. Paulson

Witnesses of rule infractions often do not choose to confront the transgressor or to report the observed infraction, and much research has been done to determine the conditions under which such whistle-blowing might occur. Individuals most vulnerable to retaliation are least likely to engage in whistle-blowing, especially when an individual acts in a subordinate role to the transgressor. The nature of the authority structure undermines the desire or ability to report infractions, even in cases when a subordinate may be held culpable for the ethical lapse. This chapter examines the relational and linguistic factors that may impact organizational influence. Influence is exerted when the recipient of a directive desires some response or reward from a superior and when noncompliance would result in punitive measures. Directives can be very direct, such as an explicit imperative coupled with a threat of retribution for noncompliance. Although this eliminates misunderstandings, the culpability for that directive rests directly on the superior. Given the downside of clear culpability for ethical infractions, authority figures may resort to implicit directives, such as hints, suggestions, or other means to mollify an instruction to bend or break ethical codes. Often, threats are not needed in such directives, for implicit in any suggestion by an authority figure is the possibility of retaliation for noncompliance. The chapter examines the coercive potential of such interaction and the role of communication in both direct and indirect imperatives. Additionally, just as unethical directives may be indirect, resistance to such directives also may be achieved by indirect means. Such measures include procrastination, partial complicity, or avoidance. Although much research has been done on direct resistance to unethical imperatives, this chapter examines hidden or passive means of resistance.

Chapter 6. Procedural Strategies for Gaining Deference: Increasing Social Harmony or Creating False Consciousness?

Tom R. Tyler

Recent studies conducted within political, legal, and managerial organizations suggest that authorities can gain deference for their decisions by making those decisions in ways that people will judge to be fair. Furthermore, an important component of procedural fairness involves treating people with dignity and respect, rather than giving them fair or favorable outcomes. Thibaut and Walker originally encouraged the study of procedural justice because they felt it suggested a way for authorities to bridge differences in interests within conflict situations and create decisions that all parties to a dispute would willingly accept. This hopeful, optimistic vision of the power of procedural mechanisms has been supported strongly by research findings. However, critics consistently have expressed concerns that the procedural justice effect provides a basis for undermining the interests of both employees and citizens by diverting attention from the nature of the outcomes they receive from organizations. The possibility of such "manipulation" is suggested by recent discussions of procedural justice as an impression management strategy. This chapter raises questions about how such social influence strategies might be viewed ethically and asks to what degree social scientists need to be concerned about these issues when conducting procedural justice research.

Chapter 7. Exit Ethics: The Management of Downsizing Among the Russian Officer Corps

V. Lee Hamilton

Research since the Great Depression has documented the sometimes severe impact that unemployment can have on mental health, physical health, and the subsequent life course. Research in the 1980s and 1990s documented the deleterious consequences that layoffs can have on workers who remain as well on those who are "downsized" out. One important topic concerns whether there are ways in which social influence can minimize the pain of such transitions.

This chapter discusses an extreme case of downsizing in which the financial and self-concept impacts of unemployment are expected to be severe: career military officers. Because the chapter further focuses on the Russian military, absolute conditions are also likely to be poor, reflecting the downgrading of the economic and social status of officers in the postcommunist economy. This chapter reports on a panel survey of Russian military officers and their wives. In all, 1,798 officers and 1,609 wives were surveyed face-to-face in early 1996, with a follow-up interview in spring and summer 1997. In this quasi-experimental design, approximately half of the officers were scheduled to be released from service shortly after the first interview and half were not. The two surveys provide (a) data on individual officers' emotional reactions to downsizing (e.g., self-esteem, distress, drinking, assessments of justice, marital satisfaction), (b) data on their labor market behaviors, (c) comparable data from wives, and (d) some data from wives about the husbands.

The chapter focuses on questions of perceived justice/injustice and how they relate to both officers' organizational commitment (a typical concern of research in management) and their mental health (a typical concern of sociological and psychological stress researchers). The chapter asks what are the ethical ways and what are effective ways to downsize a group characterized by long-standing and deep commitments to an organization.

AWARENESS OF AND RESISTANCE TO SOCIAL INFLUENCE

Chapter 8. Responses to Perceived Organizational Wrongdoing: Do Perceiver Characteristics Matter?

Marcia P. Miceli, James R. Van Scotter, Janet P. Near, and Michael T. Rehg

Whistle-blowing represents a complex example of ethical conflict in organizational decision making. Under what circumstances does one remain silent or act when faced with perceived organizational wrongdoing? To whom might one report it, and why? More than 10 years ago, researchers proposed that the process leading to the decision to blow the whistle resembles the decision process identified by many social psychologists studying bystander decision making. The process may be affected by variables pertaining to the observer (e.g., proactive personality), to the organization (e.g., unit and organizational level culture for ethical actions), to the situation (e.g., the nature of wrongdoing observed), and to person–situation (organization) interactions (e.g., perceived organizational support, self-efficacy). This chapter reviews some conceptual and empirical developments since the initial modeling. The chapter focuses primarily on variables pertaining to the observer and his or her interactions in the setting and offers suggestions for empirical research.

Chapter 9. Training in Ethical Influence

Robert B. Cialdini, Brad J. Sagarin, and William E. Rice

When sending persuasive messages, communicators often can invoke principles of social influence (e.g., authority) either ethically, in which the principle used is an inherent feature of the situation, or unethically, in which the principle is imported dishonestly. Recipients who fail to make this ethical distinction leave themselves vulnerable to misdirection by inappropriately activated principles. A training program was devised to teach participants how to differentiate between honest and dishonest uses of the authority principle in persuasive appeals and, consequently, how to protect themselves from being misled by the deceptive forms. Two experiments were designed to teach critical appraisal of authority-based messages (advertisements).

Chapter 10. Authority, Heuristics, and the Structure of Excuses

Alan Strudler and Danielle E. Warren

This chapter investigates the purely moral significance of Milgram's obedience experiments. The authors ask what, if anything, these experiments reveal about individual moral responsibility and moral assessment. After proposing a framework for evaluating the conduct of Milgram's subjects, the authors propose ways to extend the framework so that it covers managers who confront a variety of decision-making problems less exotic than the Milgram experiments. Hence the chapter discusses managerial misconduct that, unlike the misconduct in the Milgram experiments, does not consist of simply following orders. The authors examine the possibility that some managerial misconduct arises from inapt reliance on cognitive heuristics and suggest similarities between wrongly obeying orders and wrongly relying on heuristics.

SOCIAL INFLUENCE IN GROUPS, NETWORKS, AND MARKETS

Chapter 11. Golden Rules and Leaden Worlds: Exploring the Limitations of Tit-for-Tat as a Social Decision Rule

Roderick M. Kramer, Jane Wei, and Jonathan Bendor

Ethical cognitions encompass individuals' beliefs and perceptions of appropriate and inappropriate ethical behavior in social situations. Such cognitions often are codified as social decision heuristics that provide behavioral rules for evaluating and responding to various ethical dilemmas that individuals routinely confront in their social and organizational lives. For example, the belief that it is better to always give people the benefit of the doubt initially (i.e., treat them as trustworthy until evidence is presented suggesting otherwise) constitutes an ethical stance that might be codified in terms of a simple rule such as "tit-for-tat."

Tit-for-tat is a particularly interesting heuristic in this regard because considerable theory and research by Robert Axelrod and others suggest that it is a viable and sustainable heuristic across a wide range of social ecologies. Yet, most of the research on tit-for-tat has focused on ecologies in which social uncertainty (uncertainty about others' ethical cognitions and behaviors) is virtually nonexistent. Yet, some research suggests that tit-for-tat may fare less well in environments in which such social uncertainty is present. This chapter explores this important theoretical question about the potential limitations of tit-for-tat. In particular, the chapter reports the results of a large computer simulation that examines the viability of tit-for-tat and other strategies when social uncertainty is present. The results show that tit-for-tat performs poorly in such environments, especially relative to strategies that are more generous with respect to giving others the benefit of the doubt when uncertainty exists regarding their true actions. The authors discuss the implications of their findings for thinking about the viability and sustainability of various ethical heuristics, especially in so far as they are used as means of social influence to elicit and maintain cooperative relationships with others.

Chapter 12. Power Asymmetries and the Ethical Climate in Negotiations

Ann E. Tenbrunsel and David M. Messick

This chapter explores the relation between power and ethics in a negotiation context. Asymmetrical differences between negotiation opponents, including differences in resources, alternatives, and information, are argued to produce differences in power and to alter the ethical climate of the negotiation. Preliminary evidence is offered to suggest that these asymmetries can alter a negotiator's perceptions, including changing assessments of whether an act is unethical and heightening expectations that one's opponent's behavior will be unethical. The influence of asymmetries on perceptions in turn is posited to increase the prevalence of unethical behavior. Implications for negotiators and suggested directions for future research are provided.

Chapter 13. Marketlike Morality Within Organizations

Thomas W. Dunfee

The process by which moral norms are produced within organizations has the characteristics of a market. Multiple participants with varying moral preferences, roles, and endowments interact in ways that produce organizational community norms pertaining to right and wrong behavior. The chapter focuses on the nature of an internal market of morality within organizations and considers its implications for individual managers and for organizational policies. Normative dimensions also are discussed.

I

Social Influence in Hierarchies

2 Ethical Limits on the Use of Influence in Hierarchical Relationships

Herbert C. Kelman
Harvard University

In a hierarchical relationship, by definition, the superior is entitled to exert influence on the subordinate and the subordinate is obligated to accept the superior's influence. These rights and duties, however, are not unlimited. Ethical use of influence presupposes certain intraorganizational and extraorganizational limits on the demands and requests that the superior is entitled to make and that the subordinate is expected—at times, in fact, permitted—to carry out. To set the stage for a discussion of such limits, I first review some of the moral principles according to which influence attempts must be assessed and present a typology that distinguishes among different means of influence.

Influence, for the present purposes, is defined from the point of view of the target of an influence attempt. By this definition, *social influence* refers to a change in the actions, attitudes, or beliefs of a person (P) resulting from induction by another person or group (O)—the influencing agent (Kelman & Hamilton, 1989). *Induction,* in turn, refers to an identifiable act by O whereby O makes available to P a specific action, attitude, or belief, or perhaps a new pattern of responding or a different way of interpreting events that challenges habitual reactions and existing beliefs. The induction, which may take the form of a suggestion, a request, an order, a demonstration, an attempt to persuade, or an offer of information, may be accepted, rejected, adapted, or perhaps ignored by P. The induction is not necessarily deliberate and intentional; for example, O may unwittingly set an example or serve as a model for P. For present purposes, however, I largely restrict myself to deliberate induction, because this is the domain in which the most obvious ethical issues arise.

MORAL PRINCIPLES IN EVALUATION OF SOCIAL INFLUENCE

Before examining the ethical implications of different means of influence and the ethical limits on the use of influence in hierarchical settings, let me introduce some of the moral principles that are central to the evaluation of influence procedures. Beauchamp, Faden, Wallace, and Walters (1982) identified four moral principles that are especially applicable to the ethical issues that arise in social science research. These four principles seem equally applicable to the ethical issues arising in interpersonal or organizational influence attempts:

- *Autonomy or self-determination:* Does O's influence attempt respect the values and decisions of P? This principle is tantamount to Immanuel Kant's dictum of treating others as ends in themselves rather than as means to extraneous ends.
- *Nonmaleficence:* Does O refrain from inflicting harm on P in the process of exerting influence?
- *Beneficence:* Does O's conduct live up to the positive obligation of promoting P's welfare?
- *Justice or fairness:* Does O's influence attempt respect P's rights? Does O extend equal treatment to people in equal positions and ensure that people are accorded what they are entitled to?

Ethical issues arising in influence situations are most likely to implicate the principle of autonomy or freedom, because it touches the core of an influence relationship. An influence attempt, whatever its nature, represents an effort to change the other's behavior or thinking. Successful influence means that P has changed from what he or she would have done or thought in the absence of the influence attempt. Thus, the question about the extent to which the targets of influence act freely, on the basis of their own decisions and in line with their own values, automatically arises in influence situations.

It is interesting, in this connection, that some of the knottiest ethical problems often arise when influence agents claim, and indeed believe, that what they are doing is in the targets' own interest and for their own good. These circumstances are particularly conducive to guilt-free manipulation—to violation of the principle of autonomy in the name of the principle of beneficence.

MEANS OF INFLUENCE

In keeping with the central importance of the principle of autonomy, Warwick and I (Kelman & Warwick, 1977) proposed a typology of means used in implementing social intervention, which orders these means—coercion, manipulation, persuasion, and facilitation—more or less along the dimension of freedom. That is, the means of intervention vary according to the degree to which they encourage or restrict people's "capacity, ... opportunity, and ... incentive to make reflective choices and to act on these choices" (Warwick, 1977, p. 18). This typology can be generalized to distinguish the different means that can be employed in any influence situation.

At the most restrictive end of the continuum, *coercion* uses the threat of severe deprivation either to compel people to take actions that go against their preferences or to deter them from taking actions that are in line with their preferences. The next point on the continuum is *manipulation,* which can be divided into two subtypes: *Environmental manipulation* changes the structure of alternatives in the environment—for example, by creating faits accomplis that change the realities within which people have to navigate, or by changing reinforcement contingencies, as in behavior therapy; environmental manipulation leaves the person free to make choices, but within a deliberately modified framework. *Psychic manipulation* seeks to exert influence by changing people's motives, controlling the information available to them, or reducing their capacity to reason and choose. In both kinds of manipulation, the semblance of freedom is maintained, but the framework within which choices are made is modified by reducing either the capacity to choose or the availability of options.

Persuasion is a means of influence that attempts to change the target's attitudes or behavior by argument, reasoning, or debate. Although persuasion is an approach to influence that is generally consistent with the principle of autonomy or freedom, it brings its own ethical problems into play. Most notable among these is the possible asymmetry in power between O and P—between those who are in a position to exercise persuasion and those who are the targets of such an effort. Finally, the means of influence that is at the most "free" end of the continuum is *facilitation,* where influence basically involves making certain resources available to the targets. Examples might include provision of family planning services or process facilitation in decision-making groups. Although the target's freedom is maximized in this form of influence, ethical problems may well arise. The offer and availability of certain services may themselves structure people's choices and thus limit their options. Other sources of ethical concern are the possibilities that the services may be offered to some groups and not to others and that the threat of withdrawing the services may have mildly coercive implications.

Even though each of the means of influence raises its own set of potential ethical problems, the continuum from coercion to facilitation constitutes, on the whole, a rough ordering in terms of ethical acceptability, insofar as the steps on the continuum represent increasing degrees of freedom of choice for the target of influence. Nonetheless, it is not the case that coercion is never ethically justifiable or that facilitation always is. Ethical evaluation of the use of any of these means of influence in a given case may vary for several reasons. First, competing values and principles come into play in any particular influence situation and these may override the principle of autonomy. Second, each form of influence may be carried out in different ways that make a particular use of that means of influence more or less ethically acceptable. And, third, there are subtle ways in which one form of influence may shade into another. Let me comment on each of these qualifications.

Coercive or manipulative approaches often are justified by reference to competing, overriding principles. For example, restrictions on freedom may be considered necessary in the face of serious threats to public health and public safety. Indeed, a facilitative approach, in the form of a policy that responds to such threats in a laissez-faire manner—making certain services available, but leaving individuals to decide whether to use them—may be considered irresponsible. Coercion is, of course, invariably justified by its proponents on the grounds that it serves a higher value: group survival, general welfare, national liberation. It behooves us to maintain a skeptical attitude toward such justifications. But conflict between competing principles is an inevitable fact of life and, despite the ethical concerns raised by the use of coercion, it cannot be ruled out under all circumstances. There came a point, for example, when implementation of the 1954 Supreme Court ruling against school segregation required a degree of coercion. Much as I would have preferred voluntary compliance, I had no doubt that overriding values justified some curtailment of the principle of autonomy in order to put an end to racial segregation.

The fact that, in the previous example, the coercive means were used by agents of the federal government to enforce a ruling of the U.S. Supreme Court makes a considerable difference in our assessment of the ethical acceptability of the action. This brings me to my second qualification about the ethical justification of means of influence at different points on the continuum from coercion to facilitation: Our evaluation of the ethical acceptability of using a given means of influence depends on the precise circumstances under which it is used in a particular case. Who is using it, under what authority, pursuant to what procedures, and subject to what constraints? Thus, the ethical acceptability of coercive means depends, in part, on the legitimacy of the influencing agent. For example, coercion used by the agents of a democratic government is acceptable on the presumption that the government's actions ultimately represent the consent of the governed, that these actions conform to a set of clearly specified rules and procedures, and that the agents are accountable for their actions. One might, in fact, argue that the enforcement of democratically enacted laws is not even coercion: Taxation without representation is coercive and, indeed, oppressive, but taxation with representation, even though it has a coercive component, is rooted in consensual processes and thus does not quite belong in the category of coercion.

Various other features of the use of coercion in a particular case also contribute to its ethical acceptability. Take a situation in which a community is threatened by the outbreak of an epidemic to which small children are especially vulnerable. The principle of beneficence would justify some curtailment of the principle of autonomy in this case. Whether the authorities would be justified in using coercive means to confront the epidemic—such as mandating the inoculation of all vulnerable children and imposing heavy fines for failure to comply—would depend on the way in which these procedures are selected and applied. The use of coercive means would be more justified, for example, if the authorities decided on them after careful consultation within the community; if alternative, less coercive procedures had been explored and found ineffective; and if the penalties were applied fairly and equally. By the same token, a facilitative approach in this particular situation—such as opening inoculation centers in various neighborhoods—may be ethically unacceptable under certain circumstances, even though it conforms with the principle of autonomy. This would be the case, for example, if for reasons of cost or location the inoculation services were less available to some segments of the community than to others.

The ethical acceptability of manipulation also depends on the way in which this form of influence is used in a particular situation. Take, for example, a case of environmental manipulation, such as the structuring of the retirement program within an organization to encourage members to move on at a relatively early age. Environmental manipulation of this type

> would seem more acceptable to the extent that the people affected participate in the process, are free to enter and leave the program, and find their range of choices broadened rather than narrowed. Manipulation also seems more acceptable if the manipulators are not the primary beneficiaries of the manipulation, are reciprocally vulnerable in the situation, and are accountable to public agencies. (Kelman & Warwick, 1977, p. 19)

Similarly, psychic manipulation, as may occur in a therapeutic relationship or an encounter group, is more acceptable to the extent that practitioners are aware (and make their clients aware) of the manipulative potential of the situation, build protection against or resistance to manipulation into the process, and explicitly set enhancement of freedom of choice as a positive goal of the interaction (Kelman, 1965, 1968).

Finally, a word on my third qualification about the ethical acceptability of means of influence at different points on the continuum from coercion to facilitation: There are subtle ways in which one form of influence may shade into another. We cannot assume, therefore, that persuasion and facilitation, the means of influence on the "free" side of the continuum, are always devoid of ethical ambiguities. Indeed, we cannot assume that persuasion and facilitation are always consistent with the principle of autonomy.

Persuasion may take on a manipulative or coercive aspect. This is especially true under conditions of asymmetry of power between P and O. When a boss, professor, or police officer seeks to persuade a subordinate, student, or citizen, respectively, it is almost inevitable that the difference in power that characterizes the relationship will intrude on the interaction. The effect of the persuasive attempt may well be to reduce the subordinates' perceived options, or subtly change their motives, or remind them that it may be in their best interest to go along with the persuasive attempt. At the societal or organizational level, the capacity to launch a persuasive campaign is not equally distributed across the board. Thus, though the targets of persuasion may be free to choose a preferred option, the options available for choice are restricted to those that have the opportunity to be aired.

Facilitation too may take on a manipulative or coercive aspect. Let us say a religious organization makes a day-care service available to parents in a poor community. Although the parents are free to accept or reject that option, its availability may structure their choices. The very fact that it is readily available gives that option an advantage over other options that the parents potentially could explore or create. When a service is offered by an agency that represents authority, it may communicate to people that they are expected to use it or even, under certain circumstances, that they are required to use it. Thus, facilitation may shade into manipulation or coercion.

In sum, the line between persuasion or facilitation, on the one hand, and coercion or manipulation, on the other, is not always easy to draw. Regardless of the means of influence employed, therefore, there is always a need to be sensitive to the ethical implications of any influence attempt and to the ethical ambiguities of an influence relationship.

ETHICAL LIMITS OF INFLUENCE
IN HIERARCHICAL RELATIONSHIPS

The lines between facilitation, persuasion, manipulation, and coercion are particularly hard to draw in hierarchical relationships. Influence processes can become very complex and very compelling in the context of a hierarchical organization. In a hierarchical relationship within an organization, the superior is entitled, by definition, to exert influence on the subordinate—to issue demands and requests. The subordinate, in turn, is obligated to accept the superior's influence—to accede to her or his demands and requests. These rights and obligations, however, are by no means unlimited.

The ethical use of influence within an organizational hierarchy presupposes certain intraorganizational and extraorganizational limits on the demands and requests that the superior is entitled to make and the subordinate is obligated to carry out. Indeed, there are some demands and requests that subordinates are not only not expected to carry out but that they are not permitted to carry out. I refer here to superior orders that would require the subordinate to engage in or have complicity in illegal or immoral acts—in other words, to be guilty of what Lee Hamilton and I have called "crimes of obedience" (Kelman & Hamilton, 1989). Short of crimes of obedience, what are some of the ethical limits on the use of influence in hierarchical relationships?

Extraorganizational Limits

The extraorganizational limits on the use of influence are defined by precisely the kinds of considerations I raised in the preceding discussion of the moral principles by which influence attempts must be evaluated and the way different means of influence measure up against these principles. An organization exists within a larger societal context, and the principles and norms that govern social relations at large also must govern relationships within the organization, whatever the special character of the organization may be. Organizational requirements cannot be used to justify procedures that would be unacceptable elsewhere in the society. Furthermore, I maintain that an organization operating in a foreign country must adhere to the highest ethical standards of both societies. For example, an American-based multinational corporation operating a factory in a developing country cannot justify using coercive or manipulative techniques that would be unacceptable at home on the grounds that these techniques are commonly used and accepted in the country in which the factory is located. The reference point for what is ethically acceptable must be the more stringent norms of the company's home society.

As is true in society at large, the ethical use of influence within a hierarchical organization requires adherence to the principles of autonomy or self-determination, nonmaleficence, and justice or fairness. Beyond that, the principle of beneficence requires special mention, because it may be dismissed as irrelevant to the structured relationships that occur in an organization governed by rational-bureaucratic authority. The positive duty to promote the welfare of those with whom we interact, and particularly on whom we seek to exert influence, applies to the hierarchical relationships within organizations as much as it does to other human relationships.

Means of influence that are ethically unacceptable in the society at large because they violate the principles of autonomy, nonmaleficence, beneficence, or justice are also unacceptable within a hierarchical organization. Thus, organizational requirements cannot justify the use of threats or other coercive tactics, the practice of deception, the circumvention of informal consent, or the invasion of privacy. Of course, as is true elsewhere in the society, the ethical acceptability of a given form of influence may depend on the particular circumstances under which it is applied and on the precise way in which it is applied in a particular situation. Ethical evaluation takes into account the competing values and principles that come into play in the situation and the degree to which the influence attempt conforms to normatively prescribed criteria. For example, landlords are entitled to threaten tenants with eviction for nonpayment of rent, provided the landlords give the tenants sufficient warning, take account of their special circumstances, do not discriminate against them on the basis of their group membership, do not use harassment or intimidation, and do not try to short-circuit due process in other ways. In similar fashion, superiors in an organizational hierarchy have a right to threaten subordinates with termination of their employment or other status for poor performance, provided they do so in a way that is fair, considerate, nonharassing, and nondiscriminatory and that fully protects their procedural rights.

In short, I argue that the use of influence in hierarchical relationships within an organization is subject to certain ethical limits imposed by the society at large. The nature of the relationship between superior and subordinate entitles the superior to make certain demands and requests and obligates the subordinate to accede to them. The ways in which and the circumstances under which these demands and requests are made, however, are governed by the same principles and criteria that define ethical conduct in the society. These principles and criteria provide space for variations in the means of influence that are ethically acceptable under different circumstances, including the circumstances that characterize hierarchical relationships. But the ethical use of influence in hierarchical organizations means that no blanket "exemptions" from these principles and criteria can be granted to such organizations.

Intraorganizational Limits

In addition to the ethical limits in the use of influence that are extraorganizational in nature, deriving from general societal norms, there are intraorganizational limits, deriving from the framework of legitimacy that provides the moral foundation of hierarchically structured, rational-bureaucratic organizations. A hierarchical relationship is marked, by definition, by an asymmetry of power between the two parties to the relationship. This asymmetry is blunted to some extent by the shared assumption that, within the larger society, the two parties are—at least in principle—equals as citizens and human beings and hence subject to the same rights and obligations. Within the organization itself the asymmetry is controlled by the framework of legitimacy that governs the relationship. This means that there is a common set of norms and rules to which both the superior and the subordinate are subject. These norms and rules are designed to ensure that superiors do not use their power in an arbitrary fashion.

Maintaining this framework of legitimacy requires certain intraorganizational limits on the superior's use of her or his rightful power in exerting influence. The framework of legitimacy sets limits on the use of influence by specifying the domain within which the superior may exert influence, the influence tactics that are permissible, and the mechanisms of recourse available to the subordinate.

First, the legitimate use of influence implies a clear delimitation of the domain within which the superior has the right to exert influence—the areas of the subordinate's behavior and functioning in which the superior is entitled to make demands or requests. One obvious distinction here is between job-related activities and the subordinate's personal life. Moreover, on the job itself, not all demands or requests fall within the domain in which the superior can legitimately exert influence. Clearly, superiors have no right to ask subordinates to perform illegal or immoral acts. They also have no right to assign tasks to subordinates that go beyond the job description or to control subordinates' private behavior (such as the way they dress) unless it interferes with job performance.

Second, within the domain of the superior's legitimate authority, there is a set of norms specifying what influence tactics superiors are entitled to use in their relationship with subordinates. To be sure, a coercive element underlies the relationship between the parties in a hierarchical structure. The superior has the capacity to impose certain severe sanctions on subordinates whose performance is below par, including dismissing them from their jobs, terminating them from their degree programs, or giving them negative recommendations. But this reality does not justify the use of coercive tactics, such as invoking the sanctions in a manner that is harassing and insensitive, to a degree that is disproportionate, and as a device for eliciting specific behaviors. Furthermore, any use of sanctions must be subject to strict procedural rules designed to ensure that they are applied reasonably, fairly, in a nondiscriminatory way, and in accordance with due process.

The use of other means of influence, apart from coercion, is also normatively prescribed. Environmental or psychic manipulation within an organization, in the form of programs designed to channel members' choices in a certain direction, should be introduced honestly and in a way that maximizes members' freedom to participate in the program or opt out of it. Persuasion should be used with full awareness of the power differential in a hierarchical relationship and hence the possibility that it might shade into manipulation or coercion. The use of facilitation, in the form of making certain opportunities available to members of the organization, should be sensitive both to the possibility that what may be meant as an opportunity might be perceived as a requirement in a hierarchical relationship, and to the importance of making genuine opportunities available to all members who qualify, on a nondiscriminatory basis.

Finally, a third set of intraorganizational ethical limits on the use of influence—designed to ensure the legitimate rather than arbitrary exercise of power—is the ready availability of mechanisms of *recourse* and *accountability*. Subordinates who feel that their rights or expectations have been violated by their superiors—that is, that the superiors have abused their power—should have structured and accessible opportunities for a fair and attentive hearing within the organization. The office of ombudsman is an example of such an organizational mechanism. To be effective, mechanisms of recourse must be accompanied by the existence of procedures for holding superiors accountable when they overstep the limits of their authority, and by a history of using the procedures when the circumstances warrant them. Such mechanisms of recourse and accountability provide subordinates some countervailing power that allows them to protect and defend their interests in the face of demands from their superiors. The existence and use of such mechanisms within the organization are perhaps the most visible indicators of an organization's adherence to ethical norms.

CONCLUSION

Influence processes are ubiquitous in social life. People satisfy many of their own needs by exerting influence on others. Mutual influence allows people to coordinate their behavior to the benefit of both parties: Reciprocal accommodation makes it possible for each to help meet the needs and interests of the other. Social influence as such is ethically neutral. It can enhance welfare, freedom, and justice for both parties. But it also can reduce welfare, freedom, or justice—often by way of an outcome that serves the interests of O at the expense of P. Ethical evaluation of any given episode of influence depends on the form of influence used, on the

balance it achieves between competing moral principles (such as welfare and freedom), on the precise procedures involved in the influence attempt and the circumstances surrounding it, and ultimately on the relationship between the two parties.

The potential for ethical problems increases when there is a power discrepancy
between the two parties—when the influencing agent has a power advantage over
the target of the influence attempt (cf. Kelman, 1972). Thus, ethical problems almost inevitably arise in hierarchical relationships, which by definition are characterized by an asymmetry of power. The ethical use of influence in hierarchical
organizations, therefore, requires special sensitivity to the limits that must be observed when superiors exercise their legitimate right to address demands or requests to their subordinates. On the one hand, superiors are subject to
extraorganizational limits: The use of influence within an organization must adhere to the same moral principles, norms, and criteria that govern influence in the
society at large; there are no blanket "exemptions" from these principles for organizations (including organizations based in one society but operating in another
society that sets less stringent limits). On the other hand, superiors are subject to
intraorganizational limits: The framework of legitimacy that provides the moral
basis for the superior's right to make demands and the subordinate's obligation to
accede to them also sets limits on the use of influence by delimiting the domain
within which influence may be exerted, specifying the influence tactics that may
be employed, and providing mechanisms of recourse for the subordinate and accountability for the superior.

REFERENCES

Beauchamp, T. L., Faden, R. R., Wallace, R. J., Jr., & Walters, L. (Eds.) (1982). *Ethical issues in social science research.* Baltimore: Johns Hopkins University Press.

Kelman, H. C. (1965). Manipulation of human behavior: An ethical dilemma for the social
scientist. *Journal of Social Issues, 21*(2), 31–46.

Kelman, H. C. (1968). *A time to speak: On human values and social research.* San Francisco: Jossey-Bass.

Kelman, H. C. (1972). The rights of the subject in social research: An analysis in terms of
relative power and legitimacy. *American Psychologist, 27,* 989–1016.

Kelman, H. C., & Hamilton, V. L. (1989). *Crimes of obedience: Toward a social psychology of authority and responsibility.* New Haven, CT: Yale University Press.

Kelman, H. C., & Warwick, D. P. (1977). The ethics of social intervention: Goals, means,
and consequences. In G. Bermant, H. C. Kelman, & D. P. Warwick (Eds.), *The ethics of
social intervention* (pp. 3–33). Washington, DC: Hemisphere.

Warwick, D. P. (1977). Freedom. In R. M. Veatch (Ed.), *Population policy and ethics: The
American experience* (pp. 17–29). New York: Halsted.

3 Toward a More Deontological Approach to the Ethical Use of Social Influence

Randall S. Peterson

*S. C. Johnson Graduate School of Management,
Cornell University*

From the very earliest days of the field, social psychologists have actively studied social influence processes (e.g., Sherif, 1936). Social psychologists consider the empirical study of social influence processes to be a core competence for the field (see Cialdini & Trost, 1998). Indeed, social influence processes are arguably the very core of social psychology. Social psychologists have not been dispassionate observers of the social influence process, however. They have chosen specific influence processes to study as they emerge from societal trends (cf. Steiner, 1986), and they have regularly commented on the ethical and social implications of their research findings (e.g., Janis, 1982; Milgram, 1974). The first purpose of this chapter is to call attention to the ethical underpinnings of a number of the classic works in social psychology. Specifically, I discuss important early milestones in research on the ethical implications of the use of social influence by powerful people, the origins of this research in ethical concerns of the day, and the continuing effect those studies have on how social psychologists frame their research. This review is not intended to be a comprehensive look at the social influence literature (see Cialdini & Trost, 1998, for a comprehensive review). Rather, it is a reminder that interests in social influence and ethics have a long and intertwined history in social psychology.

The second purpose of this chapter is to argue for a new direction in research on the ethics of social influence. I argue that a dominant theme in this literature is the suggestion that the most ethical use of social influence is not to exercise direct social influence at all. Group leaders should be impartial (e.g., Janis, 1982), legal authorities should be neutral (e.g., Tyler & Lind, 1992), and those who give direct orders should never go beyond normative boundaries (e.g., Milgram, 1974). I maintain that these recommendations do not solve the ethical dilemmas associated with the exercise of social influence; they simply pass them elsewhere. Influential people can have enormous impact on others through indirect means (e.g., deciding who will be empowered to make a decision rather than accepting group membership as given and trying to influence the members directly). In fact, a number of scholars recently have drawn attention to indirect and procedural uses of influence in authority relations and the ethical issues associated with that practice (e.g., Belliveau, 1995; Hoyt & Garrison, 1997; Peterson, 1997; Tyler, this volume). I conclude by arguing that the study of ethics and social influence should be expanded to consider the ethics of such indirect social influence attempts.

HOW SOCIAL INFLUENCE AND ETHICS ARE INTERTWINED IN CLASSIC SOCIAL PSYCHOLOGY

Ethics and the Use of Group Membership Pressure

The power of group membership to alter attitudes and behaviors is documented in a number of classic studies beginning with Sherif's (1936) work on the autokinetic effect (i.e., judging the distance a stationary spot of light appears to move in an otherwise dark room). Sherif became interested in this problem in part as a result of the great debates taking place both inside and outside of academe at the time about the role of culture and the evolution of social norms. He was very interested in how people's opinions and attitudes could be manipulated through group process. His research was the first to convincingly document that people look to others for information about the correctness of their attitudes. Beyond documenting social comparison behaviors, however, one of the most significant findings from Sherif's studies was that an extreme and confident individual could have a disproportionate effect on others' attitudes under conditions of uncertainty. According to Sherif, the implications of these findings are profound; they go to the very heart of how we understand human nature. If the most confident and persuasive people in a society value individual competition and personal gain, then "a person of the J. P. Morgan type will be among the great and envied heroes. In a society where the supreme values are the reverse, a person like Stakhanof will be hailed among the public heroes" (Sherif, 1966, p. 197). Strong political ideologues, by implication, are likely to be among the most persuasive and potentially divisive in society. In short, Sherif's research on the development of cultural norms strikes at the very nature of how people define themselves and what is considered ethical.

Sherif later became interested in understanding conflict among groups within a society after observing the problems he saw with race relations in the United States and elsewhere. Sherif, Harvey, White, Hood, and Sherif (1961) reconfirmed the general notion that individual attitudes can be manipulated powerfully via group pressure but also found that competition induced stereotyping, prejudice, and violence toward outgroup members. At Robber's Cave, Sherif divided groups of boys at a camp into the "Eagles" and "Rattlers" and put the groups first into competition and then into a situation that required cooperation (i.e., a superordinate goal). Results revealed that competition encouraged violence toward and stereotyping of outgroups. These behaviors later stopped when the groups worked together toward a superordinate or shared goal. For Sherif, this mimicked the kind of competition one expects between individuals and groups versus the need for nations to work together. He also believed that his findings reflected how conflict between national subgroups can flare up under normal circumstances and disappear during periods of national crisis (Sherif et al., 1961). These research findings and implications inspired a generation of social psychologists to study how to avoid the hatred and violence created by intergroup competition (e.g., Aronson, Blaney, Stephan, Sikes, & Snapp, 1978; Brewer & Miller, 1984; Cook, 1985; Wilder, 1984, 1986).

Sherif was by no means alone in his interest in the ethics of employing group power. Asch (1955, 1956) also was interested in the power of the group to change public attitudes, as a result of having witnessed the rise of fascism in Europe. He initially believed that people would say what they believed to be true if the subject of discussion were objectively true (i.e., the witnessed behavior of someone else, or in the case of his later studies, the comparative length of lines). The results of his classic conformity experiments showed that Asch's initial hypothesis was wrong. Seventy-five percent of participants in his studies conformed at some point in the experiment when faced with a unanimous and incorrect majority. Although Sherif (1936) had demonstrated that group pressure could change attitudes in ambiguous situations, Asch's (1955) results demonstrated that people were willing to alter their public position on a task with an objective reality. Of course, participants did not necessarily believe the incorrect answers they gave. The powerful point Asch made is that most people are willing to publicly state something that they know to be objectively false. The ethical implication of these findings, according to Asch, is that an authority figure can entice people to make a false statement, in turn pressuring others into acting on that false statement. As Adolf Hitler (1938/1971) noted, "The great masses of the people will more easily fall victims to a big lie than to a small one" (p. 22).

Even more, there is evidence that these group membership processes work for good as well as evil in two other classic social psychology studies. The first example is in Lewin's (1943) use of this tactic to get women to prepare more organ meats during World War II. Neither rational nor emotional appeals persuaded women to change their behavior. Public discussion and commitment to each other following an appeal did, however. The women in the public commitment condition reported cooking more organ meat in the follow-up interview than any other condition. Similarly, Festinger, Riecken, and Schachter (1956) found such dynamics at work in their observational study of Marian Keech's "seekers" cult. They infiltrated the cult to find out how a cult leader maintains control when his or her "big lie" or prophecy fails. In this case, Marian Keech had predicted that the world would flood, but the few faithful would be saved. When the flooding failed to materialize, cult members who had the social support of other believers not only continued to profess belief in the prophecy but began to recruit new members to the cult based on the belief (i.e., caused by cognitive dissonance) that their faith had saved the earth. On the other hand, cult members who found themselves isolated without the social support of other members began to question their beliefs.

Tajfel's (1978, 1982) minimal group studies also show the power of group membership to create unethical behavior. In his effort to understand why inter-group hostility maintains itself over generations, Tajfel attempted to create the most "minimal" groups possible. His intention was to create a control condition for comparison with other groups based on more substantive criteria to better understand the foundations of intergroup hostility. His findings revolutionized the way social psychologists think about the power of group membership. Ingroup favoritism was found even in groups where there was no basis for discrimination between ingroup and outgroup members (i.e., random selection to membership). The ethical implications of this finding are profound; ingroup favoritism and prejudice do not need any basis in history of intergroup conflict. Simple categorization of people invokes differentiated behavior. The psychological and ethical implications of this seminal work have been pursued by a number of social psychologists (e.g., Abrams & Hogg, 1990; Brewer, 1979; Turner, Hogg, Oakes, Reicher, & Wetherell, 1987).

Group membership, in sum, is a powerful force that can be used to apply social influence. More specifically, the ethical concern running through these studies is the notion that social pressure can be used to influence others to (a) state something they would otherwise not have said (Sherif, 1936), (b) engage in behavior that they would not initiate on their own (Festinger et al., 1956), and even (c) say things they do not believe (Asch, 1955). All of these studies suggest that people are loathe to deviate from others, even when it involves evaluating objective stimuli. Schachter's (1951) classic study on opinion deviance suggests a possible reason why it is difficult for an individual to resist such group pressure. He found that deviants are disliked intensely and are subject to enormous scrutiny, followed by shunning if they fail to comply with the group. By implication then, groups wishing to be ethical ought never to allow extreme and/or overly confident people to sway their group and thus apply this kind of pressure to others. The extreme version of this recommendation is the notion that leaders or authority figures ought to be closely monitored, or even barred from emerging at all, for fear that they may use the power of group pressure to press an unethical agenda. That fear is illustrated in the next group of classic social psychology studies.

Ethics and Leadership in Small Groups

Lewin's (1935; Lewin, Lippitt, & White, 1939) work on small-group leadership is also a classic example of ethical interests motivating social influence research.

Having seen the rise of fascism and its effect on the scapegoating of Jews, Lewin became interested in the role of leadership style on the ethical behavior of followers. He asked whether experiencing "authoritarian," "democratic," or "laissez-faire" leadership makes it more or less likely that group members would scapegoat outgroups, rebel against authority, or engage in violent behavior. In these classic studies of leadership styles, Lewin compared leadership climates (social influence styles) of adults working with groups of 11-year-old boys. He found that if leaders simply told group members what to do, the authoritarian style, group members (a) engaged in varying types of rebellion (e.g., passive or active aggression toward others in the group, destroying their own work, and extreme dislike of the leader), (b) practiced scapegoating of both outgroups and marginal ingroup members, and (c) reported extreme displeasure with the work environment. Democratic leadership, including discussing all issues with the boys, led to virtually no acts of scapegoating, rebellion, or violence. In short, the ethical behavior of group members was better under democratic rather than authoritarian leadership.

Lewin's seminal studies inspired a half-century of research implicating authoritarian or directive leaders as the cause of a variety of ethical concerns ranging from suppression of minority dissent and scapegoating to excessive leader influence on group decisions. (e.g., Callaway, Marriott, & Esser, 1985; Esser & Lindoerfer, 1989; Flowers, 1977; Harper & Askling, 1980; Hirokawa & Pace, 1983; Janis, 1972, 1982; Leana, 1985; Maier, 1950, 1963; Maier & Solem, 1952; Moorhead & Montanari, 1986). A great deal of subsequent research consistently implicated directive leaders as the cause of unethical group decisions. Maier (1950; Maier & Solem, 1952), for example, found that authoritarian leadership that suppressed dissent was associated with minority ideas being systematically ignored and ultimately worse solutions to problems being found.

Irving Janis' (1972, 1982) groupthink theory also suggests that directive leadership causes unethical group behavior (these decisions are also often ill-conceived, but see Sims, 1992, for a full justification of the unethical label). Specifically, Janis argued that "a lack of tradition of impartial leadership" was an antecedent cause of groupthink that resulted in unethical group behavior such as "stereotypes of outgroups," "belief in the inherent morality of the group," and "direct pressure on dissenters" to conform (Janis, 1982, pp. 244). In each of the 21 case studies listed in Table 3.1, the authors found support for the notion that directive leadership is a prime cause of groupthink and specific unethical outcomes.

Experimental studies investigating the leader directiveness component of the groupthink hypothesis also support the notion that authoritarian leadership is a significant cause of unethical behavior. For example, Courtright (1978) found that imposition of a restricting set of directions by the experimenter (a leader substitute) resulted in significantly less discussion of alternatives, especially in highly cohesive groups. Flowers (1977) found a similar effect by manipulating group cohesiveness and leadership style. She found no effect for group cohesiveness but found that a "closed" (partial and directive) leadership style engendered lesser acceptance of minority ideas, leading to decreased use of available information and

TABLE 3.1

A List of Case Histories of Groupthink-Induced Disasters
Where Directive Leadership Was Cited as a Cause

No.	Author	Case
1	Janis (1982)	Chamberlain cabinet's decision to appease Hitler and Nazi Germany
2	Janis (1982)	Truman cabinet's decision to cross the 38th parallel in the Korean conflict
3	Janis (1982)	Kennedy cabinet's decision to support and launch the invasion of Cuba at the Bay of Pigs
4	Janis (1982)	Johnson cabinet's decision to escalate the Vietnam War
5	Janis (1982)	Admiral Kimmel's lack of readiness for the Japanese attack on Pearl Harbor
6	Janis (1982)	Nixon cabinet's decision to engage in a cover-up of the break-in at the Watergate complex
7	Janis (1982) Smith (1985)	Carter administration's failed attempt to rescue hostages in Tehran
8	Janis (1982)	Ford administration's decision to attempt to rescue the crew of the Mayaguez
9	Janis (1985)	Ford Motor Company's decision to build the Edsel
10	Janis (1985)	Buffalo Mining Company's decision to ignore warnings about their dam bursting
11	't Hart (1990)	Irangate decision to support the rebels in Nicaragua
12	't Hart (1990)	Failure to prevent the Nazi invasion of Holland
13	Kroon, 't Hart, Crouch, & van Kreveld (1991)	Variety of dutch government operations
14	Heller (1983)	Thatcher administration's conduct of the Falkland Islands War
15	Hensley & Griffen (1986)	Kent State University Board of Trustees' decision to build on site of shooting
16	Huseman & Driver (1979)	Small and large business groups
17	Manz & Sims (1982)	Groupthink in autonomous work groups
18	Sims (1992)	Beech-Nut's decision to sell "phony" apple juice
19	Sims (1992)	Fraud at E. F. Hutton
20	Sims (1992)	Salomon Brothers' illegal purchase of government securities
21	Metselaar & Verbeek	Dutch government's conduct of the West New Guinea Conflict

ultimately to fewer solutions being suggested than with an "open" leadership style. The closed leader in her study strongly advocates a position on the issue being considered and discourages discussion of alternative solutions. Open leaders give a position on the issue only after others have given theirs (impartiality) and encourage discussion of all potential solutions.

Nonexperimental studies also have implicated directive leadership as the cause of unethical group behavior. The results of a descriptive study by Hirokawa and Pace (1983) suggested that influential group members (especially leaders) can often get others to accept invalid "facts" and lead their groups to unethical and poor group decisions (cf. Sherif, 1936). Similar results were reported in a study by Harper and Askling (1980), who found that directive leadership often results in conflict and poor decision making. Similarly, Moorhead and Montanari (1986) found that directive leadership and insulation from dissent generally led to poor decision process with teams of business students in a competitive 3-month management simulation.

Tetlock, Peterson, McGuire, Chang, and Feld (1992) employed a q-sort analysis of historical case studies to assess the internal logic of the groupthink model. They tested antecedent causal claims made by the groupthink model by using structural equation modeling across all eight of the groups Janis (1982) studied, plus two additional cases suggested as possible examples of groupthink. Consistent with other studies already discussed here, results revealed that structural and procedural faults of the organization, not group cohesiveness or situational stressors, were potent predictors of group process among the 10 political decision-making groups. Leader directiveness specifically was associated with truncated group discussion, suppression of dissent, a less extensive search for information, and a lack of contingency planning. Leader directiveness was found to be a significant cause of defective group process leading to a high likelihood of poor, often unethical, group decisions. In sum, research consistently supports the notion that directive leadership leads to unethical group member behaviors and poor quality group decisions.

Ethics and Obedience/Compliance With Authority

A third classic line of social influence inquiry that was motivated by ethical concerns is the literature on obedience to authority. Stanley Milgram (1963) was concerned with the capacity of everyday people to engage in unethical behavior they would never initiate on their own—all in the service of obedience to someone in a position of authority. He became interested in the subject as result of the Nuremberg trials, where German citizens defended their participation in the Holocaust by arguing that they were simply following others' orders. Milgram (1974) explicitly argued that Nazi Germany was not the exception but an extreme example of the general rule that people will engage in unethical behavior when ordered. He also cited the actions of soldiers in the Vietnam War as further examples of the continuing ethical problem of obedience to authority. Indeed, his studies documented the willingness of people in a democratic society (i.e., the United States) to follow unethical orders to administer extreme electric shock to an innocent victim.

The ethical problems associated with obedience to authority in Vietnam were powerfully described and studied in Herbert Kelman and V. Lee Hamilton's (1989) *Crimes of Obedience*. Specifically, they were interested in public response to the trial of Lieutenant Calley for giving orders in the My Lai massacre of civilians in Vietnam. Kelman and Hamilton found evidence to suggest that most people could imagine themselves engaging in criminal behavior if ordered to do so by a "legitimate" authority. The best way to avoid this ethical dilemma is, of course, to be sure that officers do not put soldiers in this kind of predicament, or more generally, to ensure that authority figures never request "nonnormative" (i.e., unethical) behavior from followers.

Standing the obedience literature on its head, procedural justice researchers more recently have looked for unethical behavior in disobedience to authority. Procedural justice researchers ask why people sometimes do not comply with the directives of legitimate authorities (i.e., police, judges, etc.) rather than why people do comply with the unethical directives of authorities. In other words, the concern is about engaging in unethical or antisocial behavior as a result of disobedience rather than obedience. Tyler and Lind (Lind & Tyler, 1988; Tyler & Lind 1992) suggested that authorities must treat people with respect to gain legitimacy and compliance. In a study of citizen interaction with the Chicago police force, for example, Tyler (1990) found that people obey the law voluntarily (a) when laws are made and enforced by impartial authorities, (b) when laws are enacted in procedurally fair ways, and (c) when the police force treats people with respect. Together, these two literatures on compliance or obedience to authority (which one you chose depends on your perspective) suggest opposing sources of unethical behavior (obedience vs. disobedience). However, they agree that ethical or "fair" authority is content neutral. Either an authority should refrain from encouraging people to engage in unethical acts (i.e., the obedience paradigm) or the authority should enforce rules in a neutral manner (i.e., the procedural justice paradigm).

EXERCISING SOCIAL INFLUENCE ETHICALLY

As diverse as the social influence literature is, it shares two interrelated ideas. The first is the focus of attention on the direct exercise of social influence. In other words, these studies all focus on the use of persuasion or threat aimed at changing the public attitudes and behaviors of the less powerful. The second and related commonality in the literatures is the call for restraint in exercising social influence as the most ethical course of action. Milgram (1974), for example, recommended that authorities not demand "nonnormative behavior." He argued that it is unethical to ask someone to do something out of the everyday norm. Similarly, Festinger et al. (1956) suggested that cults are the product of a charismatic individual without whom cults and their potentially unethical behavior would not exist. Lind and Tyler (1988) likewise argued that fair procedures require "neutral" authorities. If an authority favors one position over another before hearing from both sides, one cannot expect full compliance with the directives of the authority. In group decision making, Janis (1982; Janis & Mann, 1978, 1989) argued that leaders should set broad parameters and limitations but refrain from advocating specific actions or decisions. He argued strongly that leaders ought to refrain from communicating policy preferences to achieve an atmosphere of open communication and problem solving. Expressing a clear policy preference, he argued, discourages the group from seriously examining all aspects of a problem and is likely to lead to disastrous, often unethical, outcomes. In sum, the consensus view on ethics and social influence appears to be that powerful people ought not to exert direct influence to be ethical in their use of power—they should stick with indirect forms of control such as facilitating decision making.

Is Refraining From Direct Social Influence Attempts the Best Advice We Can Offer?

Does the existing advice to refrain from engaging in direct social influence attempts fully address all of the ethical issues inherent in the exercise of social influence? Is it reasonable and advisable to expect powerful people to refrain from engaging in social influence attempts? Two strands of work suggest an alternative point of view. First, recent findings in the procedural justice literature strongly suggest that people care deeply about being treated with respect (e.g., Tyler & Lind, 1992). People care about how they are treated by authority figures because that treatment conveys to them that they are valued socially. This effect is so strong, in fact, that it can be found even after controlling for any effect that procedure has on perceptions of control over the outcome of the decision (e.g., Lind, Kanfer, & Earley, 1993). In other words, people derive self-esteem from respectful treatment, not control over the process as a means to obtain a favorable outcome.[1]

The second strand of work that questions the advice for influential people to refrain from direct social influence is my own more specific work on process and outcome directiveness. Recently, I have argued that the negative effects associated with directive leadership reviewed earlier actually result from process directiveness (i.e., the regulation of the process by which the group reaches a decision) rather than outcome directiveness (i.e., the degree to which a leader advocates a favored solution; Peterson, 1997; Peterson, Owens, Tetlock, Fan, & Martorana, 1997). The problem with directive leadership as it has been studied in the past is not promotion of the leader's own point of view as much as if the leader genuinely encourages additional perspectives through the process of decision making. Past studies of leader directiveness have confounded "process" and "outcome" directiveness. Those studies have operationalized leader directiveness by

---

[1]Thibaut and Walker (1975) originally suggested that people cared about procedural justice and treatment by authority figures because these concepts allowed for indirect control over the outcome of the decision.

manipulating whether the leader strongly advocates a specific position and whether the leader encourages discussion of all possible alternatives. "Open" or "democratic" leaders do not advocate a position of their own (low outcome directiveness), but they do encourage discussion of alternative ideas (high process directiveness). "Closed" or "authoritarian" leaders are the reciprocal, strongly advocating their own solution (high outcome directiveness and low process directiveness). That study (Peterson, 1997) tested the hypothesis that process directiveness would be a potent predictor of group process and decision quality, whereas outcome directiveness would not. Results of studies from an experiment, archival analysis of the case histories Janis studied, and an observational study of city councils in the San Francisco Bay Area all confirmed this prediction.

In a more recent study of seven top management teams of seven large companies in successful and unsuccessful times, Peterson, Owens, Tetlock, Fan, and Martorana (1998) found compatible results. We found that successful decision-making teams had strong leaders who were more likely to try to persuade others in the corporation to share their views than were leaders of unsuccessful teams. Moreover, leaders of successful teams were more likely to be explicit about their policy preferences with others. This finding clearly contradicts the advocates of impartiality. Importantly, however, successful chief executive officers were also more open to minority dissent than their unsuccessful counterparts. This combination of findings is consistent with my argument here that people respond as strongly to how they are treated by authority figures as much as to the specific outcomes that come from a decision-making process. In short, process behaviors of leaders are significant and reliable predictors of group member satisfaction, acceptance of minority rights, and acknowledgment of trade-offs in the decision making of presidential cabinets, city councils, top management teams, and experimental subjects.

The message of this larger pattern of results is, in short, that influential people concerned about their ethical impact on an organization should focus on the process by which decisions are made as much as on the actual decisions themselves (a more deontological or process-oriented approach). These results suggest that people care deeply about indirect social influence attempts as well as the direct attempts. That is, people care deeply about how they are treated by people in positions of authority (cf. Lind & Tyler, 1988; Tyler & Lind, 1992).[2]

Toward a More Deontological Approach to Research on the Ethical Use of Social Influence

The call for more attention to process and indirect social influence attempts raises three interrelated research problems. The first and most thorny of the problems is defining what an ethical or fair process entails. From a social science perspective,

---

[2]In many respects this was a lost point from Lewin et al. (1939), who argued that the decision-making climate matters more than specific orders that followers are given (i.e., process matters more than outcome).

this presents a formidable challenge because people's perceptions of what constitutes a fair process are affected by their personal values (Feather, 1994, 1996; Peterson, 1994; Rasinski, 1987). For guidance on the question of implied social values (i.e., ethical norms), one can turn to a variety of normatively important historical and philosophical treatises such as Aristotle's *Politics*, Hamilton, Madison, and Jay's *The Federalist*, Mill's *Essay on Liberty*, and the *United States Constitution*. All of these documents emphasize the importance of protecting minority rights and engaging dissent directly and genuinely. This is not to say that the majority ought to be prohibited from acting without the consent of the minority, just that dissent ought to be honestly engaged. How it is to be engaged is a more difficult problem, however (e.g., Jost & Ross, 1999).

The difficulty of defining fair process notwithstanding, scholars interested in procedural justice have made significant attempts to address this problem. Early theoretical work was done by Leventhal (1980), who suggested six rules of justice, consistency (across people and over time), bias suppression (i.e., no self-interest on the part of authorities), accuracy (use of accurate information), correctability (opportunities to modify the actions of a single individual), representativeness (concerns considered), and ethicality (compatibility with social values). Tyler and Lind (1992) found empirical support for their three-part model of neutrality, standing (the degree to which the authority treats others with respect and dignity), and trust (the degree to which the authority tries to account for the individual needs of others) as the key aspects of fair process. Belliveau (1995) also pointed to social identity issues as being a significant predictor of what constitutes fair process. Specifically, she argued that universalistic standards of interpersonal treatment determine perceptions of procedural fairness. All three of these perspectives offer important beginnings to understanding what constitutes fair process, but clearly more work needs to be done.

Progress in defining fair process also would be aided by work describing how influential people engage in indirect social influence attempts and the effects of these tactics on followers. Here again, there is some significant beginning work in the area. Hoyt and Garrison (1997), for example, suggested three ways in which leaders can indirectly influence decisions. The first is structural manipulation—this involves changing the physical composition of the deliberating group. Highly influential people often have the power to determine who will be included in any decision-making process. Unethical leaders can handpick their group to favor the outcome they desire or systematically exclude an individual or perspective. They usually also have the power to add others midway through the process if they realize they could be defeated by the existing configuration of people.

Influential people also have the power to change discussion through agenda setting, framing, and control of information. Leaders have enormous impact on the direction of the group by what they declare off-limits or priority. A carefully crafted set of parameters virtually can predetermine the outcome of a meeting. People also may choose to influence others by deciding what information to disclose or hide from others. All of this can be done while staying within Janis' (1982) directive to leaders to restrict themselves to setting broad parameters and limitations for decisions.

Finally, indirect influence also can occur through interpersonal manipulation. That is, influential people often are able to shape the dynamics between individuals (e.g., playing one person against another). They may use threats to discourage dissent. They may also use the coalition-building process in groups to their advantage (e.g., let others fight their battles for them). Influential people also may be in a position to either choose their own "expert" or designate someone in the group as a technical expert not to be questioned on some important matter. All of these tactics have been demonstrated in the cabinets of Presidents Nixon and Carter (see Garrison, 1996). However, more work needs to be done to fully understand the effects of these tactics on the ethical behavior of other team members.

A third research issue for a deontological perspective on the ethical use of social influence derives from the second, that is, influential people who act or "look" fair and inclusive but are not. Greenberg (1990), in particular, suggested that the notion of impression management vis-à-vis "fairness" is understudied. He suggested that "looking fair" is a highly desirable social identity that people seek to achieve.[3] In fact, Belliveau and Cook (1999) further suggest that when given the opportunity to appear procedurally fair, managers and leaders may actually behave less fairly. That is, they may behave in a distributively unfair way where otherwise, in the absence of an opportunity to demonstrate their procedural fairness, they would have acted with distributive fairness. Leaders need not necessarily actually be fair. As Machiavelli (1531/1979) noted in *The Discourses,* "The people are often deceived by a false appearance of good unless they are persuaded otherwise by someone worthy of their confidence" (p. 274). Indeed, as Brockner, Tyler, and Cooper-Schneider (1992) discovered, when loyal people discover that they have been deceived by someone in a position of authority, they react extremely negatively. That is not to say that trying to be perceived as fair is itself inherently unethical. Even those who strive to be ethical and fair usually need others to see them as fair if they are to be effective. The important point is that leaders can give "window dressing" to fair procedure but actually work toward unethical ends. We know very little about how this occurs in the real world and what its effects are.

CONCLUSION

In sum, I make two interrelated arguments in this chapter. First, I argue that the recommendation to restrict the use of direct social influence by the powerful does not solve the ethical dilemmas associated with the exercise of social influence. Such recommendations for impartiality, neutrality, and normative behavior simply pass the dilemmas to more indirect forms of social influence. Influential people are able to manipulate others indirectly as well as directly if they choose.

---

[3]Indeed, this is one important reason that authoritarian political regimes engage in periodic "elections" with no choice: Such elections enhance the notion that the dictatorship is legitimate.

The second argument I make here is that the study of the ethics of social influence would be greatly enhanced and enriched by directing more attention to indirect forms of social influence. To that end, I have suggested a research agenda that includes defining fair process (cf. Tyler & Lind, 1992), explicating how influential people use indirect tactics of social influence (cf. Hoyt & Garrison, 1997), and studying impression management tactics in authority relations (cf. Greenberg, 1990). Each of these areas has important early work already underway. However, many important things are yet to be learned about what people believe about fair process, how influential people manipulate process to personal advantage, and the impression management process.

One note of clarification should be made. I am not arguing that direct attempts at social influence do not pose ethical problems. Most of the literature reviewed here and in the other chapters in this volume speak to the importance of these problems. Rather, I am arguing for the need to consider the social science implications of the following argument (Perrault, 1990): "In actuality, the means that we use do shape who we are. We cannot separate the means from the end ... we become whatever we do." (p. 2)

ACKNOWLEDGMENTS

I thank John Darley, Dave Messick, and Pam Owens for thoughtful comments on earlier versions of this chapter presented at the Conference on Social Influence and Ethics in Organizations at Kellogg Graduate School of Management, Northwestern University, January 1998.

REFERENCES

Abrams, D., & Hogg, M. A. (1990). *Social identity theory: Constructive and critical advances.* New York: Springer-Verlag.

Aronson, E., Blaney, N., Stephan, C., Sikes, J., & Snapp, M. (1978). *The jigsaw classroom.* Beverly Hills, CA: Sage.

Asch, S. E. (1955). Opinions and social pressure. *Scientific American, 193,* 31–35.

Asch, S. E. (1956). Studies of independence and conformity: A minority of one against a unanimous majority. *Psychological Monographs, 70* (9, Whole No. 416).

Belliveau, M. A. (1995). Understanding employee reactions to affirmative action implementation: Identity versus interest effects on procedural fairness judgments. *Dissertation Abstracts International, 57,* AAI9621053.

Belliveau, M. A., & Cook, K. (1999, August). *Engendering inequity? The contribution of procedural justice and workgroup sex composition to the gender wage gap.* Paper presented at the Academy of Management national meetings, Chicago, IL.

Brewer, M. B. (1979). In-group bias in the minimal intergroup situation. A cognitive-motivational analysis. *Psychological Bulletin, 86,* 307–324.

Brewer, M. B., & Miller, N. (1984). Beyond the contact hypothesis: Theoretical perspectives on desegregation. In N. Miller & M. B. Brewer (Eds.), *Groups in contact: The psychology of desegregation* (pp. 281–302). New York: Academic Press.

Brockner, J., Tyler, T. R., & Cooper-Schneider, R. (1992). The influence of prior commitment to an institution on reactions to perceived unfairness: The higher they are, the harder they fall. *Administrative Science Quarterly, 37,* 241–261.

Callaway, M. R., Marriott, R. G., & Esser, J. K. (1985). Effects of dominance on group decision making: Toward a stress-reduction explanation of groupthink. *Journal of Personality and Social Psychology, 49,* 949–952.

Cialdini, R. B., & Trost, M. R. (1998). Social influence: Social norms, conformity, and compliance. In D. T. Gilbert, S. T. Fiske, & G. Lindzey (Eds.), *The handbook of social psychology* (vol. 2, pp. 151–192). New York: McGraw-Hill.

Courtright, J. A. (1978). A laboratory investigation of groupthink. *Communication Monographs, 45,* 229–246.

Cook, S. W. (1985). Experimenting on social issues: The case of school desegregation. *American Psychologist, 40,* 452–460.

Crouch, C., & Heller, F. A. (1983). *Organizational democracy and political processes.* Chichester, UK: John Wiley & Sons.

Esser, J. K., & Lindoerfer, J. S. (1989). Groupthink and the space shuttle Challenger accident: Toward a quantitative case analysis. *Journal of Behavioral Decision Making, 2,* 167–177.

Feather, N. T. (1994). Human values and their relation to justice. *Journal of Social Issues, 50,* 129–151.

Feather, N. T. (1996). Reactions to penalties for an offense in relation to authoritarianism, values, perceived responsibility, perceived seriousness, and deservingness. *Journal of Personality and Social Psychology, 71,* 571–587.

Festinger, L., Riecken, H. W., & Schachter, S. (1956). *When prophecy fails.* Minneapolis: University of Minnesota Press.

Flowers, M. L. (1977). A laboratory test of some implications of Janis's groupthink hypothesis. *Journal of Personality and Social Psychology, 35,* 888–896.

Garrison, J. A. (1996). The games advisers play. *Dissertation Abstracts International, 57,* AAI9637119.

Greenberg, J. (1990). Looking fair vs. being fair. In B. M. Staw & L. L. Cumings (Eds.), *Research in organizational behavior* (Vol. 12, pp. 111–157. Greenwich, CT: JAI.

Harper, N. L., & Askling, L. R. (1980). Group communication and quality of task solution in a media production organization. *Communication Monographs, 47,* 77–100.

Hensley, T., & Griffen, G. (1986). Victims of groupthink: The Kent State University board of trustees and the 1977 gymnasium controversy. *Journal of Conflict Resolution, 30,* 497–531.

Hirokawa, R. Y., & Pace, R. (1983). A descriptive investigation of the possible communication-based reasons for effective and ineffective group decision making. *Communication Monographs, 50,* 363–380.

Hitler, A. (1971). *Mein kampf* (R. Manheim, Trans.). Boston: Houghton Mifflin. (Original work published 1938)

Hoyt, P. D., & Garrison, J. A. (1997). Political manipulation within the small group: Foreign policy advisers in the Carter administration. In P. 't Hart, E. K. Stern, & B. Sundelius (Eds.), *Beyond groupthink: Political group dynamics and foreign policy-making* (pp. 249–274). Ann Arbor: University of Michigan Press.

Huseman, R. C., & Driver, R. W. (1979). Groupthink: Implications for small group decision making in business. In R. C. Huseman & A. B. Carroll (Eds.), *Readings in organizational behavior: Dimensions of management actions.* Boston: Allyn & Bacon.

Janis, I. L. (1972). *Victims of groupthink.* Boston: Houghton Mifflin.

Janis, I. L. (1982). *Victims of groupthink (2nd ed.).* Boston: Houghton Mifflin.

Janis, I. L., & Mann, L. (1978) *Decision making: A psychological analysis of conflict, choice, and commitment.* New York: The Free Press.

Janis, I. L., & Mann, L. (1989). *Crucial decisions: Leadership in policymaking and crisis management.* New York: The Free Press.

Jost, J. T., & Ross, L. (1999). Fairness norms and the potential for mutual agreements involving majority and minority groups. In E. A. Mannix, M. A. Neale, & R. Wageman (Eds.), *Research on managing groups and teams: Context* (Vol. 2), 93–114. Greenwich, CT: JAI.

Kelman, H. C., & Hamilton, V. L. (1989). *Crimes of obedience: Toward a social psychology of authority and responsibility.* New Haven, CT: Yale University Press.

Kroon, M. B. R., 't Hart, P., & van Kreveld, D. (1991). Managing group decision making processes: Individual versus collective accountability and groupthink. *The International Journal of Conflict Management, 2,* 91–115.

Leana, C. R. (1985). A partial test of Janis' groupthink model: Effects of group cohesiveness and leader behavior on defective decision making. *Journal of Management, 11,* 5–17.

Leventhal, G. S. (1980). What should be done with equity theory? New approaches to the study of fairness in social relationships. In K. Gergen & R. Willis (Eds.), *Social exchange* (pp. 27–55). New York: Plenum.

Lewin, K. (1935). *A dynamic theory of personality: Selected papers.* Translated by P. K. Adams & K. E. Zener. New York: McGraw-Hill.

Lewin, K. (1943). Forces behind food habits and methods of change. *Bulletin of the National Research Council, 108,* 35–65.

Lewin, K., Lippitt, R., & White, R. K. (1939). Patterns of aggressive behavior in experimentally created 'social climates.' *Journal of Social Psychology, 10,* 171–199.

Lind, E. A., Kanfer, R., & Earley, P. C. (1990). Voice, control, and procedural justice: Instrumental and noninstrumental concerns in fairness judgments. *Journal of Personality and Social Psychology, 59,* 952–959.

Lind, E. A., & Tyler, T. R. (1988). *The social psychology of procedural justice.* New York: Plenum.

Machiavelli, N. (1979). The discourses. In P. Bondanella & M. Musa (Eds.), *The portable Machiavelli* (pp. 167–418). New York: Viking. (Original work published 1531)

Maier, N. R. F. (1950). The quality of group decisions as influenced by the discussion leader. *Human Relations, 3,* 155–174.

Maier, N. R. F. (1963). *Problem-solving discussions and conferences: Leadership methods and skills.* New York: McGraw-Hill.

Maier, N. R. F., & Solem, A. R. (1952). The contribution of a discussion leader to the quality of group thinking: The effective use of minority opinions. *Human Relations, 5,* 277–288.

Manz, C. C., & Sims, H. P. (1982). The potential for "groupthink" in autonomous work groups. *Human Relations, 35,* 773–784.

Metselaar, M. V., & Verbeek, B. (1994, July). *The Dutch government and the 1959–1962 Western New Guinea conflict.* Paper presented at the International Society of Political Psychology annual conference. Santiago de Compostela, Spain.

Milgram, S. (1963). The behavioral study of obedience. *Journal of Abnormal and Social Psychology, 67,* 467–472.

Milgram, S. (1974). *Obedience to authority.* New York: Harper & Row.

Moorhead, G., & Montanari, J. R. (1986). An empirical investigation of the groupthink phenomenon. *Human Relations, 39,* 399–410.

Perrault, G. (1990). *Ethical leadership—Ethical followership.* Minneapolis: University of Minnesota.

Peterson, R. S. (1994). The role of values in predicting fairness judgments and support of affirmative action. *Journal of Social Issues, 50*, 95–115.

Peterson, R. S. (1997). A directive leadership style in group decision making can be both virtue and vice. Evidence from elite and experimental groups. *Journal of Personality and Social Psychology, 72*, 1107–1121.

Peterson, R. S., Owens, P. D., Tetlock, P. E., Fan, E. T., & Martorana, P. (1998). Group dynamics in top management teams: Groupthink, vigilance, and alternative models of organizational failure and success. *Organizational Behavior and Human Decision Processes, 73*, 272–305.

Rasinksi, K. (1987). What's fair is fair—Or is it? Value differences underlying public views about social justice. *Journal of Personality and Social Psychology, 53*, 201–211.

Schachter, S. (1951). Deviation, rejection, and communication. *Journal of Abnormal and Social Psychology, 46*, 190–207.

Sherif, M. (1936). *The psychology of social norms.* New York: Harper & Row.

Sherif, M. (1966). *The psychology of social norms (2nd ed.).* New York: Harper & Row.

Sherif, M., Harvey, O. J., White, B. J., Hood, W. R., & Sherif, C. W. (1961). *Intergroup conflict and cooperation: The Robbers Cave experiment.* Norman, OK: Institute of Group Relations.

Sims, R. R. (1992). Linking groupthink to unethical behavior in organizations. *Journal of Business Ethics, 11*, 651–662.

Smith, S. (1985). Groupthink and the hostage rescue mission. *British Journal of Political Science, 15*, 117–123.

Steiner, I. D. (1986). Paradigms and groups. *Advances in Experimental Social Psychology, 19*, 251–289.

Tajfel, H. (1978). *Differentiation between social groups: Studies in the social psychology of intergroup relations.* London: Academic Press.

Tajfel, H. (1982). *Social identity and intergroup relations.* Cambridge, UK: Cambridge University Press.

Tetlock, P. E., Peterson, R. S., McGuire, C., Chang, S., & Feld, P. (1992). Assessing political group dynamics: A test of the groupthink model. *Journal of Personality and Social Psychology, 63*, 403–425.

't Hart, P. (1990). *Groupthink in government: A study of small groups and policy failure.* Amsterdam: Swets & Zeitlinger.

Thibaut, J., & Walker, L. (1975). *Procedural justice: A psychological analysis.* Hillsdale, NJ: Lawrence Erlbaum Associates.

Turner, J. C., Hogg, M. A., Oakes, P. J., Reicher, S. D., & Wetherell, M. S. (1987). *Rediscovering the social group: A social categorization theory.* Oxford, UK: Blackwell.

Tyler, T. R. (1990). *Why people obey the law.* New Haven, CT: Yale University Press.

Tyler T. R., & Lind, E. A. (1992). A relational model of authority in groups. *Advances in Experimental Social Psychology, 25*, 115–191.

Wilder, D. A. (1984). Intergroup contact: The typical member and the exception to the rule. *Journal of Experimental Social Psychology, 20*, 177–194.

Wilder, D. A. (1986). Social categorization: Implications for creation and reduction of intergroup bias. *Advances in Experimental Social Psychology, 19*, 291–355).

4 The Dynamics of Authority Influence in Organizations and the Unintended Action Consequences

John M. Darley
Princeton University

The general processes by means of which social influence has its effects in nonhierarchical settings are reasonably well documented experimentally and well understood theoretically by social psychologists. But to have applications within the world of organizational behavior, these principles need to be contextualized for that hierarchical world. This is perhaps a harder task than the social psychologist imagines, or to put it another way, it requires us to move farther from our nonhierarchical models than we imagine. In this chapter, I begin that task.

In this chapter I consider acts in which individuals in an organization act, knowingly or unknowingly, to bring about unjustified harmful consequences for others or for themselves. Examples include organizations that illegally dispose of toxic waste, harming the environment; organizations that manufacture and sell dangerous products, harming customers; and organizations that have dangerous workplace practices, harming their workers. These are socially influenced acts. To begin to develop a vocabulary, they are products of "organizational social influence."

THE DYNAMICS OF ORGANIZATIONAL SOCIAL INFLUENCE

To a social psychologist, coming from the egalitarian world of the 40-min experiment on the interaction patterns of college sophomores, and living in the anarchic world of the academic community, the hierarchical and coordinated nature of the organizational world is striking but requires some serious thought before its implications become apparent. Four connected implications strike me as particularly important for considering social influence processes in organizations. The first, and most obvious, is that hierarchies are authority hierarchies; the exercise of authority within them is legitimated by the context. Second, communication of directives in organizations often is done in a compact and incomplete way; subordinates are expected to fill in the implications of directives and behave accordingly. Third, organizations often control the behavior of their members by using incentive systems, in which rewards are specified and earned for certain behaviors or outcomes. Fourth, ethically appropriate behavior in organizations often is designed to be produced by such mechanisms as the communication of corporate codes of conduct, and we need to examine the ways that the existence and communication of the code fit into or clash with other aspects of the authoritative communication structures of the organization.

My central contention here is that these four facts in interaction create a gestalt in which what we might call "organizational social influence" works and works in very powerful ways. I attempt to demonstrate this by citing a number of instances in which these intertwined forces of social influence lead the influenced individuals to commit actions that they would not ordinarily commit if they were functioning as independent actors. Many of these actions are both organizationally useful and morally appropriate. Others can be seen from an outside perspective as intending to fit the goals of the organization but having little hope of doing so—they turn out to be organizationally dysfunctional. Others are simply stupid. Others, we see, are morally dubious or simply morally outrageous.

Organizations Are Authority Hierarchies

I consider the ramifications of the hierarchical structure first. As Simon (1997) remarked, "of all of the modes of influence, authority is the one that chiefly distinguishes the behavior of individuals as participants of organizations from their behavior outside such organizations" (p. 177). The central aspect of authority in organizational structures is that the subordinate regards it as legitimate for the superior to give "commands" or "directions." These commands are thought to specify the actions of the subordinate that will fulfill the overall plan of the organization.

A further assumption lies behind the willingness to obey authority, and this centers around the "expertise" function that was so usefully discriminated in French and Raven's (1959) taxonomy of grounds for granting authority to individuals. Within an organization, it will not be apparent to middle-level managers which of the various choices available are the best choices to maximize the overall productivity of the organization. Should an assembly line be speeded up with the inevitable increase in production errors that might entail? The answer to this depends to some extent on the degree to which the eventual consumer is thought to be conscious of quality considerations in the long term. There is no way that the plant managers can assess this. If they receive an order to speed the lines, they do so, judging that those giving the orders have made the appropriate calculations and that sales of the product will be relatively robust to the increase in product defects that will be caused by speeding the lines.

To generalize this, the requirements of coordination create a certain kind of expertise. Those who are the developers and custodians of the overall plan are the experts in what actions need to be taken, when those actions need to be taken, what actions can be substituted for the planned ones, and what actions, although apparently profitable, useful ones, cannot be substituted because they would destroy the overall plan. The need for organizations to coordinate activities generates an incontrovertible position-based expertise among those assigned the coordinating function. The requirement of coordination guarantees the existence of organizational authority.

To sum this up, authority in organizations is legitimate, is expert, and stems from the requirements of complex task coordination. As is often the case when many independent principles flow together to support each other, the whole is greater than the sum of the parts. Authority in organizations is habitually, reflexively obeyed.

The Characteristics of Organizational Communication

Turn next to the process of communicating decisions and orders in an organizational setting. Although this is a general impression of mine that is difficult to document, I think that those who study this process often find it wanting. I suspect that if one were to study the transfer of plans, goals, commands, and task delegations, that would also be found to be greatly flawed. That is, often the subordinate does not emerge from the communication interaction with a picture of his or her responsibilities that is either clear or congruent with the image that the superior is trying to convey. There are, of course, a number of reasons for this. Not everyone is able to produce clear oral or written directives.

Recent research in cognitive components of communication suggests a quite central and perhaps not well enough recognized reason for this characteristic communication slippage. The research has been characterized as discovering "the illusion of transparency" (Keysar, Barr, & Horton, 1998; Keysar, Ginzel, & Bazerman, 1995) that leads to "the curse of knowledge" (Camerer, Loewenstein, & Weber, 1989).

Superiors are likely to give action orders that assume too much knowledge on the part of subordinates, and the lack of critical knowledge means that the subordinates must carry out their orders in a mechanical rather than plan-guided way. Thus, they are unable to modify their actions to save or salvage the successful outcome.

And, of course, the situation is worse; the curse of knowledge will ensure that the superior, who may be out of touch with ongoing activities which would include signs that things are going wrong, assumes that the subordinates are acting in a plan-governed way and will not contemplate the possibility that they are not; will not, in other words, realize that the plan is being fatally harmed in its execution because the subordinates do not have "a grasp" of the plan; will not, in the cases of especial interest to me, realize that the subordinates' actions are now harming others, fellow workers, bystanders, or consumers of the products manufactured.

The Role of Incentive Systems

Modern management systems tend to rely on defining what they want workers to do and then providing incentives for the workers who take the desired actions or reaching the desired goals. The most familiar model for that situation is some version of the ever-popular, ever-changing, "management by objectives." This is the world of the "sales commission structure," or the "bonus for reaching goals" compensation system.

The point of all of this for our purposes is that incentive systems have an elevated status for communicating what the organization "really wants" and "really values." In a world in which talk is regarded as cheap, bonuses, promotions, and other tangible marks of valuing are what really matter. Speaking more precisely, talk is meaningful to the extent that it connects with the incentives eventually provided through the incentive system.

Codes of Conduct and Corporate Procedures

Organizations, and particularly corporations, are well aware of the possibilities of violating legal or ethical standards and how that might harm them. As a response to this, corporations increasingly are adopting corporate codes of conduct, in an attempt to guide the behaviors of the corporate employees. The purpose here is to make clear to employees that the corporation seeks to have them behave in an ethically appropriate fashion. From the perspective of the behavioral scientist, knowledgeable about the control of human behavior in complex settings, some obstacles to codes providing effective controls on human behavior are noticeable.

The first one involves the necessarily general way in which the codes must be couched. One code I have examined reads "all company personnel are expected to observe high standards of business and personal ethics in the discharge of their assigned responsibilities." This is not without content but does not answer an employee's question about the moral appropriateness of any specific act (March & Heath, 1994).

A second problem with controlling conduct by the necessarily general codes is that it is often not possible for a subordinate to understand that an action he or she is directed to take may have harmful consequences. Therefore, the subordinate does not realize that an ethical issue arises when he or she decides whether to take that action. The problem arises because the subordinate's actions have their effects not simply, but in coordination with other actions, taken by other people. What is not communicated, because it is something that the superior understands clearly and wrongly expects that the subordinate understands or at least has the information to assemble, is what specific aspects of the actions that the subordinate is directed to take can cause hazard. I suspect that this is a common source of organizational malfeasance. One individual seals the hazardous waste in drums, unaware that it will not be marked as hazardous; another transports the unmarked drums to the waste dump.

Third, the existence of corporate codes can cause superiors to assume that the codes are much on the minds of subordinates, and of course this assumption may not be true. The superior may believe that any directive he or she gives carries with it the unstated but understood addition of "do this in a way that is allowed by the corporate codes." The superior assumes that he or she has communicated such ethical precautions far earlier; therefore, they do not need to be a part of the present communication. Absent that part of the communication, when the subordinate recognizes the ethical concerns that taking an action raises, he or she will not necessarily assume that the superior has communicated that those actions must be "within code." And recall that applying the generalities of the code to the specific actions possible is problematic. The subordinate may believe the superior is saying that the most obvious actions that fulfill the directive are "business ethical."

For all of these reasons, it is difficult to imagine that the role of corporate codes is going to be powerful in preventing organizational harms.

CASE STUDIES: EXAMPLES OF DIFFICULTIES

Next I present examples of how these four streams of information, which give subordinates apparently or genuinely contradictory messages, are resolved into action orders by those subordinates. I do not demonstrate how one stream of information, in isolation, brings subordinates to take morally ambiguous or wrong actions. That is a story that we already understand. We have had numerous examples of subordinates in organizations who carry out directives that proved to produce morally disastrous results. We also are aware of examples in which superiors have communicated directives that were insufficiently responsive to what subordinates knew and didn't know and caused them to unknowingly take actions that had harmful consequences to workers or the clients of the organization. We also are well aware of ways in which incentive systems have caused those governed by them to behave in less than ethical ways. Instead, I discuss examples in ways that reveal the psychological dynamics of the interpretative process that the subordinate goes through when the streams of information provide conflicting action implications.

Dishonesty From the Top Down

Assume that you are an authority. Take as your task bringing the workers in your organization to perform harmful actions to outsiders, even though those actions are banned by any normal ethical rules. (The social psychologist thinks of the

Milgram research in this context.) The point of the example is this: Authoritative communications directing actions that initially seem morally acceptable but later are revealed to be harmful and counter to the organization's code of ethics can be surprisingly effective. This is so because they are often used in tandem with the workings of the financial incentive system. Financial incentive systems, with the signals they give about the behavior that the organization finds appropriate, and the dependence they create on the part of the organization members on those incentives, can be quite destructive of the ethical stance of the organization members. Good people can become first entrapped in and then active in perpetuating ethically wrong and destructive actions on innocent victims.

Eichenwald (1995) demonstrated how this took place recently at the stock-brokerage unit of the Prudential Company. The end state involved Prudential-Bache stockbrokers selling investment products that were guaranteed to fail to naive customers who trusted the advice they were getting from the Prudential-Bache stockbrokers.

Of course, this was in the face of, and in direct opposition to, the behavior specified in the firm's much-publicized code of ethics and its ethical directives to the stockbrokers. Both of those asserted the duty to give primacy to the interests of the firm's customers. The leaders of the firm were complicit; making huge profits by selling scam investments was a result they desired and encouraged. Therefore, we are not examining the actions of a few dishonest brokers. The question is how it was possible for the higher-ups to get large numbers of initially honest brokers to go along with these practices. Whatever they did, the authorities did it successfully. The Prudential-Bache sales actions produced huge losses for large numbers of clients.

How did this come about? Stockbrokers are the link between the central administration of brokerage firms and their customers. The brokers are to some extent salaried, but they get commissions and advancement within the firm for selling products to their stable of customers. The corruption starts when the incentives to the sales force become nonlinear to the benefits to the customers. A common pattern begins when the organization provides large rewards to the sales force for selling certain products. The sales force is then motivated to sell those "high-bonus" products to customers rather than standard bonus products.

There are a number of reasons that a firm creates "high-bonus" products. There may be legitimate reasons for doing so, but often the reasons, from the point of view of the clients, are illegitimate. We see several such illegitimate reasons as the stories unfold.

Usually the stockbrokers selling these high-bonus products initially believe that these products are good for the customer to own. Brokers assume that the higher management that designed these products did so with an appropriate concern for the financial well-being of the clients who buy these partnerships. Brokers often are provided information from the research group of the organization that claims to document this. They then can do well by doing good, by selling these products to their customers.

Over time, the sales force slowly accumulates information that could indicate that the higher levels of the organization do not have the best interests of the clients in mind. In the stock-brokerage business, this information comes in the form of drops in value of the products and anguished calls from customers. There is an initial reluctance to come to this conclusion, because it means that the incentives already earned by the sales force were tainted by the harmfulness of the products sold. Instead of doing good for their customers, the brokers have done them real harm.

To come to the belief that the products were dangerous or doomed to fail is psychologically very difficult. One would conclude that he or she had been gullible about the assurances given, or, worse, negligent in believing them, that one certainly had not lived up to any fiduciary responsibilities to the customers. And, of course, to conclude that these products are harmful would be to lose a lot of very attractive commissions. The psychological state induced in the brokers here can be described as at the intersection of commitment processes and resistances produced by a psychological version of "sunk costs" (Staw, 1997). Given these processes, naturally one resists concluding that the private placements or the real estate packages are toxic and continues to sell substandard product for high commissions.

Furthermore, even when this conclusion is reached and the sales force generally knows that the products are designed to produce high commissions for the firm and to fail for the customers, the sales force and the sales managers of those forces may find themselves so implicated in dishonest practices that they continue them. They then become the sources of continuing corruption pressure on others who would act ethically. Here the corrupt organization can muster strong economic pressures to bring the sales force to continue the dishonest practices and hide past evidence of those practices. Those who behave honorably lose their jobs, and attempts are made to destroy their careers. Others, seeing what happens to those people, buckle under the pressure and continue to be complicit in cheating clients.

Socialization Into Corruption

Sometimes the workings of psychological principles can be seen with textbook clarity in organizational settings. This example makes clear the ways in which social influence processes cause a dichotomous shift in the ways participants construe their goals and relationships to their organization. Occasionally, this comes in the form of a revelation to some participants, leading them to feel that they now understand for the first time "what is really going on." In Goffman's (1971) useful terminology, they now have a key that enables them to frame the situation. Michael Lewis is the author of *Liar's Poker* (1989), the rueful and terribly funny story of the few years he spent in the training programs and on the trading floors of Salomon Brothers, a then powerful brokerage house. Lewis was a novice salesman for Salomon Brothers; his task was to learn from the traders in the firm which were good bonds to sell and to push those bonds on the small institutional clients whom he was allocated to contact. Lewis had been through a training program and heard the standard material about the corporate code of conduct, duties to customers, and so on.

As Lewis remarked, "I was ignorant and malleable when I advised my first customers.... The people who suffered as a result were, of course, my customers" (Lewis, 1989, p. 163). The customers suffered? Yes. The Salomon Brothers' stance toward novice brokers, called "geeks," had a realpolitik cast:

> There was an excellent reason my jungle guide-manager didn't let me lay my hands on the larger investors. He knew that soft-brained as I was, I was dangerous. His plan was for me to learn on the small clients so that if disaster struck, the effect on overall business of Salomon Brothers would be negligible. It was assumed that I might well put a customer or two out of business. That was part of being a geek. (p. 164)

A Salomon Brothers trader convinced Lewis that AT&T bonds would be good ones to sell to his customers, and Lewis relayed the trader's assurances to a customer, who bought 3 million dollars worth. This triumph was announced on the loudspeaker system—the "hoot" that did a good deal to promote a competitive atmosphere among the sales force.

> The AT&T trader's voice came loudly over the hoot: "Mike Lewis has just sold three million of our AT and T's for us, a great trade for the desk, thank you very much, Mike."

> I was flushed with pride.... But something didn't quite fit. What did he mean, "Our AT and T's"? I hadn't realized the AT&T bonds had been on Salomon's trading books. [Meaning that Salomon owned the bonds and stood to lose its own money if the bonds dropped in price.] I had thought my trader friend had snapped them up from stupid dealers at other firms. *If the bonds were ours to begin with ...*

It began to dawn on Lewis that the trader had tricked Lewis into selling the bonds by saying that the bonds would be a good investment for the customer. A more experienced salesman told Lewis what had really happened, which was that the bonds were terrible investments, that Salomon was dying to get them out of their inventory so they wouldn't take the loss. In the language characteristic of the testosterone-driven culture of the trading floor, the experienced salesman explained what would happen: "'You are going to get fucked,' Dash [experienced trader] said again. 'That's all right because you're just a geek. Geeks were born to be fucked.' He meant this in a nice way, to absolve me, as it were."

Just what had happened to whom, and for what did Lewis need absolution? In the long haul, the customer took the ultimate loss. By selling the bonds to his customer, Lewis had harmed the customer. Lewis had also potentially destroyed his relationship with the customer and ruined chances of future sales to him. Lewis taxed the trader who had lied to him about the bonds, pointing out how it had burned the customer.

"Look," he [the trader] said, losing his patience, "who do you work for, this guy or Salomon Brothers?"

"Who do you work for?" That question haunted salesmen. Whenever a trader screwed a customer and the salesman became upset, the trader would ask the salesman, "Who do you work for anyway?" The message was clear. *You work for Salomon Brothers. You work for me. I pay your bonus at the end of the year. so just shut up, you geek* (p. 167).

As Lewis pointed out, "A policy of screwing investors could lead to ruin. If they ever caught on, we'd have no investors" (p. 167). However, this is the policy that the firm adopted.

Let's go back to "absolution" for a moment. It is a remarkably well-chosen word. Unknowingly, Lewis had committed an act of dubious morality, abusing the trust of a person who depended on him. But Lewis realized this while also discovering that he had an immediate self-presentational choice to make, and that his bonus and other aspects of his future at Salomon might ride on his choice.

I was at once furious and disillusioned. But that didn't solve the problem. Bellyaching to the trader wasn't going to get me anywhere. That much was clear. He'd just dock my bonus at the end of the year. Bellyaching would also make me look like a fool, as if I had actually thought that the customer was going to make money on the AT &Ts. How could anyone be so stupid as to trust a trader? the best thing I could do was to pretend to others at Salomon that I had meant to screw the customer. People would respect that. It was called jamming. I had just jammed bonds, abet unknowingly, for the first time. I had lost my innocence.

Examine this from a psychological perspective. The prototypical geek, at this crossroads, was presented with a complex self-definitional choice but was surrounded by a culture that all but guaranteed the choice he would make. Surrounded on the trading floor by others ready to savagely ostracize a fool, he solved the self-presentational problem of the moment, which was that he looked suspiciously like a fool. He presented himself to his group as a person willing to harm customers—a "jammer" rather than a fool. After he had done so, by processes familiar to psychologists, his self-definition followed. The socialization apparatus of the firm had produced what it was designed to produce, which was a person who would harm clients for the benefit of the firm. As the song says about somebody else, Salomon Brothers gets the gold mine, the customer gets the shaft.

The role of the conformity pressures put on by more experienced sales representatives and traders is critical here, and it is reinforced by the bonus system. As the preceding quotes indicate, to present oneself as unwilling to jam, and to criticize either the wisdom or the morality of jamming customers, would jeopardize one's bonus. Why? Because Salomon Brothers, like many other firms, paid high bonuses, designed to motivate behavior of the sales force. The bonuses were awarded not solely on the basis of objective criteria, such as sales volume, but on more intangible and undefined criteria as well. So there was good reason to suspect that a person would lose money for making waves within the organization. This is an effective way of causing people to self-monitor to avoid committing possible deviant actions. People are loss averse, and for them to lose bonus money that their sales volume had already "earned" for them by some actions that the group judged deviant or disloyal would be very painful indeed. Salomon Brothers, by tying bonuses to vague criteria of "loyalty," had created an extremely powerful engine for socialization into immorality.

To sum up, the Prudential-Bache and Salomon Brothers cases are both examples of the ways in which superiors in an organization, working through perverse incentive systems, can create an organizational culture that puts high and highly destructive pressures on the subordinate actors, pressures designed to get them to willingly take unethical actions that damage innocent people. The corporate code of conduct, if it exists, plays little role in these cases. In fact, both corporations had codes of conduct, high-sounding principles about working for the benefit of the clients. What the workers for the corporation learned, as they observed the actions of those more experienced who had advanced within the corporation, was that the code of conduct was "nonoperational."

The Salomon Brothers case also shows us how the corporate culture offered a perspective that hid from the actors the fact that their behavior was immoral by giving them a vocabulary that provided an alternative interpretation of their actions. The perspective was strikingly similar to the one that sometimes prevails in the locker rooms of professional sports teams, testosterone laden and full of justifications for aggression against other groups, and contempt for those "softies" who might advance moral counterarguments against current practices. The Prudential case shows us how a reign of terror administered from the upper levels of the hierarchy, and ruthlessly amplified down the chain of command, can crush most moral opposition.

It would not be unreasonable for the reader to complain that the cases I have presented so far have stacked the deck toward producing immoral behavior by organizational members because that is what the organizational superiors desired. True. So next I consider a case in which the organizational superiors did not wish to produce the exploitative sales behavior that emerged and indeed made major efforts to move to an ethically based sales system. And yet, because of the message-conveying attributes of the old sales incentive system that the organization had left in place, the sales force took it as appropriate to revert to older sales practices that were exploitative. The "villain" in this story is the incentive system, which overrode the restraints intended to be provided by the operation of ethical good judgments of the acting individuals, by the careful communication of action purposes by superiors, and by the existence of a corporate code of ethics.

The Force Is Against Us: The Xerox Case

The Xerox Corporation not surprisingly rents and sells copiers, using regional sales forces that make sales calls on large accounts and small, mom-and-pop stores that make only a few Xerox copies a day. The sales staff is, as they say, "on commission," which is corporate shorthand for the fact that their compensation is partially wage-based but also partially based on some metric of the sales they make and the rentals they arrange. The account I give here of the ways in which their incentive system overcame the marketing philosophy of the corporation in one district comes from David Dorsey's (1994) *The Force,* a book he wrote based on his observations of one of the sales teams in action. Dorsey observed the team with the permission of the Xerox Corporation, who expected the story to be about the unequivocal success of their new, ethically based marketing strategy. Instead it is a story of the perversion of the marketing strategy brought about by the workings of the incentive system, and the tendency of people to revert to old habits. Because the marketing strategy was based on "total quality" principles, it had a strong ethical component.

The sales representatives were partially salaried, but what really loomed large in their cognitive maps was the bonus system in place. The bonus system stretched out over the year and culminated not only in end-of-the-year prizes but in end-of-the-year rewards that were tied to achieving those prizes.

And not only end-of-the-year prizes. What the book reveals, and what I had not realized, is the incredibly powerful forces that are unleashed by sales competitions between different units of the sales staff. The corporation cleverly controls behavior by making the sales competition immediate, rather than simply a final target many months in the future, thus keeping a constant pressure on the staff to make sales now rather than tomorrow.

> The contests, the parties, the skits, the whole act—it turned work into a fantasy, draining away the monotonous reality of the daily labor, giving managers an excuse to post everyone's results on a wall. It was all out in the open. The very look and feel of the office became a constant pinprick, an endless emotional goad, pushing everyone toward greater results. You couldn't walk into the office without seeing your face or your name posted beside a number—and everyone could mock your failure or envy your success. The very walls themselves taunted and triggered emotions. The building seemed to be built not of wood and nails but of mirrors. Everywhere you looked, you saw yourself exposed as a loser or a winner, a Nobody or a Somebody. (Dorsey, 1995, p. 77)

It is not that the units (and individuals within those units) compete just for the bonuses associated with reaching and surpassing sales quotas. It is rather that they compete for the glory, the self-validation, the acclaim of others, the often alcohol-propelled fun of the parties given for those who "do best," and the extended party atmosphere of the week at a resort that the best sales force wins. The financial bonuses, although important for the salespersons and often counted on to maintain their lifestyles, are only a necessary but rather pale validation of these other events. This is what a well-administered bonus system does, and it is very powerful in controlling human behavior, especially the behavior of those who gravitate to the life of a salesperson and self-select themselves for these rewards.

In the bad old days before the Xerox Corporation revised its marketing strategy, the sales force did what they perceived as their job; they traveled to large, medium-size, and small companies and sold or rented Xerox machines for the use of those companies. Using their charm, what trust they could develop in their counterparts in the companies, and back of the envelope calculations, they recommended Xerox machines to their customers, and their recommendations were often accepted. The costs of the rentals to the companies often could be obscured by shifting lease lengths, bundling in or out the cost of replacement cartridges, front loading or back loading the leases, and so on. The per month expense, which was what the small company often focused on, could be made to come out to just under what the company could afford. Sometimes the company decided it could afford the machine because of the presumed savings it would produce in related expenses such as printing, which might or might not come true.

Often in their evening unwindings with others on the sales force, the sales representatives admitted, or bragged, that they had rented copiers with capabilities and capacities far in excess of what the customer really required. Often the costs of the rentals to the companies, stretching many months into the future, were a considerable burden to those companies. Some companies, perhaps those who relied most heavily on the "expertise" of the sales representatives, went under.

> Fred sold for Xerox for many years when the only guiding principle was to write as much business as possible, as early as possible, by any means possible. They stopped at nothing; they did whatever it took to make their goals. When he arrived in Cleveland, reps were bending rules to get orders and then forcing the company to accommodate the orders. Customers were unhappy. (Dorsey, 1995, pp. 134–135)

Of course, there were consequences. Small companies discovered that their businesses did not grow at the rate they had been led to project and that their rental expenses were a major drain on their resources. The salesperson who had so confidently joined in their growth predictions "regretfully" could not change the conditions of the rental deal for the oversized copier gathering dust in the corner. In larger companies, other negative aspects of the leases became apparent. Cynicism about the Xerox Corporation developed, along with resistance to signing further leases with them. Other copier companies competed for sales and leases and, increasingly, won the competitions.

Faced with this, the Xerox Corporation foresightedly changed their marketing goals, based on the principles of total quality management (TQM). In this instance, that involved putting the needs of the customer first and counting on the successful filling of those needs to build the trust and credibility that would produce long-term profitable relationships with those customers.

The task of the salesperson, then, was to become a source of analysis for the customer company, suggesting ways to achieve what the customer needed to achieve, ways to make new and innovative use of Xeroxes to reduce materials that needed to be sent to outside printers, ways to achieve savings by tying into existing computer networks. Putting the needs of the customer first would build long-term relationships that would give Xerox a profit that was not only "decent" in the slang sense of the term but also decent in an ethical sense. "Treat your customer as you would treat yourself. Give your customer exactly what your customer needs to improve his business of his life. Don't just sell a product, *satisfy a customer*" (Dorsey, 1995, p. 133).

As Dorsey makes clear, this kind of approach is an ethical one.

But back to the Xerox sales force: There the standard incentive system stayed in place, with all of the pressures and joys that I have described. Nor, as far as I can tell, was any system established for determining when a salesperson was deviating from the TQM approach to the needs of the customer. Lease agreements were written and put into action by the Xerox Corporation without any scrutiny about whether the order was plausible on TQM grounds. In other words, the incentive system could deliver rewards for performances that the Xerox Corporation did not wish to happen.

As one could expect, over time, the incentive system influenced the practice of the new, ethical, system for the analysis of customer needs. We can imagine what happened to the teams of salespersons. A rumor spread that another regional group was back to jamming product, and the next reporting period that force led the competition. Closer to home, on one's own sales force, another salesperson was observed stretching the rental period of the copier out to near infinity, so that the monthly payments would be lower but the machine would become obsolete before it was paid for. And so on. And the company did nothing. The inference was that the company approved. What may actually have been the case was that the company leaders were unaware that these things were happening, because they did not have the acumen to see that they needed to monitor for them.

Increasingly, as the end of the year came closer, and the big contest came near an end, the old sales routines broke through. Sales representatives sold or rented oversized machines to small stores; hid the price of supplies in the rental, which were then "given free" to induce sales; wrote leases disadvantageous to Xerox to squeeze the last orders out of the quarterly period and win sales contests. The company was back to square one with its sales practices. In fact, it was worse off: The vocabulary of TQM was used to cover jamming product on the customers, causing another layer of mistrust in the customers.

SUMMARY

I began by sketching four interlocking facts about influence patterns in organizations. In organizations, hierarchical structures of legitimate authority exist and it is generally acceptable for subordinates to follow the directives they receive from superiors. The directives are assumed to be first the most effective way of fulfilling the organization's goals and, second, a morally acceptable way of doing so.

Because organizational communication patterns are often radically incomplete, the directives given may not fully specify either how a directive is to be fulfilled or the precautions and limits that need to be placed on its fulfillment. Given "the curse of knowledge," many superiors assume that subordinates know the context that lies behind the directives they give, which is assumed to fill in what the subordinate needs to know to guide those actions. But the subordinate, in fact, does not know these contextual pieces of information.

Perhaps because they have had disturbing experiences with actions taken by subordinates that do not fit ethical standards, modern organizations often try to avoid future immoral actions by propagating an organizational code of conduct. The problem with organizational codes is twofold: First, they must be written at such a high level of abstraction that they cannot unequivocally generate a decision about whether at least some particular concrete actions are "against the code" or not. Second, and relatedly, many organizational actions that prove to be morally wrong are the products of individual actions by many persons, each of whom may not have been able to see the wrongness of his or her own actions. Thus the code is not seen as having relevance for their actions. This is one of the consequences of the fragmentation of production introduced by many modern manufacturing methods, for instance.

All of this means that subordinates are left to choose among a range of actions that are consistent with the directives they are given, without being sure if the actions they choose are either the maximally efficient actions or the morally appropriate ones. Given this, they look to what feedback they receive after they have taken a certain action to guide them about its efficiency and appropriateness. In organizations, the feedback that often disambiguates the value of the actions that were taken is given by the corporate incentive system. An imaginative sales representative works out a new way of approaching potential markets for the company's products, or a new discount structure to offer a customer, and the entire sales force watches to see if she receives the end-of-the-quarter bonus on the discounted sales. A vice president of manufacturing reduces costs by reducing the rate of inspection of products, which saves money in the present but may lead to a higher rate of defective product in the future. Does the company approve of this? A large end-of-quarter bonus to the vice president will be interpreted as signaling corporate approval. Sometimes, interpreting the workings of the incentive system as signaling approval is a correct interpretation. Other times, the corporate structure may not be aware of the particular action taken by the subordinate to reach the goal and would be outraged if they did know. But there will be a tendency for the subordinates, gripped in their own "curse of knowledge," to assume that the superiors were cognizant of the exact nature of the actions taken to fulfill the goal, and thus to assume that the organization not only approves of those actions but actively desires others in the organization to take similar actions.

I then told stories in which two or more of these systems were in operation, governing the behavior of persons in subordinate positions in organizations. The stories were designed to lead you to this conclusion: The system in place is often insufficient to prevent behavior that cuts ethical corners, harms the consumer of the organizational output, hides from the upper levels of the organization the real practices of the staff, and otherwise inflicts damage.

Of course, sometimes this is exactly what the organization in question desires. The management of Prudential clearly desired to swindle those who bought their products. Company leaders have bonused sales forces for selling dubious or harmful products to customers, cut costs in ways that reduce future profitability, turned in high quarterly earnings, cashed in options on the stocks that have soared in price as a function of the inflated quarterly earnings, and moved on to other companies.

But these are not the analytically most interesting cases. The most interesting cases involve the inadvertent workings of the dynamics that I have sketched here. These are the organizations in which the management does not desire the system to take actions that will harm workers, clients, customers, or the public, and yet the organization travels down a path in which those sorts of actions are taken, become routine, and eventually are discovered, to the detriment of the organization. I have tried to show that the combination of the complex communication characteristics of the organization, which is relatively weakly controlled by the existence of the necessarily general and abstract code of conduct, is responsible for this inadvertent drift into practices of dubious ethicality. To conclude, I simply want to highlight the role of the incentive system in producing these destructive consequences. An incentive system is designed to cause actions that maximize the incentives that the organizational workers receive, and it generally succeeds in that design. The messages conveyed by the incentive system, at the extreme, have the power to cause people to take actions that they would not regard as ethical. However, these messages perhaps more often shape workers' definitions of actions that are acceptable or "ethical" in the context in which they are uttered. We all know the ways in which this works, the ways in which the customer is cast as the enemy or the dupe, the organizational competitors as behaving in much worse ways, and so on.

REFERENCES

Camerer, C., Loewenstein, G., & Weber, M. (1989). The curse of knowledge in economic settings: An experimental analysis. *Journal of Political Economy, 97,* 1232–1254.

Dorsey, D. (1994) *The force.* New York: Random House.

Eichenwald, K. (1995). *Serpent on the rock.* New York: Harper Business.

French, J. R. P., Jr., & Raven, B. (1959). The bases of social power. In D. Cartwright (Ed.), *Studies in social power* (pp. 150–167). Ann Arbor, MI: Research Center for Group Dynamics, University of Michigan.

Goffman, E. (1974). *Frame analysis: An essay on the organization of experience.* New York: Harper & Row.

Keysar, B., Barr, D., & Horton, W. (1998). The egocentric basis of language use: Insights from a processing approach. *Current Directions in Psychological Science, 7,* 46–50.

Keysar, B., Ginzel, L., & Bazerman, M. (1995). States of affairs and states of mind: The effect of knowledge of beliefs. *Organizational Behavior and Human Decision Processes, 64,* 283–293

Lewis, M. (1989). *Liar's poker.* New York: Norton.

March, J., & Heath, C. (1994). *How decisions happen: A primer on decision-making.* New York: The Free Press.

Simon, H. (1997). *Administrative behavior: A study of decision-making processes in administrative organizations* (4th Ed.). New York: The Free Press.

Staw, B. (1997). The escalation of commitment: An update and appraisal. In Z. Shapira (Ed.), *Organizational decision making: Cambridge series on judgment and decision making* (pp. 191–215). New York: Cambridge University Press.

5 Confronting Organizational Transgressions

Michael E. Roloff
Northwestern University

Gaylen D. Paulson
University of Texas at Austin

To enhance the quality and survivability of a social system, societies generate rules of conduct that further the interests of the members and that inhibit disruptive, exploitative, and nonsupportive actions (Shimanoff, 1980). Unfortunately, individuals' behaviors do not always conform to such codes. For example, although social systems typically condemn telling lies, lying appears to be relatively common, with individuals reporting that they tell one or two falsehoods each day (DePaulo, Kashy, Kirkendol, Wyer, & Epstein, 1996). Moreover, more than 70% of those who have told a lie report that if given a chance to do it over again, they would still choose to deceive (DePaulo et al., 1996). Even though deception can be detected and when discovered can have negative consequences (McCornack & Levine, 1990), individuals often do not regard their lies as serious, engage in very little planning prior to lying, and do not expect to get caught (DePaulo et al., 1996).

Businesses are not immune from such everyday questionable conduct. Organizational members engage in a wide variety of wrongful actions, including some that are explicitly illegal (Harper, 1990; Robinson & Bennett, 1995). Although formal organizational rules and professional codes of conduct inhibit some undesirable actions, they do not guarantee their elimination. In a survey of human resource professionals, only 50% reported that they frequently used their company's written standards for ethical conduct to guide their behavior and decisions (Institute of Management and Administration, 1998). And in a survey of office professionals, 17% of the respondents indicated that they had notarized a document that they had not witnessed being signed (DeMars, 1997).

These various rule violations do not always go unnoticed. In the aforementioned survey of human resource professionals, 54% reported that they had observed workplace conduct that violated the law or the organization's standards of ethical business conduct (Institute of Management and Administration, 1998). More than 30% of office professionals indicated that they had seen others engage in transgressions ranging from filing falsified time sheets and travel expenses to releasing confidential information about hiring, layoffs, salaries, and performance evaluations (DeMars, 1997). Yet noticing transgressions does not mean that they are always confronted. For example, in a survey of federal employees, slightly more than 70% of respondents failed to report an observed transgression to another individual or group (Miceli & Near, 1984). Because unethical actions may lead to long-term negative consequences (Murphy, 1993), and because organizational codes of ethics mandate that observed violations should be reported (Mathews, 1988), such inaction itself may constitute an ethical breach. Moreover, some individuals might act in a way that directly supports a wrongful action. In a survey of secretaries, 88% reported that they had lied on behalf of their bosses (Mulrine & Schrof, 1998) and more than a third of office professionals indicated that they sometimes or often lied to others about their supervisors' whereabouts and activities (DeMars, 1997).

The aforementioned research begs the following question: Why do individuals act in a manner that ignores, or even supports, the ethical violations of others and thereby run the risk of being held accountable should such transgressions be discovered? Intuitively, one might expect that involvement in a "conspiracy of silence" results from the direct orders of authority figures and/or from job requirements. Both experimental studies and historical cases document that subordinates sometimes comply with the orders of their superiors even when they believe the orders to be morally wrong (see Kelman & Hamilton, 1989). However, although one can find evidence of such processes, they do not seem to be common. When office professionals were asked why they went along with an unethical action, the aforementioned survey found that only 2.2% reported that the action resulted from a direct order, 0.4% reported that their compliance resulted from fear of reprisals from their supervisor, and 8.8% indicated that it was part of their job description (DeMars, 1997). Moreover, survey and experimental evidence indicates that threatened retaliation for reporting transgressions is not significantly related to the willingness to report wrongdoing (Miceli, Dozier, & Near, 1991; Near & Jenson, 1983; Near & Miceli, 1986). These findings suggest that the decision to remain silent about witnessed transgressions typically arises from factors other than authority-based compliance. Hence, to better understand such inaction, we need to more fully explore the factors that influence a person's decision to directly confront observed wrongdoing. In this chapter, we do so by adopting a social confrontation framework. We first highlight some of the unique insights offered via this perspective, examine critical processes evident at each stage of a social confrontation, and identify issues for future consideration by organizational scholars.

A SOCIAL CONFRONTATION APPROACH

Newell and Stutman (1988) broadly defined a social confrontation as "a particular kind of communication episode initiated when one person communicates to another that his or her behavior has violated (or is violating) a rule or expectation for appropriate conduct within the relationship or situation" (p. 271). Individuals who initiate a confrontation report that they wish to accomplish a variety of strategic goals, including ending the objectionable behavior, venting frustration about the rule violation, maintaining a strong relationship with the transgressor, seeking retribution, and obtaining information about the reasons for the transgression (Stutman & Newell, 1990). Once the confrontation is initiated, both the confronter and the alleged transgressor engage in a variety of interaction behaviors that to some degree are aimed at resolving the issue at hand (Newell & Stutman, 1991).

The notion of a social confrontation differs from frameworks typically used to analyze how individuals respond to witnessed transgressions. For example, Kelman and Hamilton (1989) used a social influence model to explain crimes of obedience. They characterized social influence situations as those in which "an influencing agent offers some new behavior or attitude to a person and somehow communicates that the person's chance of achieving his goals depend on whether or not that he adopts the behavior" (p. 79). In the context of crimes of obedience, a superior's orders cause a subordinate to enact a behavior that he or she views as wrong or to take an action with which he or she agrees but does not feel empowered to enact. Such influence processes can play a role in social confrontations. Illegitimate orders to a subordinate could prompt a social confrontation just as a social confrontation could prompt authorities to direct the subordinate to comply. However, social confrontations could take place with little attempted social influence from authorities. As we noted earlier, not all transgressions arise from direct orders from authorities. A person could simply observe a transgression (e.g., observe a superior sexually harassing someone) and then choose to confront the transgressor. Furthermore, not all transgressions are enacted by authority figures. For example, in the previously cited survey of human resource professionals, 45% reported that they had observed subordinates lying to their superiors (Institute of Management and Administration, 1998). In such cases, either a coworker or a superior could initiate a social confrontation with the lying subordinate. Hence, social confrontation episodes may include interactions of a different nature than those involving social influence from authorities.

In addition to providing insight into a wider range of transgression situations, models of social confrontation provide a different perspective into the processes that drive such encounters. Social influence models focus on the transgressor as the primary source of influence as he or she attempts to induce a subordinate to follow an order. Social confrontation frameworks characterize the witness of a transgression as being more active, as he or she attempts to convince the transgressor to explain or cease the objectionable action. Thus, influence messages should originate from the confronter rather than the transgressor.

Near and Micelli (1987) developed a model of whistle-blowing that also conceives of the witness of a transgression as an active change agent. They define whistle-blowers as follows:

> organizational members (including former members and job applicants) who disclose illegal, immoral, or illegitimate (i.e., not legitimate within the authority structure in the Weberian sense) practices under the control of their employer to persons or organizations who may be able to effect action. (p. 330)

Although the processes involved with whistle-blowing are similar to those observed in social confrontations, they differ in at least one critical respect. The focus of research on whistle-blowing is on the antecedents and consequences of reporting observed transgressions to groups or individuals other than the transgressor. Although the person being confronted may be responsible for those who committed the transgression, that individual is not accused of having enacted the wrongdoing. Hence, there is little analysis within that literature focused on whether the witness confronted the transgressor and, if such a confrontation occurred, what took place during the encounter. By contrast, social confrontation research is focused primarily on the interaction between the witness and the transgressor. This difference is not inconsequential. By directly confronting a wrongdoer, the witness sacrifices anonymity. Although organizational procedures may not be able to protect the anonymity of a whistle-blower, a social confrontation ensures that the transgressor can identify the witness. Consequently, the witness invites scrutiny of his or her own motives and behaviors. Indeed, for face-saving reasons, the transgressor may counterattack, putting the accuser on the defensive.

With these alternative approaches in mind, we see research on social confrontations as providing relevant and unique insights into the processes related to how witnesses respond to observed transgressions. Although social confrontation research has not focused specifically on ethical breaches within business contexts, we believe that this scholarship may suggest new insights and directions for these areas. Accordingly, we examine this literature with an eye toward highlighting such linkages.

STAGES OF SOCIAL CONFRONTATION

Although the notion of a social confrontation episode implies a bounded time sequence, most researchers who adopt this framework conceive of stages within the episode. In studying relational transgressions, Roloff, Soule, & Carey (in press) found that social confrontation could be divided into three stages: preconfrontation, initial confrontation, and postconfrontation. We organize our literature review around these stages.

Preconfrontation

By definition, a social confrontation begins when a witness initiates contact with a transgressor about some wrongdoing. However, researchers also have focused on the processes that occur before the initiation. Although some confrontations occur immediately after observing wrongdoing, some individuals report that they wait an extended time before initiating a confrontation (Johnson & Roloff, 1998). Scholarship informs as to two processes that occur before confrontation: sense-making and action formation.

Sense-Making. For a social confrontation to occur, a witness must first perceive that a rule violation has taken place. To some degree, this implies that witnesses act in a manner similar to a jury. In effect, they combine relevant information about an action sequence into a story that is then compared to legal, organizational, or lay conceptions of rules of conduct (e.g., Pennington & Hastie, 1992). If the action sequence is inconsistent with rules, witnesses can feel confident that wrongful action has taken place.

However, this process can be fraught with ambiguity. Not all potentially transgressive behaviors are sufficiently direct so that one can confidently label them rule violations. For example, authority figures may construct messages for their subordinates that are sufficiently ambiguous that one cannot tell whether the target is being ordered to enact wrongdoing or merely is being requested to do so and/or what exactly the target is being ordered or requested to do (Kelman & Hamilton, 1989). Furthermore, not all sexually harassing comments explicitly demand sexual activity from the target (McCann & McGinn, 1992). Hence, when speech acts are indirect, observers look for contextual features to judge their coercive (Vollbrecht, Roloff, & Paulson, 1997) or harassing (Solomon & Williams, 1997) nature.

In addition, individuals may not have witnessed directly wrongdoing but were told about it from others. In such cases, the individual may second-guess the veracity of the report until he or she can verify it (cf. Hewes & Graham, 1989). In such cases, the individual may wait to act until he or she actually observes evidence of a transgression or directly witnesses a new case.

When trying to make sense of a transgression, individuals may engage in three types of information seeking. First, they may consult their memory of the event to determine whether they have accurately interpreted the action. Research indicates that individuals sometimes replay conflict episodes in their memories (Zagacki, Edwards, & Honeycutt, 1992) to make sense of them, and mulling about a conflict can impact judgments of the severity of the event and the degree to which the partner is blamed for the problem (Cloven & Roloff, 1991). Second, individuals may monitor the ongoing behavior of the transgressor for information about the observed event. In some cases, witnesses may observe the wrongdoer's action passively but in other cases may manipulate circumstances actively so as to gauge the person's reaction. Indeed, Baxter and Wilmot (1984) found evidence that individuals sometimes put their relational partners through "secret tests" or "experiments" to reduce their uncertainty about the partner's affection for them. Finally, witnesses may turn to others for information about the event and/or alternative perspectives. If others observed the event, they may be able to verify the observer's perception. Even if they did not observe the specific action, they may be able to provide insight into its frequency, cause, and consequences.

Although the aforementioned research was conducted on transgressive episodes within interpersonal relationships, it is likely that witnesses of organizational wrongdoing also may go through a period in which they delay confrontation until they feel more confident of their perceptions. For example, Near and Miceli (1987) noted that whistle-blowers go through a stage in which they recognize and assess wrongdoing. In some cases, witnesses turn to others for their opinion of the event, and when the event is viewed by the group as ambiguous or not serious, witnesses become convinced that there is insufficient basis for action and even may ignore future instances of similar behavior. Hence, sense-making activity plays a critical role in determining whether a person will confront a transgressor. Next, we amplify on the decision to confront.

Action Formation.   Assuming that an individual is sufficiently confident that wrongdoing has occurred, he or she faces the question of what to do about it. Fundamentally, this question requires the person to decide whether to confront the wrongdoer. Newell and Stutman (1991) asked individuals to report the kinds of situations in which they would be inclined to confront a rule violator. Their analysis of open-ended responses indicates that individuals react to seven situational features. First, individuals focus on the degree to which the transgression requires urgent action. If a transgression might result in serious harm or has been frequent, then the pressure to confront increases. Second, individuals cue on the nature of their relationship with the transgressor. They consider their relative power as well as the intimacy of the relationship. Third, they consider whether they have a responsibility to confront the other person. If they perceive that their role requires confrontation, they will do so. Fourth, individuals use their impressions of the transgressor to forecast how that person will react when confronted. The more negative the anticipated reaction, the less likely a confrontation will take place. Fifth, a witness considers how much of his or her personal resources will have to be committed in the confrontation. A confrontation may require psychological, emotional, physical, time, and even financial investment, and not all witnesses are willing to undergo such costs. Sixth, individuals seem to consider the appropriateness of the time and place when deciding whether to confront wrongdoing. Some individuals choose to wait for more appropriate settings. Seventh, individuals consider the rewards and costs of the confrontation, including the likelihood that a confrontation will cause the rule violation to cease and what effect the confrontation might have on their relationship with the transgressor. In the same study, Newell and Stutman conducted a discriminant analysis to determine which factors best predicted the initiation of a confrontation. The five best predictors of choosing to confront were (a) the witness felt a responsibility to say something to the transgressor, (b) the witness felt that a confrontation would personally benefit himself or herself, (c) the witness felt he or she had the ability to confront the transgressor, (d) there was no person other than the witness who could better handle the problem, and (e) the witness could no longer tolerate the transgression.

Assuming that a person chooses to enact or to avoid a confrontation, he or she then considers how to operationalize that choice. Research suggests that individuals who intend to confront a rule violator develop a plan of action designed to achieve three performance goals (Stutman & Newell, 1990). First, during the confrontation, they want to present all of the relevant arguments related to the wrongdoing. Second, individuals want their presentation to be clear and organized. Third, they want to enact behaviors that will prevent the transgressor from countercomplaining and thereby turning the tables on them. To accomplish these goals, individuals often report that they practice what they will say hours and sometimes days before the confrontation. Confronters report that when time permits, they consider and evaluate alternative word choices and arguments, often rehearsing them in their minds out loud to themselves, or in front of friends. Such elaborate preconfrontation planning is most likely with serious transgressions and with confrontations involving an authority figure. Confronters report that practice results in a variety of benefits, including greater ability to control their emotions during the confrontation, improved confidence, more articulate presentation, and better ability to counter the responses of the transgressor.

Although the decision to avoid a confrontation might be seen as a simple, passive response, such is not the case. A person who chooses to remain silent may anticipate having to learn to cope with an ongoing objectionable action that he or she might even be seen as tacitly endorsing. Such a future might well be stressful. Hence, the person who chooses to be nonconfrontational may engage in a variety of behaviors to help alleviate his or her stress. For example, the person might look for reasons to justify his or her inaction. When asked why they have not confronted their relational partner over a negative behavior, individuals report a variety of reasons, frequently citing the unimportance of the behavior (Solomon & Roloff, 1996). Although it is possible that some objectionable actions are indeed unworthy of confrontation, such a judgment could be a rationalization for powerlessness. Recently, Solomon and Samp (1998) found that individuals who are relationally dependent, or who perceive their partner as having coercive potential, are more likely than relationally powerful individuals to justify nonconfrontation on the basis of problem insignificance. Alternatively, passive observers of transgressions may alleviate their stress by complaining to significant others. Individuals report that they often turn to friends and family to complain about the behavior of others, most often with the goal of venting frustration (Alicke et al., 1992).

In addition to coping with stress, nonconfrontational individuals may formulate a strategy designed to distance themselves from an objectionable action. For example, Belk and Snell (1988) interviewed individuals about how they avoided complying with a relational partner's requests. An analysis of the responses yielded 24 avoidance strategies, of which 7 appear to be nonconfrontational: dodging the request by changing the subject, avoiding the requester, procrastinating until it is too late to comply with the request, ignoring the request or the requester, withdrawing emotionally from the requester, fabricating excuses for noncompliance, and pretending that one is unable to comply. Although such indirect strategies may not end an objectionable behavior, they may provide a means by which an individual can limit his or her involvement with it.

As in the case of sense-making, most of the aforementioned research has been conducted in relational contexts. However, similar processes may be at work in organizations. For example, Near and Miceli (1987) argued that when deciding whether to blow the whistle on wrongdoing, individuals account for how coworkers will react to their disclosure. Indeed, anticipating negative group reactions has a chilling effect on expressing complaints. In the earlier mentioned survey of human resource professionals, of those who witnessed wrongdoing but did not report it, 96% cited a fear of being accused of not being a team player, and 38% indicated that their inaction was due, in part, to fear of retaliation or retribution from coworkers (Institute of Management and Administration, 1998). Even perceived group indifference to ethical violations may chill the expression of complaints. Of those human resource professionals who withheld complaints, 58% did so because they felt that nobody else cared about business ethics (Institute of Management and Administration, 1998), and in a survey of office professionals, 8% said they went along with an unethical practice because everybody else did and 3% did so because they believed nobody else cared about the practice (DeMars, 1997).

Furthermore, Near and Miceli (1987) argued that witnesses of organizational wrongdoing must decide how to confront it. In some cases, they may choose to confront the problem through political activity designed to enlist the support of more powerful others. A recent dissertation (Van Camp, 1997) found that organizational members may have a rather wide range of resistance strategies. When faced with a wrongful order from a superior, organizational members sometimes enact rather direct strategies such as explicit refusals or objections, but in other cases they enact the same nonconfrontational strategies identified by Belk and Snell (1988).

Thus, when allowed sufficient time, individuals who observe organizational wrongdoing may engage in extensive sense-making and action formation before initially confronting the transgressor. Indeed, we suspect that some individuals go through several cycles of sense-making and action formation as they internally and externally deliberate about what to do. However, at some point, circumstances may force the witness to make a decision and some may choose confrontation. We turn to that next.

Initial Confrontation

Newell and Stutman (1989/90) argued that a social confrontation begins when a person complains to another that his or her behavior violates a rule or expectation for appropriate conduct. Their analysis of accounts of social confrontations indicates that complaints vary in the degree to which they are focused on the behavior of the transgressor or the emotional reactions of confronter, and the degree to which the message content is implicit or explicit. When complaining about a specific behavior, confronters may be extremely indirect by hinting that there is a problem, moderately indirect by asking if a problematic behavior occurred, or highly direct by blaming or accusing the transgressor of acting inappropriately. When expressing emotional reactions, confronters are often indirect by nonverbally displaying emotions (e.g., acting upset) or more direct by making emotional statements (e.g., telling the transgressor they are upset).

The type of complaint that is used to initiate a confrontation can set the tone for the encounter. For example, hinting, asking if a transgression occurred, or "acting out of sorts" are so indirect that another might not understand them to be complaints (Newell & Stutman, 1989/90). However, to directly accuse another of a transgression may be insulting and may cause the receiver to become defensive (Stamp, Vangelisti, & Daly, 1992). Although individuals report that they prefer people who confront them to be specific about the undesirable behavior, they dislike personal attacks (Alberts, 1989). Hence, researchers have attempted to find ways in which a confronter might be sufficiently direct so as to be understood to be complaining without being perceived to be offensive. For example, complaints that have an assertive rather aggressive tone and that express less intense negative emotions prompt fewer negative emotional reactions and behavioral resistance than do complaints that are accusatory or express more intense negative emotional reactions (Kubany, Richard, Bauer, & Muraoka, 1992). Moreover, Benoit and Benoit (1990) found that forms of complaints that mitigate against loss of face (e.g., statements that acknowledge shared responsibility for a transgression, polite requests to stop the transgression) are judged to be more appropriate and effective than are those that aggravate face loss (e.g., insults, accusations, commands to stop).

A complaint requires a response, and analyses of complaint sequences suggest that a transgressor may respond in three ways (Newell & Stutman, 1989/90). First, the transgressor might acknowledge the validity of the complaint and offer sympathy, a remedy, or an excuse. Second, the transgressor might attack the validity of the complaint by ignoring the complaint, countercomplaining against the confronter, or challenging whether the action occurred or whether it violated a rule. Third, the transgressor might argue that he or she is not responsible for the transgression and direct the confronter to talk to another. Not surprisingly, confronters report that the desired responses to a complaint include acknowledgment and agreement that there is a problem, remaining calm, and offering to work toward a constructive solution (Alberts, 1989). The least desirable responses include ignoring the complaint, arguing, denying the complaint, or countercomplaining (Alberts, 1989).

Examination of transcripts of complaint sequences within marital interactions suggests that initiations and responses can combine into six interaction patterns (Alberts & Driscoll, 1992). First, a complaint may be met initially with resistance, and after some arguing, the individuals may refocus the responsibility for the transgression away from the person who was confronted toward some third party. Second, individuals may enact a responsive pattern in which each engages in information seeking followed by validation of the expressed opinion. Third, the target of the complaint may provide excuses for the behavior that causes the confronter to downplay the seriousness of the transgression. Fourth, the target may choose not to address the complaint by ignoring it, shifting the topic, or telling an unrelated joke. Fifth, the target may respond to the complaint by denying its validity or by trying to ignore it, but the confronter is unresponsive to either move and continues to hold the partner responsible for the transgression. Sixth, partners may escalate their confrontation by repeating complaints and denials, countercomplaining against one another, and generally becoming more hostile as the confrontation unfolds.

As a confrontation continues, individuals seek some way to close it off (Vuchinich, 1986). Newell and Stutman (1988) hypothesized that confrontations may end in a variety of ways. In some cases, a transgression is acknowledged and some remedy is offered to the aggrieved party. In others, individuals may create legislation to prevent future transgressions, revise existing rules to adapt to new circumstances, or reaffirm commitment to conform to the existing rules. Of course, some confrontations end with no agreement at all. Indeed, when individuals enact interaction patterns in which they mitigate the seriousness of their problems, refocus the cause of the problem on third parties, and are responsive to each other's points of view, they are more likely to reach an agreement than are those who pass on commenting about the complaint, or those who press or escalate their attacks on each other (Alberts & Driscoll, 1992).

Thus, the nature of the initial confrontation can be crucial in dealing with transgressions. If handled in an appropriate fashion, undesirable behavior might be ended with minimal problems. Guides to establishing ethical organizations often prescribe confrontational actions that are consistent with the aforementioned research (e.g., DeMars, 1997). Unfortunately, the absence of research focused on ethics-based confrontations within organizations makes it difficult to evaluate the efficacy of such prescriptions.

Postconfrontation

Even when the initial confrontation has been closed, one should not assume that no other confrontations will occur. As noted earlier, some confrontations end with no agreement, and the problematic behavior continues. Even when reaching an agreement, some individuals may find their accords to be unworkable or undesirable, such that further transgressions occur. Thus, individuals may re-engage one another. These behaviors might be conceived as linked confrontational episodes or what Trapp and Hoff (1985) called "serial arguing."

One can identify two patterns across linked confrontations. First, individuals may find themselves caught in an "argumentative rut" in which their statements become predictable (Johnson & Roloff, 1998). When individuals perceive their serial arguments to have become predictable, they become pessimistic about ever being able to resolve them, which erodes relational satisfaction and commitment (Johnson & Roloff, 1998).

Rather than becoming scripted, confrontations may become increasingly coercive. Pruitt, Parker, and Mikolic (1997) found that a person who violated a rule to share supplies often was subjected to increasing pressure by other group members. A linear progression of confrontational messages was observed beginning with polite requests and followed by complaints, angry statements, threats, and harassment, with some sequences culminating in abuse. Hence, in initial confrontations, individuals may remain relatively civil. However, in subsequent confrontations, individuals may start in a civil manner but quickly move to insulting, coercive, and aggressive tactics. Indeed, a similar escalatory pattern has been observed in the confrontations that lead to physical violence (Felson, 1984).

For organizational transgressions, the aforementioned research suggests that witnesses and transgressors may become locked in a series of confrontations. When the pattern becomes scripted or increasingly coercive, the witness may give up and may even quit the organization. Alternatively, the witness may turn to others for support and, in essence, blow the whistle on wrongdoing to internal or external sources. Indeed, Pruitt et al. (1997) found that after several encounters with a rule violator, individuals often appealed to third parties for assistance before they moved to more coercive actions directed at the transgressor.

Thus, social confrontations might play an important role in organizational life as individuals attempt to deal with witnessed wrongdoing. Unfortunately, such confrontations seem not to have been extensively researched. If we are to do so, we believe that a number of fundamental questions should guide our inquiry. We turn to those next.

IMPLICATIONS AND DIRECTIONS

Our first and perhaps most important question concerns the desirability of confronting organizational wrongdoing. In other words, is it necessary to confront all transgressions to improve organizational quality? Not all deviant behavior is viewed as harmful to the company, organizational members, or their clients, and only the most serious offenses, most of which are illegal, are considered severe ethical violations (Robinson & Bennett, 1995). Although relatively minor transgressions (e.g., leaving work early, taking excessive breaks) could accumulate to the point where organizational functioning is threatened, occasional rule violations may yield benefits. For example, Downs (1967) argued that what appears to be wasted effort (e.g., socializing at work, improving personal comfort) may increase the morale of organizational members and their commitment to the organization. If so, a system that encourages confrontations could produce a more ethical, but less satisfying work environment, ultimately leading to less efficient organizational outcomes.

The aforementioned analysis implies that organizational members may adopt a contingency approach when deciding what to do about a witnessed ethical breach. If the violation is not large (e.g., the practical consequences are minor, it is a one-time occurrence, it may have been unintentional), the observer lets it pass without comment. Alternatively, the person may ask the transgressor about the action but avoids directly criticizing it or informing superiors. In that way, the witness has met the obligation of raising the issue but without appearing to condemn the action or the actor. It is the actor's decision whether he or she should make amends and alter his or her actions. However, if the ethical breach is serious, a more assertive response is required and others must be informed.

Such a contingency approach could be problematic. Simply asking questions may not be sufficient to stop ethical breaches. Moreover, it seems unlikely that an organization would construct formal rules and procedures that permit its members to overlook some ethical violations. Instead, we suspect that organizational rules often dictate "zero-tolerance" for ethical violations even though the members adhere to a contingency approach. Hence, the latter may reflect a negotiated order of things created by members as they interpret and live within formal organizational rules and procedures (e.g., Strauss, 1979).

Second, are social confrontations the most effective means of controlling transgressions? By their very nature, social confrontations imply that witnesses and transgressors should attempt to resolve problems without resorting to third parties. Indeed, one could argue that the individuals who are most knowledgeable of the situation should be best able to resolve it, and therefore many issues should be resolved without involving other parties. However, can all transgressions best be resolved by the parties who are directly involved? For example, in cases in which the witness is of lower authority than the transgressor, might it not be more effective to have a person with greater authority perform the confrontation? In effect, might a "level playing field" be more desirable than requiring a subordinate to be confrontational?

Third, if social confrontations are indeed desirable, what factors would facilitate their occurrence? Newell and Stutman (1991) created a scale that would differentiate among individuals who are predisposed to confront wrongdoing as opposed to those who are inclined to avoid confrontations. These authors found that individuals who are predisposed to be confrontational see confrontations as strategic means of accomplishing their personal goals, and they have high self-efficacy with regard to their ability to confront others. By contrast, individuals who are not confrontational see confrontations as harmful and uncomfortable and have little confidence that they can be effectively confrontational (Makoul & Roloff, 1998). This implies that systems that wish to encourage confrontations must convince individuals that confrontations can work, and that the individuals can carry out confrontations. This seems to suggest that assertiveness training is desirable.

However, simply convincing organizational members to be confrontational may not be sufficient. We must also answer one additional question: What skills are necessary to effectively perform a social confrontation? If individuals confront others inappropriately, the benefits of confrontation will not be realized. However, what constitutes an appropriate confrontational style may be complex. On one hand, the style must be sufficiently direct so that the target understands that a challenge is being made, but it must not be so direct as to be offensive. For example, individuals often do not directly oppose a peer's objectionable remark due to a desire to be polite and to avoid retaliation (Swim & Hyers, 1999), and it seems reasonable that such concerns would be heightened when the speaker is of greater authority.

Fortunately, research informs as to effective and socially appropriate ways in which a confrontation may be enacted. As noted earlier, one way is to employ mitigating linguistic devices that soften the loss of face to the person being confronted. Hence, initiating a confrontation with a request or with a statement in which the speaker shares responsibility for the transgression with the target is perceived to be more effective and appropriate than beginning the confrontation with an insult, imperative, or accusation (Benoit & Benoit, 1990). Furthermore, group members perceive expressed resistance to offensive speech to be more polite and less likely to prompt retaliation when it is grounded in the task that is being discussed than when it simply characterizes objectionable statements as inappropriate (Swim & Hyers, 1999). This latter finding may mean that individuals should be trained to be argumentative and to control their verbal aggressiveness. Infante and Rancer (1996) distinguished between individuals who are predisposed to be argumentative and those who are inclined to be verbally aggressive. Argumentative individuals attack the positions taken by others, whereas verbally aggressive individuals attack the self-concepts of others. Argumentative individuals, compared to those who are not argumentative, prepare more arguments before a confrontation (Rancer & Infante, 1985), are less likely to be provoked by their partner's verbal aggression (Infante, Trebing, Shepherd, & Seeds, 1984) and appear to be more competent during an argument (Onyekwere, Ruben, & Infante, 1991). In contrast, verbally aggressive individuals primarily rely on character and competency attacks to convince others (Infante, Riddle, Horvath, & Tumlin, 1992). Not surprisingly, argumentativeness in the workplace enhances organizational quality, whereas verbal aggressiveness reduces it (Infante & Rancer, 1996). Fortunately, individuals can be trained to be argumentative and to control their verbal aggressiveness (Infante & Rancer, 1996).

As these questions point out, the study of social confrontations could serve as a potentially productive and important area for organization research. A more complete understanding of the processes and problems associated with directly confronting wrongdoers provides insight into some of the bases for sustained unethical actions. Ultimately, by addressing the issues we identify in this chapter, we might move toward realizing a more ethical and positive workplace.

REFERENCES

Alberts, J. K. (1989). A descriptive taxonomy of couples' complaint interactions. *Southern Communication Journal, 54,* 125–143.

Alberts, J. K., & Driscoll, G. (1992). Containment versus escalation: The trajectory of couples' conversational complaints. *Western Journal of Communication 56,* 394–412.

Alicke, M. D., Braun, J. C., Glor, J. E., Klotz, M. L., Magee, J., Sederholm, H., & Siegel R. (1992). Complaining behavior in social interaction. *Personality and Social Psychology Bulletin, 18,* 286–295.

Baxter, L. A., & Wilmot, W. W. (1984). "Secret tests": Social strategies for acquiring information about the state of the relationships. *Human Communication Research, 11,* 171–201.

Belk, S. S., & Snell, W. E., Jr. (1988). Avoidance strategy use in intimate relationships. *Journal of Social and Clinical Psychology, 7,* 80–96.

Benoit, W. L., & Benoit, P. J. (1990). Aggravated and mitigated opening utterances. *Argumentation, 4,* 171–183.

Cloven, D. H., & Roloff, M. E. (1991). Sense-making activities and interpersonal conflict: Communicative cures for the mulling blues. *Western Journal of Speech Communication, 55,* 134–158.

DeMars, N. (1997). *You want me to do what? When, where and how to draw the line at work.* New York: Simon & Schuster.

DePaulo, B. M., Kashy, D. A., Kirkendol, S. E., Wyer, M. M., & Epstein, J. A. (1996). Lying in everyday life. *Journal of Personality and Social Psychology, 70,* 979–999.

Downs, A. (1967). *Inside bureaucracy.* Boston: Little, Brown.

Felson, R. B. (1984). Patterns of aggressive social interaction. In A. Mummendey (Ed.), *Social psychology of aggression: From individual behavior to social interaction* (pp. 108–126). New York: Springer-Verlag.

Harper, D. (1990). Spotlight abuse—Save profits. *Industrial Distribution, 79,* 47–51.

Hewes, D. E., & Graham, M. L. (1989). Second-guessing theory: Review and extension. *Communication Yearbook, 12,* 213–248.

Infante, D. A., & Rancer, A. S. (1996). Argumentativeness and verbal aggressiveness: A review of recent theory and research. *Communication Yearbook, 19,* 319–352.

Infante, D. A., Riddle, B. L., Horvath, C. L., & Tumlin, S. A. (1992). Verbal aggressiveness: Messages and reasons. *Communication Quarterly, 40,* 116–126.

Infante, D. A., Trebing, J. D., Shepherd, P. E., & Seeds, D. E. (1984). The relationship of argumentativeness to verbal aggression. *Southern Speech Communication Journal, 50,* 67–77.

Institute of Management and Administration (1998). Written ethical standards: An "intangible" that helps discourage internal fraud. *Preventing business fraud* [On-line]. Available FTP:http://www.ioma.com/newlsetters/pbf/articles/0498.shtm

Johnson, K. L., & Roloff, M. E. (1998). Serial arguing and relational quality: Determinants and consequences of perceived resolvability. *Communication Research, 25,* 327–343.

Kelman, H. C., & Hamilton, V. L. (1989). *Crimes of obedience: Toward a social psychology of authority and responsibility.* New Haven, CT: Yale University Press.

Kubany, E. S., Richard, D. C., Bauer, G. B., & Muraoka, M. Y. (1992). Impact of assertive and accusatory communication of distress and anger: A verbal component analysis. *Aggressive Behavior, 18,* 337–347.

Makoul, G., & Roloff, M. E. (1998). The role of efficacy and outcome expectations in the decision to withhold relational complaints. *Communication Research, 25,* 5–29.

Mathews, M. C. (1988). *Strategic intervention in organizations: Resolving ethical dilemmas.* Thousand Oaks, CA: Sage.

McCann, N. D., & McGinn, T. A. (1992). *Harassed: 100 women define inappropriate behavior in the workplace.* Homewood, IL: Business One Irwin.

McCornack, S. A., & Levine, T. R. (1990). When lies are uncovered: Emotional and relations outcomes of discovered deception. *Communication Monographs, 57,* 119–138.

Miceli, M. P., Dozier, J. B., & Near, J. P. (1991). Blowing the whistle on data fudging: A controlled field experiment. *Journal of Applied Social Psychology, 21,* 271–295.

Miceli, M. P., & Near, J. P. (1984). The relationships among beliefs, organizational position and whistle-blowing status: A discriminant analysis. *Academy of Management Journal, 27,* 687–705.

Mulrine, A., & Schrof, J. M. (1998, September 28). Coping with a crooked boss: How to protect yourself from becoming an accessory to office crimes. *U.S. News & World Report, 125,* 76.

Murphy, K. R. (1993). *Honesty in the workplace.* Belmont, CA: Brooks/Cole.

Near, J. P., & Jenson, T. C. (1983). The whistle-blowing process: Retaliation and perceived effectiveness. *Working and Occupations, 10,* 3–8.

Near, J. P., & Miceli, M. P. (1986). Retaliation against whistle-blowers: Predictors and effects. *Journal of Applied Psychology, 71,* 137–145.

Near, J. P., & Miceli, M. P. (1987). Whistle-blowers in organizations: Dissidents or reformers. In B. M. Staw & L. L. Cummings (Eds.), *Research in organizational behavior* (Vol. 9, pp. 321–368). Greenwich, CT: JAI.

Newell, S. E., & Stutman, R. K. (1988). The social confrontation episode. *Communication Monographs, 55,* 266–285.

Newell, S. E., & Stutman, R. K. (1989/90). Negotiating confrontation: The problematic nature of initiation and response. *Research on Language and Social Interaction, 23,* 139–162.

Newell, S. E., & Stutman, R. K. (1991). The episodic nature of social confrontation. *Communication Yearbook, 14,* 359–392).

Onyekwere, E. O., Ruben, R. B., & Infante, D. A. (1991). Interpersonal perception and communication satisfaction as a function of argumentativeness and ego-involvement. *Communication Quarterly, 39,* 35–47.

Pennington, N., & Hastie, R. (1992). Explaining the evidence: Tests of the story model of juror decision making. *Journal of Personality and Social Psychology, 62,* 189–206.

Pruitt, D. G., Parker, J. C., & Mikolic, J. M. (1997). Escalation as a reaction to persistent annoyance. *International Journal of Conflict Management, 8,* 252–270.

Rancer, A. S., & Infante, D. A. (1985). Relations between motivation to argue and the argumentativeness of adversaries. *Communication Quarterly, 33,* 209–218.

Robinson, S. L., & Bennett, R. J. (1995). A typology of deviant workplace behaviors: A multidimensional scaling study. *Academy of Management Journal, 38,* 555–572.

Roloff, M. E., Soule, K. P., & Carey, C. M. (in press). Reasons for remaining in a relationship and responses to relational transgressions. *Journal of Social and Personal Relationships.*

Shimanoff, S. B. (1980). *Communication rules: Theory and research.* Newbury Park, CA: Sage.

Solomon, D. H., & Roloff, M. E. (1996). *Reasons for withholding complaints in dating relationships*. Unpublished manuscript, University of Wisconsin at Madison.

Solomon, D. H., & Samp, J. A. (1998). Power and problem appraisal: Perceptual foundations of the chilling effect in dating relationships. *Journal of Social and Personal Relationships, 15,* 191–210.

Solomon, D. H., & Williams, M. L. M. (1997). Perceptions of social-sexual communication at work: The effects of message, situational, and observer characteristics on judgements of sexual harassment. *Journal of Applied Communication Research, 25,* 196–216.

Stamp, G. H., Vangelisti, A. L., & Daly, J. A. (1992). The creation of defensiveness in social interaction. *Communication Quarterly, 40,* 177–190.

Strauss, A. (1979). *Negotiations: Varieties, contexts, processes, and social order.* San Francisco: Jossey-Bass.

Stutman, R. K., & Newell, S. E. (1990). Rehearsing for confrontation. *Argumentation, 4,* 185–198.

Swim, J. K., & Hyers, L. L. (1999). Excuse me—What did you just say?! Women's public and private responses to sexist remarks. *Journal of Experimental Social Psychology, 35,* 68–88.

Trapp, R., & Hoff, N. (1985). A model of serial argument in interpersonal relationships. *Journal of the American Forensic Association, 22,* 1–11.

Van Camp, K. (1997). *Noncompliance among subordinates in organizations.* Unpublished doctoral dissertation, Northwestern University, Chicago.

Vollbrecht, J. L., Roloff, M. E., & Paulson, G. D. (1997). Coercive potential and face-sensitivity: The effects of authority and directives in social confrontation. *International Journal of Conflict Management, 8,* 235–251.

Vuchinich, S. (1986). On attenuation in verbal family conflict. *Social Psychology Quarterly, 49,* 281–293.

Zagacki, K. S., Edwards, R., & Honeycutt, J. M. (1992). The role of imagery and emotion in imagined interaction. *Communication Quarterly, 40,* 56–68.

6 Procedural Strategies for Gaining Deference: Increasing Social Harmony or Creating False Consciousness?

Tom R. Tyler
New York University

My work has been concerned with issues of social justice; in particular, I have been interested in understanding the role of procedural justice in organizational dynamics (see Lind & Tyler, 1988; Tyler, Boeckmann, Smith, & Huo, 1997; Tyler & Smith, 1997). Thinking about my research from the perspective of social influence has been an interesting experience, because social justice research typically has not been thought of as being research about social influence. However, thinking about social justice research in this new way is valuable and leads to a number of new and interesting insights about social justice. In particular, it makes clear the importance of discussing ethical issues when considering social justice research and its findings.

This is also an interesting time for me to think about the ethical implications of procedural justice research, because those ethical implications are being raised by others. I was recently on a panel discussing the ethical implications of procedural justice research that was held at a meeting of the American Psychological Association (August 1998). Most of the other panelists took the position that at least some aspects of procedural justice research or the application of that research were unethical. This criticism initially surprised me and has led me to consider my own views about the ethics of the work in my field.

Let me begin by raising what I regard as the key question: Why has the study of social justice become so important in organizational settings? Over the past several decades, a large literature has developed exploring people's feelings of justice and injustice in legal, political, and work organizations. This work has become so important because people's views about what is fair or unfair have been found to influence what they think and do in organizational settings. In other words, it is clear that people are influenced by their justice judgments, responding to their own sense of what is fair or unfair, right or wrong (Tyler, 1999; Tyler et al., 1997; Tyler & Smith, 1997).

The question is how to think about the ethical implications of the empirical finding that people are influenced by their assessments of fairness and unfairness. Is it wrong for authorities, whether managers, judges, or politicians, to act based on the knowledge that presenting their actions in ways that will lead them to be viewed as fair increases their influence over others? Is it in some way inappropriate or unethical to "play on" people's sense of justice by giving them what they think is fair? Is there a perverse way in which treating people fairly actually can be unethical?

Let me begin to address this question by giving some background information about social justice research in organizations (see Tyler et al., 1997). There have been two major waves of such research. The first involved the study of equity or inequity in the distribution of pay and promotions. This research began in response to concerns about employee dissatisfaction with their pay and promotion opportunities within work organizations. Such employee dissatisfaction was found to decrease work efforts, increase turnover, and sometimes lead to sabotage. Hence, it interfered with the viability of work organizations. The problem was that work organizations had only limited resources and could not give employees as favorable a level of outcomes—amount of pay, promotion opportunities—as they wanted, so organization leaders had to think of other approaches to managing the problem of employee discontent. They could not resolve problems of discontent by giving workers everything they wanted.

Equity theory suggested that employees would accept outcomes that were less than they desired if they felt that the levels of the outcomes they received were fair. Hence, equity theory suggested a way to distribute limited resources among employees without creating or intensifying discontent. And, in fact, the findings of equity theory have supported the basic equity theory argument. People were found to be more willing to accept an outcome if that outcome seemed fair to them.

An example of research demonstrating this equity theory finding is a study conducted by Pritchard, Dunnette, and Jorgenson (1972). That study paid employees a fixed amount of money to do a job. However, it varied how that salary was described to the employees. In some cases employees were told it was a fair wage. In other cases they were told they were being underpaid or overpaid. Reasons were given for the necessity of this unfair treatment, but employees in two conditions still realized that their pay was not fair. The study shows that the most satisfied employees were those who felt that they were being fairly paid. Interestingly, those employees were more satisfied than employees who thought they were being overpaid. Findings of this type support the argument that employees will respond to judgments about the fairness of their pay when evaluating their jobs.

The equity theory findings suggest a clear social influence strategy for managers: Tell employees that their pay and/or promotions are fair. This suggests that equity theory can, indeed, help to solve a problem that management regards as important—lessening employee discontent. Hence, it is not surprising that equity theory research was pioneered by a management school professor—Stacy Adams. It addresses a problem that management views as important: minimizing employee unhappiness with existing pay and promotion opportunities.

Over time, equity research has become less influential. This declining influence is not, however, due to ethical concerns about the implementation of equity-based social influence strategies. Instead, it is due to the ineffectiveness of equity-based approaches in dealing with key organizational problems. There are two reasons for this failure.

First, studies of discontent have found that dissatisfaction with issues of allocation, such as those involved in pay and promotion, is not central to the issues that trouble people in organizational settings (Messick, Bloom, Boldizar, & Samuelson, 1985). When people are asked to describe instances of injustice from their own experience, they seldom mention problems with pay or promotion. Hence, people's workplace grievances center on issues besides pay and promotion.

Second, there are difficulties involved in effectively enacting equity-based strategies. Equity theory is based on the effects of people's subjective feelings of being fairly or unfairly treated. It suggests that people will feel more satisfied when they believe that their outcomes are proportional to their inputs. However, research shows that people overestimate their contributions to groups—that is, their inputs into the equity equation (Schlenker & Miller, 1977). Hence, people feel entitled to more than is objectively warranted. This makes it difficult for managers to persuade people in real-world settings that they are receiving fair levels of rewards. Instead, people typically believe that their pay is too little to match the value of their contributions. And managers are not able to match people's expectations without providing unreasonably high levels of rewards, rewards not matched by an employee's actual contributions to the organization.

More recently, a second wave of organizational justice research has focused on procedural justice. Procedural justice research is concerned with the fairness of group decision-making procedures. As with earlier work on equity, research on procedural justice shows that people are more satisfied with decisions that are made through procedures that they view as fair. A number of studies have demonstrated this procedural justice effect in both experimental and field settings (Lind & Tyler, 1988; Thibaut & Walker, 1975; Tyler et al., 1997; Tyler & Smith, 1997).

As with equity theory research, procedural justice research originally developed out of the concerns of organizational authorities. In this case, those authorities were legal authorities. The relationship of this work to legal problems may stem from the fact that Laurens Walker is a law school professor whose work addresses legal issues. The legal system is concerned about how to effectively resolve conflicts. In particular, the legal system seeks to resolve conflicts by using third-party authorities, such as judges or mediators. It wants those authorities to make decisions that will be accepted voluntarily by the disputants. If decisions are not accepted, then the legal system must engage in costly efforts to enforce compliance. Hence, finding ways to facilitate the voluntary acceptance of decisions is important to legal authorities. Although the system can deal with some people through coercion, it would be overwhelmed rapidly if it had to compel obedience from most of the people who appeared before it (Tyler, 1990). Instead, the system relies on voluntary cooperation from most of the people, most of the time.

In addition, the legal system is interested in finding ways for third-party authorities to make decisions without being disliked by the parties to a dispute. To be effective, the legal system needs to maintain its legitimacy in the eyes of citizens. If citizens come to dislike legal authorities whenever those authorities try to resolve problems, then the system will lose its legitimacy and, hence, its effectiveness as an agency that can help to resolve disputes. Legal authorities typically fear the potential loss of legitimacy, because they often must provide people with decisions that do not give them what they want or feel they deserve.

Procedural justice facilitates both of the goals of the legal system. The use of procedures that people view as fair enhances people's evaluations of authorities and institutions and increases their willingness to accept the decisions of judges and mediators and to obey social rules. Hence, procedural justice suggests a viable strategy for exercising authority in legal settings, as well as more generally in any organizational setting. Authorities can bridge differences in values and interests by making their decisions in ways that people will regard as fair. Such effects have been found with legal, political, and managerial authorities, as well as with teachers and parents.

So, research suggests that the use of procedures that others will view as fair is a very effective social influence strategy. If others feel that fair procedures have been used to resolve a dispute or make a decision, they will be more influenced in what they think and do by the decisions that an authority has made about how to resolve a problem or dispute. The key question is whether encouraging authorities to try to influence others by making decisions that they will view as fair is in some way unethical.

I think the root of the argument that making use of fair-appearing procedures to influence the acceptability of third-party decisions to the parties of a dispute is unethical lies in a particular view of the relationship between organizational authorities and organizational members. This view, which is central to Marxist philosophy, is that a conflict of interest lies between authorities and organizational members. For example, there is a conflict of interest between workers and managers. Social psychologists would express this idea by saying that workers and managers have noncorrespondent interests, or are in competition, so that what is best for members of one group is not best for members of the other.

A second aspect of the Marxist philosophy is that one group, organizational authorities, typically has greater control over power and resources. By virtue of holding such power, the authorities can control the objective distribution of resources and lead outcomes to be distributed in ways that are more beneficial to their group. If authorities and those subordinate to them, for example, employees, have noncorrespondent interests, this inherently means that the objective outcomes of employees are lower than is objectively fair. Under such circumstances, employees should not be satisfied. If employees feel satisfied, this reflects "false consciousness," because employees are objectively disadvantaged.

These assumptions are inconsistent with the view of the relationship between authorities and organizational members that underlies the procedural justice research of Thibaut and Walker (1975). Their research is based on the belief that everyone—employees and managers, disputants and judges—benefits from the effective resolution of disputes. In this view, the role of third parties is to help achieve justice among organizational members (in their case, citizens bringing problems to the legal system). Thibaut and Walker believed that everyone could have a just outcome at the same time, as they indicated in the preface to their book:

> One prediction that can be advanced with sure confidence is that human life on this planet faces a steady increase in the potential for interpersonal and intergroup conflict. The rising expectations of a continuously more numerous population in competition for control over rapidly diminishing resources creates the conditions for an increasingly dangerous existence. It seems clear that the quality of future human life is likely to be importantly determined by the effectiveness with which disputes can be managed, moderated, or resolved. Procedures or methods that may be put to this task of conflict resolution therefore claim our attention. (Thibaut & Walker, 1975, p. 1)

Thibaut and Walker's perspective is rooted in the belief that society has two goals. The first is to gain the free acceptance of decisions by all parties to a dispute. To advance this goal it is important to know that research demonstrates that free (i.e., "voluntary") acceptance flows from people's judgments about the fairness of the decision-making process. This tells authorities how they should act—through procedures that those with whom they deal will judge to be fair.

The second goal is to encourage the continuation of productive relationships among people. It is important to try to heal the wounds among disputants so that they will interact in the future. It is also important to maintain a positive relationship between disputants and authorities, so that people will not become cynical about and alienated from society and its institutions.

The use of fair-appearing procedures facilitates both of these goals and, hence, is desirable. Both of these goals are viewed as being in everyone's interests, not just the interests of social authorities. Consequently, these goals are desirable from everyone's perspective. In other words, there is no core conflict between authorities and those within organizations. From this perspective, there is not a dominant and a subordinate group, with noncorrespondent interests. Instead, there is a common interest among the various people or groups involved in social interactions.

One reason that Thibaut and Walker believed that there is a nonadversarial relationship between disputants and third parties is that they believed fair procedures produce fair outcomes. Their definition of outcome fairness is an equitable outcome (Thibaut & Walker, 1978). In order for an authority to make a decision that leads to an equitable outcome in a dispute with someone else, the authority must have the most information possible about the inputs of various parties. The adversary procedure, which defines procedural fairness in Thibaut and Walker's research program, is fair because it provides disputants the maximum opportunity to present evidence about their inputs. This procedural fairness leads to outcome fairness, because the third-party authority with the most information is best able to divide resources equitably.

From Thibaut and Walker's perspective, the adversary system leads to both objective fairness and subjective fairness. That is, people want a procedure that achieves fair outcomes, and they associate fairness with procedures that provide maximum opportunities to present evidence—which maximize the attainment of actual fairness. Hence, to Thibaut and Walker, the objective analysis and the psychological analysis of procedures yield similar conclusions.

If, in fact, fair procedures produce fair outcomes, then being influenced by whether a procedure is fair seems reasonable. Employees know that in an organizational setting they cannot always have what they want. But they can expect to receive fair outcomes. If fair outcomes flow from fair procedures, then it makes sense to be influenced by the degree to which decision-making procedures appear to be fair. Consequently, influencing people by showing them that procedures are fair seems to be responding to their very reasonable social decision-making rules. It is simply telling subordinates that over time their outcomes will be fair.

And, if employees are receiving fair outcomes in the long run, then it is hard to see how they are victims of "false consciousness." If, in fact, procedural fairness is linked to outcome fairness, then there seems to be little basis for an ethical critique against using procedures that people judge to be fair to allocate resources within organizations.

An alternative basis for an ethical critique of justice research focuses on issues of distributive justice. Such a critique is based on the finding that people associate the allocation of outcomes in work settings with the use of the justice principle of equity. Because people potentially can use a wide variety of principles to judge the fairness of outcome distributions, the question is why they choose a particular one. Why not, for example, evaluate outcome distributions against the principles of equality or need?

It can be argued that people believe equity is the fair rule to use when distributing outcomes because they have been socialized into false consciousness. In other words, it could be argued that the meaning of "distributive fairness" (i.e., the principles used to define it) is socially constructed. As I noted, people could think that equality and need were the appropriate principles of distributive justice for use when dealing with others (Deutsch, 1985).

One piece of evidence supporting of this false consciousness argument is the research of Deutsch (1987). Traditionally the use of equity as a reward mechanism has been defended by suggesting that the use of equity is associated with enhancing productivity. Hence, managers are simply using the principle of fairness that works when they allocate rewards by equity and are not taking a value position beyond the desire to maximize productivity. Deutsch (1987) suggested that equality is as strongly associated with productivity in work groups as is equity. If so, then the self-evident character of equity as a reward allocation mechanism is diminished substantially. We might then ask what social factors have led to the use of equity as a "fair" principle of reward allocation.

Although Thibaut and Walker's position that procedural fairness leads to outcome fairness minimizes apparent ethical problems, subsequent research, unfortunately, has not shown that their position is correct. In particular, findings suggest that evaluations of procedural justice are distinct from, although not completely independent of, evaluations of distributive justice. People do not directly connect procedural and distributive justice in the way Thibaut and Walker assumed. This does not mean that the two judgments are unrelated. They are related, and people do associate fair procedures with fair outcomes. But the relationship is not strong, suggesting that people have more in mind when they talk about the justice of a procedure than the fairness of the outcomes it produces. Although procedural justice may lead to objective outcome fairness, as Thibaut and Walker (1975) argued, it is only loosely linked to subjective outcome fairness.

Consider a concrete example of the separation of judgments of procedural justice from judgments about outcomes. When do employees make a legal claim after a work-related loss of some type? Past discussions of this issue have suggested that people are rational in their decisions about whether to go to court (Felstiner, Abel, & Sarat, 1980/81), pursuing claims when they can reasonably expect to gain. From an instrumental perspective, people go to court when they have suffered a serious harm and/or expect to prevail in court.

Interestingly, recent research does not support this instrumental view of claiming. Lind, Greenberg, Scott, and Welchans (2000) interviewed 996 employees recently terminated by their companies. Of those employees, 23% had talked to a lawyer or government official about making a claim and 7% actually filed a formal claim. The interviews examined why such claims were filed (for a more detailed discussion of this study, see Lind, Greenberg, Scott, and Welchans, in press). The results, shown in Table 6.1, suggest that neither the degree to which employees felt that the company was to blame for the termination nor whether employees expected to win had much to do with whether former employees filed a claim. What did matter was how fairly they were treated during the termination process. What is most striking is that these procedural effects were distinct from judgments about outcomes. In other words, people were judging procedures by criteria that are not a simple reflection of outcome favorability or outcome fairness.

Bies and Tyler (1993) conducted a similar study using a sample of 409 employees who still worked for their company. The authors interviewed those employees

TABLE 6.1

Why Do Employees Sue a Company After Being Terminated?

Claiming behavior
(23% talked to a lawyer/Government official; 7% actually Filed a claim; n = 996)

Were you to blame for your termination or was the employer?	No relationship
How much do you expect to win in court?	.07
How much financial hardship has the termination caused you?	.09
Were you treated fairly when you were working for the company?	−.07
Were you treated fairly during the termination process?	−.24

Note. The numbers shown are beta weights reflecting the independent contribution of a factor when all the other factors are controlled for. All terms shown are statistically significant. The numbers were adapted from the causal model of claiming behavior presented by the authors. Based on results reported in E. A. Lind, J. Greenberg, K. S. Scott, and T. D. Welchans (2000). The winding road from employee to complainant: Situational and psychological determinants of wrongful-termination claims. *Administrative Science Quarterly, 45,* in press.

about recent conflicts with their supervisors. Of those interviewed, 141 recognized that there were external government or legal agencies to which they could appeal about the decisions their supervisors made in those recent conflicts. The study examined factors shaping whether employees considered claiming. The results, shown in Table 6.2, again indicate that employees were not very strongly influenced by the degree of harm they experienced or the likelihood of winning. Furthermore, they were not affected by whether they felt the decisions made were unfair. Again, they were influenced by issues of procedural justice and by evaluations of their treatment by the supervisor.

Why should these findings concern us? First, because they illustrate the separation of procedural justice from outcome judgments. The study by Lind et al. (1998) did so explicitly, because the beta weights shown indicate the influence of procedural assessments controlling for outcomes. These independent effects are substantial. The Bies and Tyler (1993) data did not measure independent contributions but rather measured simple correlations. But the magnitude of the contributions shown in these correlations makes clear that procedures are not simply a reflection of outcome effects, because their effects are much more powerful.

These findings show that employees react to procedural issues separately from the degree of harm they experience, the degree to which they have been treated unfairly, and/or whether they think they might win in court. Furthermore, these procedural effects are substantial and suggest that issues of procedural fairness and

TABLE 6.2

Why Do Current Employees Consider Claiming Against Their Company
in Response to a Managerial Decision?

Did you consider filing a claim?	
What was the likelihood of winning?	.09
Was the decision made by management an unfair one?	.28
What is your degree of commitment to your organization?	.08
How satisfied are you with your current job?	.21
Was the decision made in a fair way?	.46
Were you treated with dignity and respect during the decision making procedure?	.45
Do you trust the motives of the manager?	.37

Note. The numbers presented are zero-order correlations. The respondents in this sample were a subset of a larger sample of 409 employees. Those used in this analysis were 141 employees who thought that there was an external government agency to which they could make a claim about their manager's decision if they wished to do so. Because of the small sample size, it was not possible to use actual claiming behavior as a dependent variable (only two employees actually made claims). From R. J. Bies & T. R. Tyler (1993). The "litigation mentality" in organizations: A test of alternative psychological explanations. *Organization Science, 4,* 352–366.

treatment by authorities are the key issue that people consider when deciding whether to sue their current or former employer.

One clear message to authorities that is contained in these data is that social influence efforts ought to be focused on communicating to employees that decision-making procedures are fair. Clearly authorities ought to be interested in understanding how their subordinates believe decisions should be made. If the authorities make decisions in ways that are viewed as fair, they will find that people are more willing to voluntarily defer to those decisions and less likely to make claims or complaints about their experiences.

The mean judgments made by employees in the Lind et al. (1998) study suggest that this strategy does not shape current behavior by companies. The means shown in Table 6.3 suggest that employees often felt that they were not treated with respect and were not given complete and honest explanations of management actions. Hence, companies could gain substantially in enhancing the acceptability of their decisions by more effectively communicating to employees that the procedures they use are fair. These findings suggest that companies should use fair-appearing procedures much more than they currently do.

Findings of this type lead directly to the suggestion that managers should focus on developing the appearance of fairness as an impression management strategy

TABLE 6.3

Employer Behavior When Dismissing Employees

	Mean
Did they give you advance notice?	29 days
Did they help you find another job?	1.48
1 = A great deal	
2 = Some	
3 = Slightly	
4 = No help at all	
Were they sympathetic to your needs?	1.93
1 = Very	
2 = Somewhat	
3 = Slightly	
4 = Not at all	
Were you given a complete explanation?	3.40
1 = Very complete	
2 = Somewhat complete	
3 = Somewhat incomplete	
4 = Very incomplete	
Was the explanation honest?	2.45
1 = Very	
2.5 = Somewhat	
4 = Not honest at all	

Note. Based on results discussed in E. A. Lind, J. Greenberg, K. S. Scott, and T. D. Welchans (2000). The winding road from employee to complainant: Situational and Psychological determinants of wrongful-termination claims. *Administrative Science Quarterly, 45, in press.*

(Greenberg, 1990). In other words, they should shape their communications and decision implementation strategies to explicitly create fair-appearing procedures. Furthermore, the results I have outlined suggest that managers can do so without providing employees with favorable or even fair outcomes. Consider the concrete example just presented. The data suggest that companies can terminate employees without being particularly concerned about whether the employees have behaved in a way that merits termination and without much concern about whether the employee has a legally valid claim that might prevail in court, if they manage the termination procedure in ways that seem fair to employees. If managers do manage the process in a fair way, employees generally will accept termination decisions without formal protest. The key point is that such a process of impression management via the use of fair procedures can be substantially distinct from providing people with fair or favorable outcomes.

This potential separation of process judgments from evaluations of the outcomes of a process connects procedural justice findings to an earlier literature in the political and legal arena—the literature on "symbolic" politics (Edelman, 1964; Scheingold, 1974). That literature argued that political and legal authorities typically provide people with symbolic (i.e. non-outcome-related) benefits to maintain their satisfaction and support. Authorities are believed to keep the better outcomes for themselves (Tyler & McGraw, 1986).

More recently, social psychologists have made a similar argument about procedural justice strategies, through articles with titles such as "Let Them Eat Due Process" (Fox, 1993; Haney, 1991). Their argument is that fair process and treatment with respect are provided to subordinates instead of fair outcomes or favorable distributions of resources.

Recent research on procedural justice strongly supports the argument that providing people with respectful and decent treatment leads them to feel that the procedures they are experiencing are fair (Tyler & Lind, 1992). This suggests that there is considerable possibility of creating fair-appearing procedures that are influential without reference to the favorability or fairness of the outcomes people receive through them. The potential for creating satisfaction and securing acceptance without providing resources is quite robust.

Underlying the suggestion that influencing people by treating them with respect and dignity might in some way be unethical is the assumption that what really matters is receiving fair or favorable outcomes. This critique implicitly assumes that outcomes are the primary issue and being satisfied without receiving favorable outcomes is bad. Hence, it is unethical to use a strategy that creates satisfaction without providing fair or favorable outcomes. Because research suggests that satisfaction can be created in this way, the question is whether to accept the argument that to do so is unethical.

FREE CHOICE AS A STANDARD

One way to consider the ethicality of social influence strategies is by evaluating those strategies against objective standards that often are applied to evaluate the ethicality of influence attempts. One such standard is whether the behavior of accepting a decision is freely chosen. That is, if people willingly and freely embrace a settlement, encouraging them to accept it is more ethical than if they are in some way pressured or intimidated to accept the decision. From this perspective, procedural justice approaches to social influence are very ethical. When people feel that a decision is fairly made, they freely accept it. Furthermore, the method of influence that leads to such feelings is persuasion, not coercion.

If employees are treated with dignity and respect, judge their experience to be fair, and then indicate that they feel satisfied, it is hard to understand the framework from which we can say that such happiness is unreasonable. The problem with political analyses of the type I have associated with Marxist thought is that these analyses suggest that social scientists know better than the people they are studying what these people really should be feeling. Those people say they feel satisfied, and they freely embrace decisions, but social scientists suggest that they really should feel unhappy and should reject the decisions.

The root of the problem may lie in the implicit assumption I have already mentioned: that outcomes are more important than anything else. This idea is rooted in the belief that the fundamental reason that people deal with organizations is to exchange resources. Consequently, the quality of the resources given and received defines the quality of the relationship. This assumption underlies theories of social exchange and realistic group conflict (Taylor & Moghaddam, 1994).

However, another body of theory might be applied to the situation: social identity theory (Tajfel & Turner, 1979). Social identity theory says that people interact with others to create a social identity. This process involves two stages. The first is categorization. People create their social selves by drawing on the groups to which they belong. For example, I may think of myself primarily in terms of where I work. Second, people evaluate their self-esteem and self-worth by assessing the status associated with the groups through which they define themselves.

If we accept the social identity view of the relationship between people and organizations, then what people actually want from organizations is identity-relevant information. Hence, procedural justice and treatment with dignity and respect are important because they tell people that they have status within the group. This, in turn, facilitates the creation and maintenance of high self-esteem and encourages feelings of self-worth. People may value this favorable identity-relevant information more than they value receiving fair or favorable outcomes.

Evidence supports this identity perspective by showing that the quality of treatment people experience when dealing with authorities has an important effect on people's feelings about their status, as well as on their feelings of self-esteem and self-worth (Smith & Tyler, 1997; Tyler, 1999; Tyler & Blader, 2000; Tyler et al., 1997; Tyler, Degoey, & Smith, 1996). Hence, research supports the argument that people use the quality of the treatment they receive from authorities, including the fairness of the procedures experienced, to evaluate their status.

AWARENESS OF PROCEDURAL JUSTICE
EFFECTS AS A BASIS FOR EDUCATION

Another approach to understanding the implications of the findings that link procedural justice to freedom of choice is to accept the traditional social psychological argument that outcomes are the ultimate concern, as suggested by social exchange theory, but to use the procedural justice findings I have outlined as an education tool.

Research suggests that most people accept the "myth of self interest" (Miller & Ratner, 1998). They believe that they are concerned about outcomes. Hence, the procedural effects outlined here are not part of people's self-awareness. People do not realize how much they react to the quality of the treatment they receive from others. If directly presented with these findings, in other words, people would find them surprising and difficult to accept. The findings would not seem consistent with their own image about human nature. Hence, procedural justice findings could be used to educate people about the "truth" concerning human nature. These findings could help people to understand how much their own subjective reactions depart from their self-perceived "desirable" goal of interacting to gain valuable resources from others.

My own experience is that knowing about procedural justice findings has led me to be much more aware of the influence of fair treatment. Nowadays when I deal with authorities, for example, my department chairman, I recognize when I have been treated politely but not given what I want. I try to focus on the actual outcomes I am receiving, knowing that I have a natural tendency to lose that focus and focus, instead, on how I am being treated by others.

In other words, these findings could be used to educate employees or citizens to evaluate authorities more critically by questioning the favorability of their outcomes. In this way, people could be discouraged from accepting treatment with dignity and respect instead of a raise or a bigger office.

Of course, as noted previously, this assumes that outcome favorability is what people really care the most about when dealing with authorities—an assumption questioned by recent research. If, in fact, people actually are concerned about issues of identity and status, then the outcomes they do or do not receive are not central to their evaluations of their experiences.

Tyler (1994) supported the argument that outcomes are not central to issues of identity by showing that outcomes do not shape judgments of procedural justice, although they do influence distributive justice judgments. Procedural justice judgments, in turn, are central to self-esteem and social identity (Tyler et al., 1996). In other words, if people want a favorable identity, the question is what leads to such a favorable social identity. Interestingly, research suggests that fair treatment with respect and dignity shapes status, rather than outcomes such as a larger office or a pay raise.

Recent research suggests that an educational effort designed to communicate to people that they actually do not value maximizing their gain of resources when dealing with others might make people's social interactions more personally satisfying. In a series of studies, Tyler, Huo, and Lind (1999) explored the psychology of preference and of evaluation. They found that people with disputes chose which of many procedures should be used to resolve a dispute based on their expectations about their likely personal gain through the use of various procedures. In other words, they wanted to resolve the dispute in the way that made it most likely that they would win. However, after experiencing an actual dispute resolution procedure, they evaluated that procedure in terms of the quality of their treatment by others.

These findings suggest that people are continually dissatisfied and frustrated through the failure to pick procedures that give them what they really want. Why? Because they do not know what they really want. Instead, they believe that they want favorable outcomes (i.e., they believe the "myth of self interest" about themselves; see Miller & Ratner, 1998). If people understood their own psychology better, they could pick procedures that would give them what they "really" want and they would emerge from the dispute resolution situation happy. To do so, they should pick procedures in which they would be treated with dignity and respect.

The key point is that social scientists can empower those who might otherwise be disadvantaged because they accepted fair-appearing procedures. Such empowerment efforts would counteract the tendency for organizations and their authorities to have greater awareness of social science findings and their potential use in organizational settings than do ordinary people. Through education, everyone would learn about procedural justice effects.

The problem with this educational approach already has been outlined. It assumes that people really want outcomes. Hence, we can educate them to ignore procedures and focus on outcomes, assuming that this will lead to greater satisfaction. However, we know that this flies in the face of the procedural justice findings. In other words, when my chairman treats me politely, listens to my arguments, and then refuses to give me a raise, perhaps I should simply accept the high self-esteem that develops from this favorable treatment. Perhaps this is truly what I want, rather than the raise itself. By educating myself to focus on whether I get the raise, I may be simply leading myself down a path to unhappiness, because I will be creating a situation in which I learn to avoid focusing on those elements in social interaction that research suggests actually are linked most strongly to social identity (i.e., the fairness of one's treatment by others).

As these arguments make clear, the empirical findings that people care about procedural justice are distinct from the social implications that social scientists or social critics draw from those findings. Their social implications depend on who uses the findings and for what purposes. One natural use of these findings is by existing organizational authorities eager to find tools to solve organizational problems. To the degree that such authorities have a conflict of interest with organizational members, this use might disadvantage organizational members. However, that potential disadvantage can be counteracted by social scientists' efforts to help the less powerful members of groups, societies, and organizations through education and self-awareness.

THE MOTIVATION OF THE INFLUENCE AGENT

A second criterion for judging ethicality is whether the influence agent is motivated by a concern for the welfare of others. Most social interactions involve situations with at least some degree of noncorrespondent outcomes. For example, when buying a car, the seller and buyer do not have the same interest. In such a market setting, we do not expect the buyer to have the welfare of the seller in mind. Rather, people pursue their own interests, and each is expected to protect those interests ("let the buyer beware"), rather than expecting the other parties to protect them.

Similarly, when management and workers interact, there are areas of noncorrespondent interests. In those areas, each side pursues its own interests, without focusing on the welfare of the other side. Of course, at the same time, people are cooperating with each other over other issues and mutually seeking to maintain their relationship. This cooperative–competitive "mixed-motive" situation is typical of most social interactions.

When people exert influence within such mixed-motive situations, they do not act out of concern for the welfare of the other. Yet we typically do not describe such behavior as unethical. Seeking to persuade an employee to accept a managerial decision by emphasizing that it was fairly made initially does not seem any more unethical than making any other type of persuasive arguments in bargaining.

When Thibaut and Walker conducted their initial research on procedural justice, they did so in the legal arena. Within that arena, judges are viewed as neutral authorities who have no interest in either party winning beyond the impact on the principles of law which they uphold. In fact, judges were often viewed as benevolent and caring, with a sincere interest in trying to be considerate of and fair to those with whom they deal.

Although recent radical critiques ("critical legal studies") have questioned these assumptions of neutrality and benevolence, they underlie the thinking of Thibaut and Walker, as well as many other legal scholars. Hence, legal authorities are viewed widely as acting out of concern for the welfare of the state and the parties to the dispute, to the exclusion of their own personal interests and values.

In contrast, in management settings, within which much of the recent procedural justice research has been conducted, managers are not viewed as neutral or benevolent. Managers represent those who own the companies within which they work. They enact policies designed to facilitate profitability and advance the interests of company owners. Hence, they are not neutral and clearly have possible conflicts of interest with employees. The extent of those conflicts is open to question and differs across situations, but the management situation is fundamentally different from that studied by Thibaut and Walker. Managerial authorities are often not neutral or benevolent figures. Their job often requires them to act as agents of management.

When social influence attempts based on procedural strategies are viewed from the employee's perspective, the key issue is whether the authority is motivated by a concern for the employee's needs. The degree to which an employee decides that an authority is concerned about his or her well-being is referred to as that authority's benevolence or trustworthiness (Tyler & Lind, 1992). Studies suggest that the most important factor that people typically associate with fair procedure is believing that the motives of the authorities enacting that procedure are benevolent, that is, that the authority is concerned about their needs and welfare, can be trusted to do what is right, will consider their situation, and will try to be fair to them. Hence, judgments about the motives of others are central to the effectiveness of influence strategies.

If people do not believe that an authority is motivated by a concern for their welfare, they are much less likely to accept that the decision-making procedures used by that authority are fair. Of course, concern about the motives of others is more broadly important. The ability of people to persuade others to accept their ideas, buy their products, or follow them into battle generally is linked to the message recipient's inferences about the motives of the persuader (Eagly & Chaiken, 1993).

The importance that people place on judging the motives of authorities explains two seeming paradoxes in the procedural justice literature. First, formally enacted "fair" procedures do not necessarily influence people. For example, many companies create formal grievance procedures or complaint mechanisms in hopes of heightening morale. But those procedures only have the desired effect if employees believe that managers actually are motivated to respond to their concerns.

Conversely, managers often are able to create feelings of loyalty and acceptance even when formal procedures are viewed as procedurally unfair by implementing those procedures in ways that provide informal justice. For example, managers may consult with employees over lunch before making decisions even if there are no formal mechanisms for employee input into those decisions.

How might we judge the ethicality of the influence efforts that occur when people do not have the same interests? We might draw on the negotiation literature to define unethical behavior in negotiation. That literature recognizes that people's persuasive communications are designed to shape others' behaviors to meet one's own needs. Hence, I might tell you that I love driving my car because I want you to desire the car and buy it. Emphasizing the positive features of the car and lessening its defects is an inherent part of persuading you to buy the car on terms that are favorable to me.

Furthermore, in attempting to persuade people during negotiation, bargainers not only make persuasive arguments linked to the merits of the "goods on sale" but also engage in other persuasive efforts designed to facilitate the sale. Hence, I might compliment you on your taste in music as part of a strategy to get you to sell me your home inexpensively because you like me (Cialdini, 1993). This persuasion attempt, based on irrelevant features of the situation, seems strikingly similar to treating you with dignity and respect to encourage you to view my procedures as fair and to accept my decisions. In each case, a strategy of persuasion is created through knowledge of what might influence the feelings and actions of the other. And that strategy is based on irrelevant features of the situation (at least features not linked to the issues involved). In fact, many persuasion tactics are based explicitly on efforts to build a personal connection of some type that is irrelevant to the issues involved in the persuasion to facilitate acceptance of one's message.

In negotiation, influence attempts of this type are considered both normal and ethical. It generally is not viewed as unethical to try to get the best price when trying to buy a car. People often choose how they dress and act with the goal of "softening up" the other parties to a negotiation. Furthermore, it is not unethical to use flattery to try to soften up your opponents, complimenting them for example on their appearance, their wit, or their sophistication in negotiating.

If developing and using personal connections and making statements that are flattery and "white lies" are not inappropriate tactics, what is an unethical action during an effort at persuasion? Certain more extreme tactics commonly are labeled unethical, for example, lying, telling someone that the car you are selling was not in an accident, when it was, or rolling back the odometer. In the same way, we might want to define the effort to create fair-appearing procedures to be unfair if it involved overt deception. For example, if I ask you for your opinion about an upcoming decision, knowing that I intend to ignore that opinion or that the decision has already been made, that could be viewed as an unethical influence tactic. Interestingly, these tactics are linked directly to the motives of the other party, which are so important in shaping procedural fairness judgments. Lying reveals lack of trustworthiness in one's motives. Not surprisingly, it is very difficult to recover the basis for a negotiation once evidence of lying has been obtained.

SUMMARY

This analysis suggests that we can gain a lot by thinking about procedural justice as a social influence strategy. In particular, thinking about justice in this way provides a framework for considering ethical issues in social justice research.

When we think about justice research from an ethical perspective, we need to distinguish between two types of potential critique. One type of critique is linked to sociological theories about society that see the people who occupy different positions in an organization—worker/manger, judge/citizen—as having fundamentally noncorrespondent interests. For example, managers and employees work for opposite goals. In such situations, any successful persuasion technique might be used by one group to gain its ends at the expense of the other. Creating fair-appearing procedures is clearly a successful persuasion technique, so its use to "dominate" others can be viewed as unfair.

On a psychological level, using fair-appearing procedures as an influence strategy can be viewed from the same ethical perspective that is used to evaluate negotiation tactics. There may be ways in which people can behave unethically, but in competitive situations the motivation to present one's arguments in ways that will be persuasive to others appears inevitable. What is needed is regulation of those aspects of social influence efforts that cross ethical boundaries, for example, overt lying.

REFERENCES

Bies, R. J., & Tyler, T. R. (1993). The "litigation mentality" in organizations: A test of alternative psychological explanations. *Organization Science, 4,* 352–366.

Cialdini, R. (1993). *Influence: Science and practice* (3rd ed.). New York: HarperCollins.

Deutsch, M. (1985). *Distributive justice*. New Haven, CT: Yale University Press.

Deutsch, M. (1987). Experimental studies of the effects of different systems of distributive justice. In J. C. Masters & W. P. Smith (Eds.), *Social comparison, social justice, and relative deprivation* (pp. 151–164). Hillsdale, NJ: Lawrence Erlbaum Associates.

Eagly, A. H., & Chaiken, S. (1993). *The psychology of attitudes*. New York: Harcourt Brace Jovanovich.

Edelman, M. (1964). *The symbolic uses of politics*. Urbana: University of Illinois Press.

Felstiner, W. L. F., Abel, R., & Sarat, A. (1980/81). The emergence and transformation of disputes: Naming, blaming, and claiming. *Law and Society Review, 15,* 631–654.

Fox, D. R. (1993). Psychological jurisprudence and radical social change. *American Psychologist, 48,* 234–241.

Greenberg, J. (1990). Looking fair vs. being fair: Managing impressions of organizational justice. *Research in Organizational Behavior, 12,* 111–157.

Haney, C. (1991). The fourteenth amendment and symbolic legality: Let them eat due process. *Law and Human Behavior, 15,* 183–204.

Lind, E. A., Greenberg, J., Scott, K. S., & Welchans, T. D. (2000). The winding road from employee to complainant: Situational and psychological determinants of wrongful-termination claims. *Administrative Science Quarterly, 45.*

Lind, E. A., & Tyler, T. R. (1988). *The social psychology of procedural justice*. New York: Plenum.

Messick, D. M., Bloom, S., Boldizar, J. P., & Samuelson, C. D. (1985). Why we are fairer than others. *Journal of Experimental Social Psychology, 21,* 480–500.

Miller, D. T., & Ratner, R. K. (1998). The disparity between the actual and assumed power of self-interest. *Journal of Personality and Social Psychology, 74,* 53–62.

Pritchard, D., Dunnette, M. D., & Jorgenson, D. O. (1972). Effects of perceptions of equity and inequity on worker performance and satisfaction. *Journal of Applied Psychology, 56,* 75–94.

Scheingold, S. A. (1974). *The politics of rights*. New Haven, CT: Yale University Press.

Schlenker, B. R., & Miller, R. S. (1977). Egocentrism in groups. *Journal of Personality and Social Psychology, 35,* 755–764.

Smith, H. J., & Tyler, T. R. (1997). Choosing the right pond: The influence of the status of one's group and one's status in that group on self-esteem and group-oriented behavior. *Journal of Experimental Social Psychology, 33,* 146–170.

Tajfel, H., & Turner, J. (1979). An integrative theory of intergroup conflict. In W. G. Austin & S. Worchel (Eds.), *The social psychology of intergroup relations* (pp. 33–48). Monterey, CA: Brooks/Cole.

Taylor, D. M., & Moghaddam, F. M. (1994). *Theories of intergroup relations: International social psychological perspectives* (2nd ed.). Westport, CT: Praeger.

Thibaut, J., & Walker, L. (1975). *Procedural justice*. Hillsdale, NJ: Lawrence Erlbaum Associates.

Thibaut, J., & Walker, L. (1978). A theory of procedure. *California Law Review, 66,* 541–566.

Tyler, T. R. (1990). *Why people obey the law*. New Haven, CT: Yale University Press.

Tyler, T. R. (1994). Psychological models of the justice motive. *Journal of Personality and Social Psychology, 67,* 850–863.

Tyler, T. R. (1999). Why people cooperate with organizations: An identity-based perspective. In B. M. Staw & R. Sutton (Eds.), *Research in organizational behavior* (Vol. 21, pp. 201–246). Greenwich, CT: JAI.

Tyler, T. R., & Blader, S. (2000). *Cooperation in groups: Procedural justice, social identity, and behavioral engagement.* Philadelphia: Psychology Press.

Tyler, T. R., Boeckmann, R. J., Smith, H. J., & Huo, Y. J. (1997). *Social justice in a diverse society.* Boulder, CO: Westview.

Tyler, T. R., Degoey, P., & Smith, H. J. (1996). Understanding why the justice of group procedures matters. *Journal of Personality and Social Psychology, 70,* 913–930.

Tyler, T. R., Huo, Y. J., & Lind, E. A. (1999). The two psychologies of conflict resolution: Differing antecedents of pre-experience choices and post-experience evaluations. *Group Processes and Intergroup Relations, 2,* 99–118,

Tyler, T. R., & Lind, E. A. (1992). A relational model of authority in groups. *Advances in Experimental Social Psychology, 25,* 115–191.

Tyler, T. R., & McGraw, K. (1986). Ideology and the interpretation of personal experience: Procedural justice and political quiescence. *Journal of Social Issues, 42,* 115–128.

Tyler, T. R., & Smith, H. J. (1997). Social justice and social movements. In D. Gilbert, S. Fiske, & G. Lindzey (Eds.), *Handbook of social psychology* (4th ed., Vol. 2, pp. 595–629). New York: McGraw-Hill.

7 Exit Ethics: The Management of Downsizing Among the Russian Officer Corps

V. Lee Hamilton
University of Maryland

It is particularly appropriate that the social influence and ethics conference on which this book was based was housed in the Kellogg School of Business. The business context highlights the fact that theoretical explanations of various fair or unfair procedures in the work world have two basic themes. On the one hand, it can be argued that companies should behave fairly on ethical grounds: They should do the right thing. On the other hand, it is painfully obvious that even if a company couldn't care less, it would be efficient for it to minimize the amount of disgruntled acting out, both from organizational survivors and, in the shorter term, from workers who are forced to leave. The latter argument from expediency is consistent with an *impression management* approach to the issue of what the parties do in a justice encounter (e.g., Greenberg, 1990b; Shlenker, 1980). In my view, these approaches are not mutually exclusive; people often act for multiple reasons, and if we could not be ethical and make a good impression at the same time, there would probably be a good deal less ethicality observed. For present purposes I assume that to do good and to look good are compatible goals, and that doing good is at least part of what people want.

And what about social influence? This book shows that, to paraphrase Kelman (1974), "social influence is alive and well in the sphere of ethics." Since about 1975, a great deal of social influence research has been done under the rubric of justice. Thus, more specifically, social influence research is alive, well, and flourishing in the sphere of justice. It is the question of ethics, and particularly justice, on which I dwell here. Downsizing is the specific ethical problem, and it is a problem because (or when) it is unjust.

Downsizing presents problems in what I call "exit ethics": ways of making more humane the process of disposing of people from organizations. I use the phrase exit ethics to describe the empirical focus of this chapter because ethics in corporate life involves not just the day-to-day occupancy of corporate roles but also their entry and exit. Downsizing is a modern, collective variant of losing a job. Job loss as an event and unemployment as a persistent state of affairs have long been considered stressful (see classic studies by Cobb & Kasl, 1977; Jahoda, Lazarsfeld, & Zeisel, 1933/1971; see also reviews in Kessler, Price, & Wortman, 1985; Perrucci, Perrucci, Targ, & Targ, 1988). In a famous article on "the stress process," Pearlin, Menaghan, Lieberman, and Mullan (1981) used job loss to exemplify a common, serious stressor. Not surprisingly, the stress literature also shows that unemployment is among the most potent of stressors (or "negative life events"; Dohrenwend, Krasnoff, Askenasy, & Dohrenwend, 1978).

Several characteristics of downsizing may exacerbate the ethical problems it entails. Among these are the objective circumstances, that is, level of deprivation to which job losers will be subjected; the level of commitment of the employees, in that a job treasured more is a job whose loss is more stressful (Wheaton, 1990); and the motivation of the employer, in that procedural justice can be used cynically by employers to "cover for" the lack of objective resources provided to released employees (Greenberg, 1990b). I recently had an opportunity to study downsizing in an organization whose personnel can be expected to be highly committed, in circumstances of severe deprivation in terms of objective outcomes, and where the organization has strong motives to placate both personnel who leave and those who stay. The organization is the Russian Army, and the workers are its officer corps.[1] I present some highlights from ongoing research (Hamilton, 1998, in press) to illustrate how distributive and procedural justice judgments can be, simultaneously, dependent variables shaped by social influence processes and independent variables that shape the worker's sense of well-being and organizational commitment. I briefly summarize empirical data from this study after offering a theoretical overview of issues in the interrelation of social influence and justice. I argue that justice is involved in two reciprocal relations that bear on social influence. One, a direct link, is between justice and social influence itself. The second, an indirect connection, places justice squarely within the stress literature.

---

[1]This was a collaborative project that has involved from its inception two military sociologists, David and Mady Segal of the University of Maryland; three psychologists with extensive expertise on responses to unemployment, Robert Caplan of George Washington University and Richard Price and Amiram Vinokur of University of Michigan; and three Russian experts on survey research, Gennady Denisovsky, Mikhail Matskovsky, and Paulina Kozyreva of the Russian Academy of Sciences and the International Center for Human Values. I am grateful to all of them for their contributions and advice.

JUSTICE AND SOCIAL INFLUENCE:
A RECIPROCAL RELATIONSHIP

Social psychological investigations into justice in recent decades have concentrated on two thirds of the philosopher's triumvirate of distributive, retributive, and procedural justice. Retributive justice often has been left to criminologists, although social psychologists have studied attribution of responsibility (e.g., Hamilton & Sanders, 1992; Robinson & Darley, 1995; Schlenker, Britt, Pennington, Murphy, & Doherty, 1994; Shaver, 1985; Weiner, 1995). Most of the psychological research addresses the trade-off and competition between distributive justice (ends) and procedural justice (means). Major contributions to this debate have been made by Tom Tyler, as his own chapter in this book illustrates. In this chapter I first give a brief overview of the issues.

A key finding across an array of settings, topics, and research subjects has been that the procedural justice of decisions is as important as (or more important than) the distributive outcome in producing satisfaction with an outcome and perceptions that it is fair. From a statistical point of view, this means both that the effect of outcomes on a variety of outcome-related evaluations (e.g., satisfaction, assessed fairness) flows through perceived procedural as well as distributive justice and that the bigger effect, the bigger path, runs through procedure.

Furthermore, justice perceptions not only mediate but also moderate responses to situations. Specifically, at least 45 studies have shown a pattern of results that can be described as follows: (a) Procedural justice matters particularly when outcomes are bad, (b) outcome quality matters particularly when there is little procedural justice, or (c) the combination of low procedural justice and poor outcome quality is especially pernicious (Brockner & Wiesenfeld, 1996). In each case, in this interaction one could substitute *distributive justice* for *outcome quality;* parallel results have been reported for each variable. Dependent variables in such studies have included outcome satisfaction, overall fairness, and (in the management literature) both organizational commitment and measures of job performance.

The fact that when corporations downsize they often release some employees but not others also raises questions about the reactions of what have come to be known as organizational survivors—those who survive a layoff and continue to work for the employer. Research by Joel Brockner and his colleagues has been particularly influential in highlighting the justice issues involved in job retention as well as job loss (e.g., Brockner & Wiesenfeld, 1993). Research outcomes include the standard measures such as perceived fairness (or often, in the management literature, organizational commitment), but they also incorporate such behavioral measures as subsequent performance ratings, absenteeism, and the like. Research even has focused on the extent to which disgruntled workers who feel that other workers were treated unfairly may engage in pilfering or sabotage (e.g., Greenberg, 1990a, 1990b; 1993). The outcomes of perceived unfairness—particularly procedural unfairness—include behavioral reactions of clear importance to the employer.

Thus far, it appears that perceived procedural justice modifies the response to situations, that it does so more powerfully than distributive justice, that the response to procedural and distributive justice may be interactive, and that effects of each form of injustice may be felt by those indirectly as well as those directly involved. These conclusions do not yet fully capture the complexities of the distributive justice/procedural justice debate. One issue is what is being compared with what. Distributive justice is generally a straightforward matter of applying a rule such as equity or equality to a divisible outcome. Procedural justice, however, involves a series of aspects of the case, its parties, and its judge. Researchers are still unraveling these. Among the characteristics of procedures that have been pointed to over the years are, first, the question of the participant's voice over the process or over the decision. Thibaut and Walker (1975), who helped to launch this field of inquiry, felt that voice was the key to procedural justice. Their theoretical rationale was basically instrumental; they argued that procedures that allow voice are perceived as providing the participants greater control over how things go. However, later research shows that more is at stake. Even when voice has nothing to do with outcome, voice effects can be observed (Lind, Kanfer, & Earley, 1990). Furthermore, aspects of procedure other than voice show a strong—or stronger—impact of procedure. These include the provision of information to participants and their treatment with dignity and respect, aspects of what Bies (1987) termed *interactional justice*. Interactional justice is a subcategory of procedural justice that refers to its interpersonal aspects. My focus in studying Russian Army downsizing was the trade-off between distributive justice and these latter aspects of interactional justice (information and respect), because voice is minimized in the military context.

Overlaps Between Concepts of Justice and Social Influence

Responding to the early wave of procedural justice research by Thibaut and Walker (1975), Tom Tyler and Allan Lind have been largely responsible for developing the current understanding of procedural justice, and particularly its theoretical explanation. In their book *The Social Psychology of Procedural Justice* (Lind & Tyler, 1988) and several important theoretical statements, these authors have documented the power of procedure (e.g., Lind, 1994; Tyler, 1990; Tyler & Lind, 1992, in press). Lind and Tyler (1988) proposed a "group value" theory of procedural justice judgments. In contrast with the Thibaut and Walker view, this new perspective emphasizes that procedures generate feelings of belonging to the group and of being held in regard within it. In a series of empirical studies and in a 1990 paper, Tyler specified three factors as crucial to the group value phenomenon: trust, status recognition, and neutrality. Trust captures the feeling that the authority is benevolent and trustworthy, status recognition indicates that the person is acknowledged by authorities as a bona fide group member, and neutrality stands for the evenhanded and nondiscriminatory treatment accorded the person. Tyler and Lind (1992) further labeled the phenomenon a "relational model of authority" to reflect the fact that each aspect of procedure is a judgment of and reflection on the person's relationship with authorities. Most recently, Lind (1994) attempted a theoretical explanation of why procedure makes such a difference. His "fairness heuristic theory" emphasizes that people use procedural fairness heuristically to determine their assessments of justice. Lind suggested that because procedural information is available during an event, whereas outcome information only emerges afterward, a procedural assessment becomes the basis (the anchor) for a final decision about the event.

One direction toward which these theoretical developments point is the overlap between this conception of justice and earlier theorizing about social influence. In fact, there is a suggestive correspondence between Tyler's notions of neutrality, status, and trust and Kelman's (1958) conception of compliance, identification, and internalization as bases of social influence. *Compliance,* according to Kelman, consists of responding to a social influence attempt because you perceive that you must. *Identification* means that you respond to another to help establish or retain a personal tie to the other; that is, identification as a process reflects the tie between influencer and influencee, regardless of the content of the request. *Internalization,* the third process, involves responding to an influence attempt because it agrees with your own values. The influencing agent essentially has no power at all over the outcome except by introducing the stimulus.

Initial research into the three processes, like social influence more broadly, concerned the concrete influence of a particular individual on another. Later applications of these and related concepts have opened up at least two additional meanings or applications. In a second usage, Kelman argued that we can speak of broader processes of indoctrination or socialization—what Kelman termed *integration* into the social unit—as occurring via compliance, identification, or internalization. Thus, a citizen might relate to the government or governmental authority mainly in terms of compliance, which Kelman (1969, Kelman & Hamilton, 1989) termed *rule orientation;* in terms of identification, which Kelman termed *role orientation;* or in terms of internalization, which Kelman termed *value orientation.* These can be thought of as habitual reactions. In this sense, they are akin to personality characteristics. A third potential application of the three processes refers to characteristic patterns in the environment or stimulus. Thus, for example, one might compare prisons with other settings and argue that they are organized more in terms of compliance (or more exclusively in those terms) than other settings (cf. Kohlberg, 1969, who applied moral stage concepts to such environments). In this case one would be referring to habitual or typical aspects of the setting or stimulus. My brief empirical examples from Russian Army downsizing illustrate how indicators of compliance, identification, and internalization in the setting of a real-world organization can easily take on shades of these two latter, more traitlike meanings of the concepts.

Figure 7.1 addresses relationships between Tyler's recent procedural justice theorizing and this classic trio of concepts from the social influence literature. There is no perfect one-to-one correspondence, but there are some suggestive

| | Forms of Justice | | | |
| | Distributive | Procedural | | |
		Neutrality	Status	Trust*
Social Influence:				
Compliance	X	X		
Identification			X	X
Internalization	X	X		X

Individuals who relate to the authority primarily via compliance can be expected to concentrate on such "bread-and-butter" issues as distributive justice and neutrality of the authority.

Individuals who relate via identification can be expected to concentrate on factors related to status recognition (e.g., respect shown to them).

Individuals who relate via internalization can be expected to concentrate on the authority's commitment to justice values . They should be particularly sensitive to such factors as the authority's adherence to the rules (neutrality, etc.), credibility, and motives.

---

*Effects of "voice" and of providing information may lead to consequences for perceived neutrality, status recognition, and/or perceived trustworthiness of the authority.

FIG. 7.1. Future directions in social influence studies: Overlap with research on justice.

overlaps. The figure is structured in columns showing Tyler's use of concepts from the justice literature and rows showing Kelman's concepts from the social influence literature. The text in the lower section of the figure expresses the relationships in hypothesislike fashion, phrased with the social influence concepts as the independent variables. (These "hypotheses" feature authority as the influencing agent, because that was the orientation of Tyler's explanations.) Subsequently I also illustrate how the justice concepts can be treated as the organizing principle (independent variable) in the figure and how the identity of the influencing agent can be varied. In other words, authorities are not the only sources of social influence.

From the standpoint of social influence, a person who is socially integrated—or successfully influenced—via compliance is likely to emphasize "what's in it for me" in a justice situation. Distributive justice would appear attractive to this person for practical reasons as long as he or she were viewing the situation from behind a "veil of ignorance" (Rawls, 1971, p. 12). In short, if I do not know what role I must take in a situation, distributive fairness is an outcome-maximizing strategy. Neutrality on the authority's part is attractive for similar reasons. Turning to the second row of Fig. 7.1, I concentrate on the person who is socially integrated on the basis of identification, or who responds to a particular social influence attempt on that basis. That person should orient toward the authority on the basis of that authority's status and because of factors that reflect status recognition (such as the authority's trustworthiness and show of respect to the person). Finally, the third row encompasses people who are integrated into a group or who have entered a temporary social situation for reasons having to do with their own internalized values. These people should respond to essentially all the features of the justice domain except status considerations, although for somewhat different reasons from the ones encountered thus far. That is, they should evaluate the authority's own justice values (such as their adherence to norms of distributive justice and neutrality), and they should be particularly sensitive to the authority's credibility and motives, captured here under the rubric of trust.

It is evident that there are additional principles of justice and practical procedures thereof, not all of which fit neatly into this scheme. Most prominent among them is the granting of "voice" to participants in a debate (Thibaut & Walker, 1975). Voice has long been recognized as an important element in the assessment of a situation or outcome as fair; it is not featured here because there is, in my view, no clear one-to-one correspondence between voice and either the rows or the columns of Fig. 7.1. Voice is a pervasive component of just procedure that has elements of neutrality, status, and trust, and it can be attractive to a person who orients toward persuasive messages on grounds of compliance, identification, and internalization. This pervasiveness may be part of the secret of its explanatory power in the justice literature.

The relations shown in Fig. 7.1 also can be assessed from the standpoint of the other dimension, the columns representing forms of justice. First, consider the effects of distributive justice as laid out in the first column. They lie in the areas of compliance and internalization. Distributive justice is relevant to compliance because part of the bottom line or "bread and butter" on which the person is likely to concentrate concerns getting one's fair share (outcomes). It is relevant to internalization for very different reasons: because the person who responds to influence via internalization will look for consistency between the request and ethical rules and precepts; the distributive justice of outcomes is one such precept.

Within the realm of procedural justice, the principle of neutrality stands out as relevant to both compliance (again, a bottom-line issue on which everyone would be likely to insist) and internalization (again, because neutrality stands as a moral principle of procedure). Note that neither distributive justice per se nor neutrality per se is linked to identification, whose focus is the personal connection to the allocator. In contrast, status as a procedural rule is related only to identification; the essence of both status and identification is the tie that is established to the group, authority, or other influencing agent. Trust is a procedural principle that is relevant both to internalization, because an untrustworthy influence agent violates a basic ethical principle, and to identification, because untrustworthiness undermines the influencing agent's attractiveness and connection to the influence target. Again, as the footnote of Fig. 7.1 indicates, certain "just practices" such as the provision of voice are not necessarily linked to any particular column or row in this scheme.

Figure 7.1 is a work in progress, a subject for future directions in research on social influence. The data that I discuss shortly were not gathered at a level of specificity that would enable a true test of these relations. But one of the figure's strengths is that it can lead us to think about cause and effect in the justice and social influence literatures and to consider either social influence or justice rules as causal. Fundamentally, we often assume—and sometimes set out to test—that perceived justice is produced by social influence. There is an obvious sense in which that is true in virtually every experiment on the matter. At some level, the experimenter is an authority whose goal and object are to influence the perceptions of fairness of everyone within the artificial world that is created. In that setting, the relation has a static quality, because the experimenter is the *deus ex machina* who starts a process going but generally stands outside of it. In the real world, the kind of role for authority I have in mind is one spoken of by many theoreticians of justice, including Tyler and Lind: the fact that authorities define the situation, set the rules, and establish the frameworks of justice within which citizens or group members operate. They are not a *deus ex machina*—just nearly so. In short, whether we measure the authority's social influence or not in a given case, it is there. It must be.

Reciprocity

Yet the relation of social influence to justice is reciprocal, not unidirectional, as Fig. 7.2 indicates. Consider identification as a social process:

1. Identification is logically one possible cause of perceived justice as an effect. The bottom segment of Fig. 7.2, where the social influence process is the independent variable, depicts this causal interpretation. It is noteworthy that this view also characterizes some recent justice theory. The process of identification leads to perceptions that the influencing agent is just; it includes, for example, the feeling that one is respected and is a valued member of the group (e.g., Tyler & Lind, 1992, in press).

2. The top of Fig. 7.2 depicts justice as an independent (or intervening) variable. In the justice and management literatures, this is often the focus, and one popular dependent variable is organizational commitment. As it is usually measured, organizational commitment is an affective tie to the organization that resembles Kelman's identification (e.g., Mowday, Porter, &

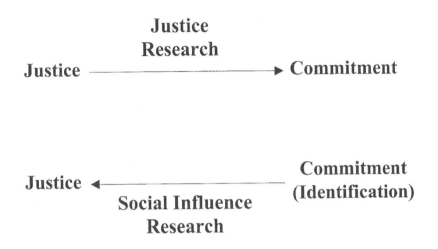

FIG. 7.2. Relationships between commitment and justice.

Steers, 1982). Thus, at least with regard to identification, it is readily possible to see justice as either cause or effect of social influence processes.

It is also possible that either compliance or internalization could take the place of identification in the framework of Fig. 7.2. Examples involving compliance might be studies of such morally related behavior as tax compliance, the issue being the extent to which the behavior is driven by self-interest (Tyler, 1990). Examples involving internalization often can be crafted by considering the inverse of compliance. Thus, the person who pays taxes for other than utilitarian reasons probably does so because of values; there is little likelihood that identification with the "tax man" is the impetus. The fundamental message is that causal ordering is potentially reciprocal in the realms of social influence and justice. Fig. 7.2 further suggests that in the long run, more complex images such as nonrecursive models may be necessary to capture the full range of the relations between perceptions of justice and processes of social influence.

OTHER RECIPROCAL LINKAGES

Justice occupies a bridge position in the social psychological literature, in that it is sometimes cause, sometimes effect. Furthermore, it holds this ambiguous position in at least two areas: social influence, as we have seen, and the burgeoning area of stress and coping research. Job loss and especially losses accompanying corporate downsizing have become popular topics among stress researchers. Both ironically and appropriately, a key developing concern in this area is the ethics of the associated corporate maneuvers: What makes exits ethical, and why should we care? In this arena perceived justice becomes more cause than effect, insofar as it shapes and even defines the person's response to a major stressor.

Downsizing and Stress

The current research into the justice of downsizing draws on a model of the stress process developed by Pearlin and colleagues (e.g., Pearlin, 1989; Pearlin et al., 1981). The basic ingredients are (a) a set of preconditions or background factors, including demographic factors, (b) a stressor, (c) mediating variables (including secondary stressors), (d) moderating variables, and (e) outcomes. In this model the justice literature provides potential mediator and moderator variables. A central basis for doing so is the argument that the perceived justice or injustice of a situation may affect its perceived stressfulness. The recent justice literature is consistent with this argument and frequently has shown how justice perceptions mediate between events and reactions. Furthermore, Brockner and Wiesenfeld's recent (1996) review found a consistent interaction effect indicating that procedural justice moderates the impact of distributive justice (or vice versa). In searching for a more satisfying theoretical framework for downsizing research, Brockner and Wiesenfeld (1993) found stress to be an appropriate organizing principle. In sum, it is natural to ask how reactions to downsizing, a stressful circumstance, may be mediated or moderated by variables characteristic of the justice literature.

As Fig. 7.3 shows, there is a potential reciprocal link between perceived justice and stress, paralleling the one that Fig. 7.2 showed for justice and social influence. The bottom panel concentrates on stress as the causal force. In the stress literature, particularly in the Lazarus and Folkman (1984) tradition, variables like justice perceptions are dependent variables, driven by the person's primary appraisal of the situation. Primary appraisals consist of judgments of the extent of threat represented by a stressor. Logically, then, primary appraisals intervene between the stressor and the justice judgment. The top panel reverses the causal emphasis to show how justice could be the causal force. In the justice literature, justice perceptions often are cast as independent or mediating variables. One popular dependent variable is usually called *outcome evaluation* (or satisfaction). Much like primary appraisal, outcome evaluation is the person's judgment of how good or bad the situation is. By definition, a primary appraisal *is* an outcome evaluation, albeit a preliminary one. I believe that it is reasonable to model a person's judgments of justice or injustice as intervening variables that are influenced by the stressor (here, impending job loss) and, in turn, that affect the primary appraisal (outcome evaluation). After all, an unjust situation is typically a more threatening one. Hence the research presented next emphasizes the causal role of justice, the top panel of this figure, just as the preceding section emphasized justice as an effect. Ultimately,

Figs. 7.2 and 7.3 both suggest that a nonrecursive model would best capture the causal role of justice judgments in relation to these processes.

Next I briefly summarize data that address this relational view of social influence and justice. In the first case I treat organizational commitment as an indicator of social influence (identification) and justice as the dependent variable. In the second, I view justice as an element in the stress process—here, a process that originates in a downsizing—that in turn shapes responses of individual distress, organizational commitment, and outcome evaluation. These ideas are exploratory, and the available data set is not always appropriate for hypothesis testing. Discussion of these preliminary findings is informal. Many details of the methods are relegated to Appendixes A and B.

THE RESEARCH PROGRAM

The Data Set

This chapter uses a portion of a quasi-experimental panel survey of Russian Army officers and their wives to illustrate points in "exit ethics." Interviews were conducted in late 1995 and mid-1997: Wave 1 approximately 3 months before some of the officers were to be released from the service, and Wave 2 approximately 18 months later. About half of the initial 1,798 officer interviews were with "leavers" and about half with officers who then planned to stay in service. An initial 1,609 interviews with wives also were conducted. This discussion focuses on Wave 1 because these were the data available at the time of this writing. (See also Hamilton,

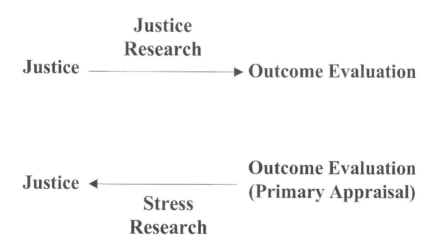

FIG. 7.3. Relationships between outcome evaluation (primary appraisal) and justice.

1998, for other aspects of the panel study.) Details of how most variables were operationalized appear in Appendix A. Next and in Appendix B, I describe the justice variables in greater depth because of their centrality to the work.

Varieties of Justice. Justice, the central construct in the analyses that follow, was measured via 18 items adapted from Joel Brockner's (personal communication, June, 1996) research on organizational survivors. Wordings were altered for the military setting. Appendix B reproduces factor loadings for these items with the wordings as they emerged from backtranslation (Russian to English).[2] Three indicators of justice emerged: distributive justice, interactional justice involving respect, and interactional justice involving the provision of information. An example of a distributive item is, "The Army is doing its best to help people discharged from the Army to find a comparable job outside the Armed Forces"; a respect item, "I am being treated with respect/People being discharged are treated with respect"; and information, "People who are discharged from the Army get very clear explanations of the reasons for the discharge."

Social Influence as Predictor of Perceived Justice

Expectations. What do the interrelationships sketched in Fig. 7.1 imply for responses to a downsizing? I suggest that the following linkages should hold (all phrased in terms of *he,* because the sample here is male):

1. To the extent that an individual is integrated into the organization via compliance, he should perceive the downsizing as distributively unjust and as procedurally unjust in such value domains as neutrality and trust, unless he is personally satisfied with his own treatment in these areas.
2. To the extent that an individual is integrated via identification, he should be likely to offer diffuse support to the institution and to see the process as fair (cf. Kelman & Hamilton, 1989). He should be particularly sensitive to

---

[2]An exploratory principal components analysis was carried out, because the 18 items had never been factor analyzed (J. Brockner, personal communication, June 1996). This analysis substituted mean values for missing data to maximize the N. An alternative factor analysis was also carried out, restricted to individuals with complete data on all items, with closely comparable results but a much smaller N. As Appendix B shows, six factors with eigenvalues greater than 1 emerged, accounting for 52.4% of the variance. Small but coherent groupings of justice questions emerged after varimax rotation of these factors. Factors 2 through 4 capture distributive justice and two facets of interactional justice (respect and information). All analyses were carried out by using first the factor scores and then scale scores based on items that loaded highly on the factors, with very similiar results (see Hamilton, in press). Results presented here use the factor scores for maximum purity of separation among the concepts tapped. On balance, the factor analysis left some ambiguity and overlap among measures. Item 12, which loads on Factor 2 (distributive justice), was originally expected to be a general procedural justice item; and Item 18, which was expected to and did load on Factor 6 (outcome evaluation), also loaded on Factor 4 (respect).

evidence that he and others are being treated as valued members of the group (i.e., Tyler's status principle).

3. To the extent that an individual is integrated via internalization, he should be more likely to apply his own value standards to assess justice versus injustice. To the extent that he evaluates the process as distributively unjust (or nonneutral, or the authorities as disrespectful or untrustworthy), the measure of internalization will be negatively related to overall perceived justice.

As suggested here, the most stable, highest perceived justice should come from those integrated via identification. They do not decrease their assessments if they are personally not favored at a given time, like the compliant, and they do not decrease them if their own values conflict with those of the authority or organization, like the internalized (cf. Kelman & Hamilton, 1989).

Predicting Justice From Compliance, Identification, and Internalization. First I attempted to form indicators of compliance, identification, and internalization from, respectively, items that concerned conformity pressures at work (Kohn, 1977), organizational commitment (Mowday et al., 1982), and complexity of the work environment (Lincoln & Kalleberg, 1990). The three compliance items did not scale well, and one (difficulty–ease of disagreeing with one's boss) was deleted (see Appendix A). The predictors therefore included two compliance items ("superior orders you versus discusses with you" and "important to do as told"), a scale tapping identification (organizational commitment), and an internalization scale. The dependent variables were distributive justice, respect, and information.

The strongest evidence of a link between social influence and justice emerged for identification, as indexed by organizational commitment. Identification was positively related to perceptions that the Army downsizing was distributively just, that those who were leaving the military were treated with respect, and that leavers were presented with prompt, appropriate information (standardized ß = .14, .10, and .15, respectively; all significant at $p < .001$). All the remaining effects were smaller. Compliance items were inconsistent predictors. Basically, "orders–discusses" seemed to pick up the reluctant "have to" nuance of compliance in that it was related negatively to distributive justice and information justice. The importance of doing as ordered, in contrast, has a more voluntaristic flavor that may tap identification. Consistent with that possibility, "important to do as told" was associated positively with both distributive justice and respect. Finally, internalization (complexity of one's job) presented a mixed picture: It was related positively to both respect and information, but the more complex the job was seen, the less distributively just the downsizing was perceived to be. It appears that both orientations of compliance and internalization, at least as measured here, were linked to a sense that the outcome was distributively unjust. Recall that in Fig. 7.1, distributive justice is an issue at both the compliance level ("where's mine?") and the internalization level ("where's justice?"). An organization can be seen as unjust for quite different reasons. These results bore a rough resemblance to the original expectations. However, Fig. 7.1 itself was a tentative exploration designed to engender debate rather than end it.

The Interrelationship of Justice and Stress. In an organizational context such as downsizing, justice—as a cognitive and emotional assessment—is a response to social influence from authority; it also, in turn, influences many other responses including the stress response. Next I turn to the potentially reciprocal relation between justice and stress, reflecting my view that in a stressful circumstance, one's perception of its justice or injustice mediates the response to the stressor. Together, these sets of potentially reciprocal relations forge a link between core social psychological theory on social influence and the wide array of research and application being done in diverse fields on the subject of stress.

Expectations

With regard to stress and justice, expectations are less speculative because both these literatures are extensive, and their intersection is growing. The current example is but an empirical generalization (to Russia and its army) and a theoretical extension (into the reciprocal relationships depicted in Figs. 7.1–7.3). In a downsizing, the fundamental comparison is between those who will leave the organization and those who will remain. The usual finding is that job loss and its anticipation are stressful (Cobb & Kasl, 1977; Hamilton, Broman, Hoffman, & Renner, 1990). Expectations include the following:

1. Those who will leave an organization will be more anxious, depressed, and hostile; will be less organizationally committed; and will evaluate their outcome more negatively. They also will see the organization as less distributively fair and as conveying less information and less respect than those who remain in the organization.[3]
2. Distributive justice, information, and respect will, in turn, affect the outcomes of this stressful event, even accounting for whether the person will or will not leave the organization. The greater the perceived justice of each type, the lower the distress (anxiety, depression, hostility) and the higher the organizational commitment (identification). According to recent re-

---

[3]In this case, the group of leavers is defined by the respondents themselves. I conservatively included officers who said in response to a follow-up question that they were leaving voluntarily as well as those who explicitly referred to the Army downsizing, because there was in fact a hazy line between the two groups; many people leaving voluntarily also were encouraged to do so. Comparison of supposedly voluntary and involuntary leavers revealed no difference on any of the dependent variables reported here; the few isolated differences were theoretically insignificant (e.g., voluntary retirees reported more somatic symptoms, but they were also older). In any case, to the extent that truly voluntary departures are less upsetting to the officer involved, this coding scheme should yield a conservative estimate of leavers' distress.

search, two aspects of procedural justice (information and respect) also should be more strongly linked to outcomes than are distributive justice judgments (Lind & Tyler, 1988; Tyler & Lind, 1992).

3. Procedural justice (information, respect, or both) also should interact with leaver status, distributive justice evaluations, or both. The most straightforward way of understanding this prediction is via the effect of justice variables for leavers versus stayers: Interactional justice should be a more important determinant of the dependent variables among leavers than stayers (Brockner & Wiesenfeld, 1996).

Key Measures

Instead of (or in addition to) being an indicator of identification with the employer, *organizational commitment* can be thought of as a dependent variable affected by the employee's perceptions of justice. Most management studies of justice have viewed affective commitment in this light. Thus, one dependent variable in this second exploration is commitment to the Russian Army.

Also prominent in the justice literature is the concept of *outcome evaluation:* how bad the person thinks the situation is. (Recall that outcome evaluation corresponds to primary appraisal in the Lazarus and Folkman, 1984, stress model.) Two items tapping outcome evaluation dominated one factor in an exploratory factor analysis (Appendix B, Factor 6); this factor was incorporated into the regressions.

Distress. Standard measures of depression, anxiety, and hostility were used (see Appendix A).

Results: Downsizing, Justice, and Distress

To summarize the basic effects of leaving, all but one effect was as anticipated. Leavers had the lowest organizational commitment, and they rated the outcome of their departure as significantly worse than stayers did. Leavers also reported themselves to be more anxious, depressed, and somewhat more hostile than stayers. Both distributive justice and information-based interactional justice were higher for the stayers, like the results for organizational commitment. Unexpectedly, officers who were leaving saw themselves as receiving more respect than the stayers thought leavers were receiving.

Testing the second and third expectations, Table 7.1 summarizes results from a series of regressions.[4] The measures of distress behave similarly to one another and

---

[4]Initial regressions (not shown) first added the justice factors to equations that included only leaver status as a predictor, to establish that they added significantly to the variance explained by leaver status alone. Second, the significance of interactions was tested. Table 7.1 presents the final equations, retaining all interactions of leaver status with justice factors for clarity of comparison. Missing interactions can be assumed to be nonsignificant.

TABLE 7.1

Justice Factors, Leaver Status, and Reaction to Downsizing

	Evaluation			Distress	
	Organizational Commitment	Outcome Evaluation	Anxiety	Depression	Hostility
Distrib. Justice	.13****	−.26****	−.11***	−.15****	−.18****
Information	.15****	−.17****	−.02	−.04	.04
Respect	.14****	.32****	−.08*	−.04	−.06
Leaver	−.23****	−.09***	.13****	.11****	.09***
Leaver× DJ	−.01	.01	−.02	−.01	.01
Leaver × Info	−.03	.02	−.00	−.01	−.00
Leaver × Respect	.12***	.08*	−.04	−.08*	−.11**
R2	.12	.21	.04	.05	.05

Note. Ns ranged from 1543 to 1648.

$*p < .05; **p < .01; ***p < .001; ****p < .0001.$

opposite to organizational commitment. That is, whatever produces high commitment also reduces distress, and vice versa. Results for outcome evaluation are less consistent, perhaps reflecting the fact that an evaluation of leaving as a negative outcome is fed by both instrumental factors such as fear of job loss and sentimental factors such as attachment to the organization. Certain conclusions also can be drawn about the relative strengths of the predictors. Together, the indicators of interactional justice (respect and information) appear more powerful than distributive justice, but only for the organizational evaluation items. The main effects of respect are more impressive than those of information, and respect has both main and interactive effects.

I explored the interactions involving leaver status and respect by running separate regressions for leavers and stayers. The impact of respect on organizational commitment was substantially larger for leavers (ß = .32, $p < .0001$) than for stayers (ß = .12, $p < .01$); results for outcome evaluation were similar. The current results show that a specific form of procedural justice—interactional justice involving respect—is a more potent predictor when the person is facing a particular negative outcome—leaving the military. These patterns are consistent with the general finding that procedural justice is a more powerful predictor when outcomes are more negative (Brockner & Wiesenfeld, 1996).

IMPLICATIONS

In this chapter I present a series of dualities. The chapter argues that social influence theorizing and justice theorizing are, or should be, reciprocal, and it illustrates, at least crudely, how measures of social influence can be shown to affect judgments of justice. A further reciprocity is found in the link between justice and stress; the chapter pinpoints injustice as a determinant of perceived stress. At the level of ethics, the chapter simultaneously argues for ethical treatment of underlings who are being "downsized" out of an organization and begins to explore what makes for more ethical treatment, from the departees' point of view.

All of this happens with the assistance of a rather unusual sample of individuals undergoing downsizing: officers of the Russian Army. Their special characteristics are not the focus of this chapter, but they are not irrelevant. Noteworthy in the present context is that these officers are likely to be extreme in a number of respects, including both the deprivations to which they have been subjected and, simultaneously, the investment they have made in their organization (see International Center for Human Values, 1997). The particular qualities of Russian Army life, family life, and the intersection of the two are the subjects of ongoing work in this project (e.g., Hamilton, Segal, Segal, & Rohall, 1999). For now, one key issue stands out that may resonate in the context of the Western business world: respect.

Respect was a significant contributor to the perceived well-being of those who were going through the downsizing of the Russian Army circa 1996. These men, in turn, were part of what had been considered a key elite in the society. By looking at them as elites rather than as soldiers we can find the clearest relevance to Western business downsizings. There is a danger that employers could take such findings as a recipe for the practice of "exit cheating" instead of exit ethics. The laid-off employee becomes a potential Rodney Dangerfield shouting, "I don't get no respect," and the employer's impression management goal becomes one of creating an atmosphere of respect, real or not. Even elite employees who are shown the door may see their treatment as fair and may exhibit fewer symptoms of distress if they are just treated with respect. And respect is cheap, at least relative to severance pay. But such theorists as Lind and Tyler, reviewed earlier, argue otherwise. At the core of their group value theory is the sense that procedure matters because it shows that the person is a respected member of the group. In this view, exiting employees ask for a simple thing: superiors who show regret that they are leaving the group. It is a challenge for business ethicists, managers, and social psychologists to explore the limits of respect as an empirical determinant of perceived justice and personal well-being and to address its theoretical contribution to a future exit ethics.

APPENDIX A

Methods

The research is a quasi-experimental panel survey of Russian military officers and their wives. Analyses concentrated on the officers, and the data were drawn from Wave 1 of a two-wave study ($N = 1,798$). I concentrate on the officers for brevity; I use Wave 1 data (before the occurrence of the downsizing in this sample) because, at the time I drafted this chapter, only the first of two waves of data were available for analysis.

Independent Variables

Compliance.   The data set included a series of questions developed by Melvin Kohn and associates (e.g., Kohn, 1977; Kohn & Schooler, 1983) to study conformity and its relation to values. These items were adapted to the military context but were otherwise virtually unchanged. Note that item wordings are reproduced as they emerged from the Russian in backtranslation. Compliance items were as follows:

1. When your immediate superior delegates a task to you, does he usually just order you to carry it out or does he, as a rule, discuss the task with you? [Options: *Gives an order, discusses it,* and *it depends* coded with the first three options 3, 1, and 2, and other options (*don't know, refusal, no answer*) deleted.]
2. Tell me please, is it very easy, easy, difficult, or very difficult for you to disagree with your superior? [Options: *Very easy, easy, difficult,* and *very difficult* coded 1–4, with other options deleted.]
3. How important is it for successful completion of your work to do exactly what you are ordered—is it very important, important, so-so, not very important, or not at all important? [Options: *Very important, important, so-so, not very important, not important;* reverse coded so *very important* = 5.]

The items did not hang together; they had a reliability coefficient alpha of –.00. An item analysis revealed that removal of one of the items, the third, improved the alpha—but only to a still-weak .25. In the analyses summarized in text, the items were entered separately rather than collapsed into a scale.

Identification.   The indicators of identification were highly reliable ($a = .72$ for a 4-item scale). These items were drawn from Porter's Organizational Commitment Scale (Mowday et al., 1982; Porter, Steers, Mowday, & Boulian, 1974; see also Lincoln & Kalleberg, 1990). They were, "I am willing to work hard to help the Army fulfill its mission," "I feel very little loyalty to the Army" (reversed), "I am proud of serving in the Army," and "I would refuse a higher paying job to remain in the Army."

Internalization. Because the military work environment is relatively constant, responses can be interpreted as at least partly reflective of the respondent's characteristic patterns of thought. People who are more likely to see their work as complex and interesting are also more likely to be involved with it for internal reasons: It resonates with their values. Four indicators of internalization originally were selected to measure the complexity of the person's work environment (Kohn & Schooler, 1983; Lincoln & Kalleberg, 1990). These items were, "My work requires a high level of skill," "My work always makes me study new things," "My work is very varied," and "My work does not let me use my skill and knowledge" (reversed). Reliability analyses indicated that a 3-item scale deleting the last item was more reliable (a = .74) than the full 4-item version (a = .63). Analyses reported here were carried out with the shorter form.

Dependent or Intervening Variables

Justice. The measured aspects of justice include the distributive justice of the outcome versus the procedural justice with which it is achieved. Furthermore, within the realm of procedural justice, at least three additional subdivisions can be made. In the military context, it is relevant to consider the extent to which individuals receive information about the downsizing and are treated with respect. Both of the latter are commonly considered aspects of "interactional" procedural justice (Bies, 1987). In contrast, probably the most commonly studied procedural variable, "voice" in the process or the decision (e.g., Folger, 1986; Thibaut & Walker, 1975), is not particularly relevant to a military downsizing, where personnel would not expect themselves to have voice in most everyday decisions, let alone the decision to be released from service. Justice measures are reproduced in Appendix B, and methodology of establishing factor scores is addressed in the text.

Distress. Mental health items came from the Symptoms Checklist 90 (SCL-90, originally the Hopkins Symptoms Checklist; Derogatis, Lipman, Rickels, Uhlenhuth, & Covi, 1974), with the exception of one item drawn from Pearlin et al. (1981). Three scales derived from these items are assessed here: depression, anxiety, and hostility. Depression refers to standard symptoms of clinical depression. Examples of the 12 depression items include "loss of sexual interest or pleasure," "feeling lonely," and "thoughts of ending your life." Cronbach's alpha was substantial (.82). Anxiety refers to clinical symptoms of high manifest anxiety. The five scale items include "nervousness" and "trembling." The four hostility items from the SCL-90 included "feeling easily annoyed or irritated" and "having urges to break or smash things." Cronbach's alphas for the shorter anxiety and hostility scales were, predictably, smaller (.59 and .65, respectively). These latter scales refer to distress in a normal population and should not be taken as indicators of psychopathology (Coyne, 1994; cf. Flett, Vredenburg, & Krames, 1997).

Sample and Survey

The research goal was to interview approximately 1,800 Russian officers, divided about 50–50 into those who would be leaving the Army within 3 to 6 months and those who would not. Army lists were used to identify and randomly sample officers who either were scheduled to be separated from the Army in the next 3 to 6 months ("leavers") or were not so scheduled ("stayers"). Sampling was clustered geographically by region. Officers came from 59 bases across seven military regions (St. Petersburg [Leningrad], Moscow, Kaliningrad, Volga, Ural, Baikal, and Far East). Sampling points (military "towns" or bases) were in locales that range from major urban centers (Moscow's outskirts) to isolated rural locales. In all, 1,798 officers were interviewed, an overall response rate of 90%. These procedures yielded a stratified random sample of those members of the Russian officer corps located in regions experiencing downsizing (seven of Russia's nine military regions) as of early 1996.

At the end of the interview, married officers were asked for permission to interview their wives. Almost all officers (96%) were married and almost all gave permission, and some 1,609 wives (93% of those asked) were interviewed. Results for wives are reported elsewhere (e.g., Hamilton, 1998).

One important consideration in evaluating the responses of leavers is, of course, the basis on which they believed themselves to have been selected to leave. The Russian Army used two methods to determine who was to be discharged: In some cases, entire bases were closed and all personnel were released; in others, officers were selectively culled from bases that were to remain open. In the latter cases, the orders came from central authority and were phrased in terms of the elimination of positions rather than persons. I attempted to obtain information about whether each respondent was part of a unit that was disbanded or was selectively released, but the Ministry of Defense would not release that information on security grounds. (Some of the closed bases were in secret locations because they housed nuclear weapons.) It appears reasonable to assume that officers were unlikely to blame themselves personally for their discharge under either procedure.

Wave 2 of the study was carried out in May through August 1997, approximately 18 months after the original interviews. As of the time of the ethics and social influence conference, this second data set was still in preparation for analysis.

Field Work

Seven field supervisors from the International Center for Human Values in Moscow traveled to various locations to train the interviewers, who were military officers from the psychological services personnel at each locale. These interviewers were used to discussing sensitive matters in a confidential manner with their fellow officers. A standard regimen of training based on the field training at the University of Michigan's Survey Research Center was followed.

Pretesting included focus group administrations of the draft instrument. Some items were modified or dropped based on these group sessions.

Instrument

Contents. The survey instrument included an array of items representing the first wave of a panel study of the downsizing experience. The officers' instrument took an average of 67 min.

Translation. The instrument initially was prepared in English, then translated into Russian in Moscow by the center's personnel, and backtranslated by additional personnel. The Russian version and backtranslation were sent to the United States, where a second independent backtranslation was prepared. The two were compared and discrepancies resolved.

Human subjects. Informed consent and confidentiality are important considerations when the subject of study is a relatively coercive organization with powers of hiring and firing. The sensitive nature of some of our questions only accentuated these concerns. Interviewers began the session with a rather lengthy description of the study, including assurances that the data would be held in confidence by the researchers. Respondents were told that the information obtained would be used to try to improve the condition of personnel who were being released from the military and their families. A warning was given that some questions might be sensitive, accompanied by the assurance that the respondent could skip or refuse to answer anything; this assurance was repeated later in the interview, just before items on mental health and drinking. Most of what our research team identified as potentially sensitive items were placed in a self-administered section that occurred partway through the interview. These included mental health, self-esteem, mastery, and drinking. Interviewers reported no complaints or difficulties with this procedure; if anything, the alternation from interview to self-administration and back to interview varied the flow and was judged to help maintain respondent interest.

Compensation. At the end of the introduction, respondents were told that they would be paid for their participation, a common procedure in Russian survey research; each respondent was paid the ruble equivalent of $8.50.

Independent Variables: Leaving the Military Impending departure from the Army was measured both as a dichotomy (leaving/not leaving) based on the Army's information and as a trichotomy (leaving/not sure/not leaving) based on the officers' own perceptions of their plans (see Table 7.A).

TABLE 7.A

Officer's Downsizing Status According to Army and as Perceived by Officer

	Army says officer will:		
Officer says he will:	Leave	Stay	Total
Leave	85.6%	0.0%	41.6%
Not sure	14.3%	2.7%	8.3%
Stay	1.0%	97.3%	50.1%
Total	48.6%	51.4%	100.0%
	(874)	(924)	(1,798)

Note. $\chi^2(2, N = 1,798) = 1,710.6, p < .0001$.

In fact, the relation between what the Army thought was going to happen to these men in the next 3 to 6 months and what they thought would happen was highly significant, but far from perfect. As Table 7.A illustrates, officers were more likely to misunderstand, distort, or simply disagree with the Army in one direction—saying they would stay or were not sure, when the Army records showed they would be leaving. It is probably safe to assume that in the climate that existed at the time, and certainly among the officer corps, the distortions/disagreements reflect the men's personal preferences for staying rather than leaving.

All analyses use the men's own characterizations of their leaver status both for theoretical reasons (because a person's perceived situation is likely to be more important than the factual one in determining attitudes) and for practical reasons (because officers were routed through the interview as a function of the responses they gave about their condition).

APPENDIX B

TABLE 7.B

Wordings and Factor Loadings of Justice-Related Items

	Gov. Blame	Distrib.	Resp.	Info.	Self Blame	Outcome Eval.
1. People who are discharged from the Army are informed about that just before the discharge. (R)				.70		
2. People who are discharged from the Army get very clear explanations as to the reasons for the discharge.				.79		
3. People who are discharged from the Army have a very good understanding of what the Army leadership took into account when deciding who would remain in and who would be discharged.				.43		
4. The Army is doing its best to help people discharged from the Army to find a comparable job outside the Armed Forces.		.52				
5. The downsizing of the Army could have been avoided. (R)	.82					
6. Among my friends and relatives there are at least a few people who are being discharged from the Army in connection with the downsizing of the Armed Forces. (R)						
7. The Army is to blame for the downsizing of the Armed Forces. (R)					-.79	
8. I share with others the blame for the downsizing of the Armed Forces. (R)					.81	
9. The government is to blame for the downsizing of the Armed Forces. (R)	.64					
10. I would, without a doubt, recommend a military career to a friend or relative.						.56

TABLE 7.B (*continued*)

Wordings and Factor Loadings of Justice-Related Items

	Gov. Blame	Distrib.	Resp.	Info.	Self Blame	Outcome Eval.
11. It was necessary to reduce the number of personnel in the Armed Forces.	.80					
12. The procedure for selecting who is to be dismissed and who is to stay in the Army is completely unjust. (R)		.56				
13. The pension [reimbursement package] that the Army will provide me is quite fair/The reimbursement package provided by the Army to the people being discharged is quite fair.		.41				
14. My immediate superiors expressed great regret about my forced retirement/ Immediate supervisors are expressing strong regret to the people being discharged.			.64			
15. My retirement from the Armed Forces will be very bad for me/Retirement from the Armed Forces will be very bad for the people being discharged.						.77
16. I am being treated with respect/People being discharged are treated with respect.			.77			
17. The government is not assisting me with finding a job or new residence or with retraining/The government is not assisting the people being discharged with finding a job or new residence or with retraining. (R)		.60				
18. My service in the Army was very important to me/Their service in the Army was very important to the people being discharged.			.54			.60

TABLE 7.B (*continued*)

Note. *N* = 1,648. *R* following an item indicates that it was reverse scored so that all items go in the direction of higher scores standing for a more pro-Army opinion. Items 1–12 appeared together in the survey instrument; Items 13–18 were asked shortly thereafter, with wordings varied as shown (leaver/stayer). Missing data for individual items are replaced by the item means. All loadings > .30 in absolute value are reproduced here. Factor names, abbreviated in the column headings, have the following meanings (high scores refer to): Government Blame (Gov. Blame) = respondent blames government for downsizing, in contrast with the Army; Distribution (Distrib.) = downsizing is distributively just; one item refers to general procedural justice; Respect = downsized personnel are treated respectfully (interpersonal justice); one item (18) refers to general negative appraisal (outcome evaluation) of being released during downsizing, double loading with Factor 6. Information = the Army provides adequate information regarding discharge (procedural justice); Self-Blame = respondent blames self and other soldiers, rather than the Army, for the downsizing; Outcome Evaluation = outcome evaluation/primary appraisal of leaving the military as negative; one of these items double loads with Factor 3, Respect; one item (10) is generally positive about the Army rather than specifically referring to departure from it. From "(In)Justice in Waiting: Russian Officers' Organizational Commitment and Mental Distress During Downsizing," by V. L. Hamilton (in press). *Journal of Applied Social Psychology.*

ACKNOWLEDGMENTS

This chapter was prepared with the assistance of Grants SBR-9402212, 9411755, and 9601760 from the National Science Foundation (Sociology Program).

REFERENCES

Bies, R. J. (1987). The predicament of injustice: The management of moral outrage. In L. L. Cummings & B. M. Staw (Eds.), *Research in organizational behavior* (Vol. 9, pp. 289–319). Greenwich, CT: JAI.

Brockner, J., & Wiesenfeld, B. M. (1993). Living on the edge (of social and organizational psychology): The effects of job layoffs on those who remain. In J. K. Murnighan (Ed.), *Social psychology in organizations: Advances in theory and research* (pp. 119–140). Englewood Cliffs, NJ: Prentice-Hall.

Brockner, J., & Wiesenfeld, B. M. (1996). An integrative framework for explaining reactions to decisions: Interactive effects of outcomes and procedures. *Psychological Bulletin, 120,* 189–208.

Cobb, S., & Kasl, S. V. (1977). *Termination: The consequences of job loss* (NIOSH Research Report 76-1261). Washington, DC: U.S. Department of Health, Education and Welfare.

Coyne, J. C. (1994). Self-reported distress: Analog or ersatz depression? *Psychological Bulletin, 116,* 29–45.

Derogatis, L. R., Lipman, R. S., Rickels, K., Uhlenhuth, E. H., & Covi, L. (1974). The Hopkins Symptom Checklist (HSCL): A self-report symptom inventory. *Behavioral Science, 19,* 1–15.

Dohrenwend, B. S., Krasnoff, L., Askenasy, A. R., & Dohrenwend, B. P. (1978). Exemplification of a method for scaling life events: The PERI life events scale. *Journal of Health and Social Behavior, 19,* 205–229.

Flett, G. L., Vredenburg, K., & Krames, L. (1997). The continuity of depression in clinical and nonclinical samples. *Psychological Bulletin, 121,* 395–416.

Folger, R. (1986). Rethinking equity theory: A referent cognition model. In H. W. Bierhoff, R. L. Cohen, & J. Greenberg (Eds.), *Justice in social relations* (pp. 145–162). New York: Plenum.

Greenberg, J. (1990a). Employee theft as a reaction to underpayment inequity: The hidden costs of pay cuts. *Journal of Applied Psychology, 75,* 561–568.

Greenberg, J. (1990b). Looking fair: Managing impressions of organizational justice. In B. M. Staw and L. L. Cummings (Eds.), *Research in organizational behavior* (Vol. 10, pp. 111–157). Greenwich, CT: JAI.

Greenberg, J. (1993). Stealing in the name of justice: Informational and interpersonal moderators of theft reactions to underpayment inequity. *Organizational Behavior and Human Decision Processes, 54,* 81–103.

Hamilton, V. L. (1998, August 13). *Unemployment as career loss: Marital adjustment to downsizing of the Russian military.* Paper presented at the International Congress of Applied Psychology, San Francisco.

Hamilton, V. L. (in press). (In)Justice in waiting: Russian officers' organizational commitment and mental distress during downsizing. *Journal of Applied Social Psychology.*

Hamilton, V. L., Broman, C. L., Hoffman, W. S., & Renner, D. S. (1990). Hard times and vulnerable people: Initial effects of plant closing on autoworkers' mental health. *Journal of Health and Social Behavior, 31,* 123–140.

Hamilton, V. L., & Sanders, J. (1992). *Everyday justice: Responsibility and the individual in Japan and the United States.* New Haven, CT: Yale University Press.

Hamilton, V. L., Segal, D. R., Segal, M. W., & Rohall, D. E. (1999, January). *Downsizing the Russian Army: Quality of life and mental health consequences for organizational leavers, survivors, and spouses.* Paper presented at international conference on Plant Closures and Downsizing in Europe, Leuven, Belgium.

International Center for Human Values. (1997). *The process of the armed forces reduction in the Russian federation and living standards of service families.* Unpublished manuscript, Moscow, Russia.

Jahoda, M., Lazarsfeld, P. M., & Zeisel, H. (1971). *Marienthal: The sociography of an unemployed community.* Chicago: Aldine. (Original work published 1933)

Kelman, H. C. (1958). Compliance, identification, and internalization: Three processes of attitude change. *Journal of Conflict Resolution, 2,* 51–60.

Kelman, H. C. (1969). Patterns of personal involvement in the national system: A social–psychological analysis of political legitimacy. In J. N. Rosenau (Ed.), *International politics and foreign policy* (2nd ed., pp. 276–288). New York: The Free Press.

Kelman, H. C. (1974). Attitudes are alive and well and gainfully employed in the sphere of action. *American Psychologist, 29,* 310–324.

Kelman, H. C., & Hamilton, V. L. (1989). *Crimes of obedience: Toward a social psychology of authority and responsibility.* New Haven, CT: Yale University Press.

Kessler, R. C., Price, R. H., & Wortman, C. B. (1985). Social factors in psychopathology: Stress, social support, and coping processes. *Annual Review of Psychology, 36,* 531–572.

Kohlberg, L. (1969). Stage and sequence: The cognitive–developmental approach to socialization. In D. A. Goslin (Ed.), *Handbook of socialization theory and research* (pp. 347–480). Chicago: Rand McNally.

Kohn, M. L. (1977). *Class and conformity: A study of values, with a reassessment* (2nd ed.). Chicago: University of Chicago Press.

Kohn, M. L., & Schooler, C. (1983). *Work and personality: An inquiry into the impact of social stratification.* Norwood, NJ: Ablex.

Lazarus, R., & Folkman, S. (1984). *Stress, appraisal, and coping.* New York: Springer.

Lincoln, J. R., & Kalleberg, A. L. (1990). *Culture, control, and commitment: A study of work organization and work attitudes in the United States and Japan.* New York: Cambridge University Press.

Lind, E. A. (1994). Procedural justice and culture: Evidence for ubiquitous process concerns. *Zeitschrift fur Rechtssoziologie, 15,* 24–36.

Lind, E. A., Kanfer, R., & Early, C. (1990). Voice, control, and procedural justice. *Journal of Personality and Social Psychology, 59,* 952–959.

Lind, E. A., & Tyler, T. R. (1988). *The social psychology of procedural justice.* New York: Plenum.

Mowday, R., Porter, L., & Steers, R. (1982). *Employee–organization linkages: The psychology of commitment, absenteeism, and turnover.* New York: Academic Press.

Pearlin, L. I. (1989). The sociological study of stress. *Journal of Health and Social Behavior, 30,* 241–256.

Pearlin, L. I., Menaghan, E. G., Lieberman, M. A., & Mullan, J. T. (1981). The stress process. *Journal of Health and Social Behavior, 22,* 337–356.

Perrucci, C. C., Perrucci, R., Targ, D. B., & Targ, H. R. (1988). *Plant closings: International context and social costs.* New York: Aldine De Gruyter.

Porter, L. W., Steers, R. M., Mowday, R. T., & Boulian, P. V. (1974). Organizational commitment, job satisfaction and turnover among psychiatric technicians. *Journal of Applied Psychology, 59,* 603–609.

Rawls, J. (1971). *A theory of justice.* Cambridge, MA: Harvard University Press.

Robinson, P. H., & Darley, J. M. (1995). *Justice, liability, and blame: Community views and the criminal law.* Boulder, CO: Westview Press.

Schlenker, B. R. (1980). *Impression management.* Monterey, CA: Brooks/Cole.

Schlenker, B. R., Britt, T. W., Pennington, J., Murphy, R., & Doherty, K. (1994). The triangle model of responsibility. *Psychological Review, 101,* 632–652.

Shaver, K. G. (1985). *The attribution of blame: Causality, responsibility, and blameworthiness.* New York: Springer-Verlag.

Thibaut, J. W., & Walker, L. (1975). *Procedural justice.* Hillsdale, NJ: Lawrence Erlbaum Associates.

Tyler, T. R. (1990). *Why people obey the law.* New Haven, CT: Yale University Press.

Tyler, T. R., & Lind, E. A.. (1992). A relational model of authority in groups. *Advances in Experimental Social Psychology, 25,* 115–191.

Tyler, T. R., & Lind, E. A. (in press). Procedural justice. In J. Sanders & V. L. Hamilton (Eds.), *Handbook of Justice Research in Law.* New York: Plenum.

Weiner, B. (1995). *Judgments of responsibility: A foundation for a theory of social conduct.* New York: Guilford.

Wheaton, B. (1990). Life transitions, role histories, and mental health. *American Sociological Review, 55,* 209–223.

II

Awareness of and Resistance to Social Influence

8 Responses to Perceived Organizational Wrongdoing: Do Perceiver Characteristics Matter?

Marcia P. Miceli
Georgetown University

James R. Van Scotter
The University of Memphis

Janet P. Near
Indiana University

Michael T. Rehg
Air Force Institute of Technology

It is not difficult to find examples of organizational wrongdoing in the private and public sectors in the United States. The crisis in the savings and loan industry in the 1980s provided one example of "massive corruption and abuse requiring hundreds of billions of dollars to correct" (Fisher, 1991, p. 358). More recently, a major internal investigation in the U. S. Army revealed widespread and serious job discrimination (Priest, 1997). Wrongdoing has negative consequences not only for the organization and its members but also for society as a whole. For example, unsafe products may cause injuries and deaths. Therefore, organization members, stockholders, and customers benefit when individuals put a stop to organizational wrongdoing such as fraud, unfair discrimination, or unsafe products or working conditions.

Wrongdoing may continue to occur in part because external regulatory agencies are limited in their ability to detect wrongdoing within organizations. Consequently, most of the responsibility for finding and reporting wrongful acts falls on individuals inside the organization, including whistle-blowers. Given society's stake in the process, it is not surprising that more than 1,000 articles describing instances of whistle-blowing appeared in 30 major newspapers from 1989 through early 1995 (Brewer, 1995). Yet, whistle-blowing can be hazardous to individuals' careers, because whistle-blowers threaten the authority structure of the organization, which may then resist and retaliate against them (Weinstein, 1979). Not surprisingly, empirical studies are quite consistent in showing that most employees who say they have observed wrongdoing in their organizations do not report it (Miceli & Near, 1992).

It often is assumed that discouraging retaliation or offering incentives is the key to encouraging whistle-blowing. Many U.S. laws proscribe retaliation or offer cash awards; for example, the False Claims Act rewards whistle-blowers who bring successful suits against recipients of federal funds who have defrauded the government (Callahan & Dworkin, 1994). Although these laws send a positive message and demonstrate lawmakers' desire to help those who try to halt wrongdoing, these provisions do not address an issue that may be more important to observers of perceived wrongdoing. Research shows that the observer's expectation of success in changing the wrongful practice or omission is a critical variable (Miceli & Near, 1992).

Although situational factors influence whistle-blowing, in most empirical investigations much variance remains unexplained (Miceli & Near, 1992). Within the same situation, some individuals blow the whistle or intervene in other ways to halt wrongdoing, whereas others do not. This suggests that individual differences may be critical. Demographic variables and beliefs about reporting channels explain some, but certainly not all, of the variance in whistle-blowing (e.g., King, 1997; Miceli & Near, 1984, 1992). Other differences in individuals' dispositions, beliefs, and relationships with their organizations also seem likely to be relevant to whistle-blowing. For instance, workers with high self-efficacy (Bandura, 1989) for whistle-blowing—that is, workers who believe strongly that they can blow the whistle successfully—should be more likely to engage in whistle-blowing than those with low self-efficacy.

The purpose of this chapter is to refine existing theory by identifying some additional personal characteristics, beliefs, and affective variables that may predict whistle-blowing. We focus primarily on individual variables that have, or are likely to have, some dispositional component. Furthermore, our objective is to build theory rather than to review existing findings regarding variables already identified as predicting whistle-blowing. Such reviews can be found elsewhere (e.g., Miceli & Near, 1992). Instead, we extend and refine an existing model to develop propositions about potentially important individual variables. Consequently, there are few if any direct empirical tests of these propositions to be reviewed; thus, we leave it to readers to debate, and future research to determine, the relative importance of the variables considered here.

Finally, to keep our scope manageable, we cannot consider all possible individual variables that might be related to whistle-blowing. Likewise, situational variables are outside our scope. Situational variables that predict whistle-blowing have been reviewed elsewhere in some detail (Miceli & Near, 1992; Near & Miceli, 1996). For example, organizational ethical climate may have effects on whistle-blowing as well as wrongdoing, although the data on climate are not straightforward (Near, Baucus, & Miceli, 1993). However, this is not the focus of the current chapter, which instead examines individual variables that predict whistle-blowing, emphasizing in particular those that are at least partially dispositional.

PLAYERS IN THE PROCESS

It is important to begin with a definition of whistle-blowing, because the term has many connotations. One widely used definition (King, 1997) is as follows: "Whistle-blowers are organization members (including former members and job applicants) who disclose illegal, immoral, or illegitimate practices (including omissions) under the control of their employers, to persons or organizations who may be able to effect action" (Near & Miceli, 1985, p. 4). This is a broad, inclusive definition. We think it important to begin with a wide net and then examine or control for variations that may appear among types of whistle-blowers (e.g., those who use channels external to the organization to report wrongdoing vs. those who use channels internal to the organization). In this way, we can determine empirically how whistle-blowers differ across situations and how they are similar across situations.

Many controversies raised by this particular definition have been discussed elsewhere (Miceli & Near, 1992); because of space limitations we do not repeat them here. However, three points should be clarified.

First, we exclude "faux whistle-blowers"—social actors who may call themselves whistle-blowers but who fail to meet one or more of the definitional requirements (Miceli & Near, 1997). For example, a faux whistle-blower may talk about wrongdoing with coworkers, family, or friends but not report it to someone who can take action; another may attempt to stop activity she or he doesn't like but doesn't judge to be truly illegitimate, illegal, or immoral.

Second, some individuals may find other ways to get wrongdoing stopped. For example, if wrongdoing terminates after an observer discusses it with the perceived wrongdoer, the observer is not a whistle-blower, because there was no report to an authority. But such persons should not be classified as bystanders or "inactive observers" (people who fail to take action), because they intervened. As we discuss later, some individual characteristics may predict intervention but not necessarily whistle-blowing, and thus it is important for researchers to include, among response choices, alternative actions along with whistle-blowing.

Third, whether whistle-blowing should include reporting wrongdoing only to a supervisor who stops it has not been determined. A scenario-based study (King, 1997) suggested that, for nurses, the act of reporting wrongdoing exclusively to supervisors may have different antecedents than reporting to other complaint recipients. Reporting a problem to one's own supervisor may be a fairly routine event within the organization's normal authority structure. It may not be viewed as whistle-blowing by either party. On the other hand, one's supervisor may react just as negatively to a subordinate's report of perceived wrongdoing as would anyone else, particularly if the subordinate is persistent or identifies wrongdoing for which the supervisor is responsible. For the present, we treat such reports as a type of whistle-blowing and encourage researchers to consider them separately. Ultimately, evidence may show that the definition should be modified to exclude these reports and to give such reporting behavior a different name, but unequivocal evidence currently does not exist.

In whistle-blowing, players besides the observer of perceived wrongdoing are important. First, the source of the wrongdoing may be other people within the organization or the organization itself. Second, it usually is assumed that the whistle-blower lacks the power to change the wrongdoing directly and must influence a potential complaint recipient to do so. Members may report questionable activities to immediate supervisors or through specific reporting channels charged with responsibility for investigating complaints.

Third, influence targets may include the dominant coalition of the organization (Thompson, 1967), operationalized in many studies as the top management team (e.g., Michel & Hambrick, 1992). It does not seem appropriate to suggest that all managers or organizations would react similarly to all instances of whistle-blowing. Some managers may be alarmed because whistle-blowing calls for changing something they don't want to change, or because it raises moral and ethical questions that are not easily resolved. They may object to anonymous whistle-blowing because it does not provide the accused with the opportunity to face their accusers (Elliston, 1982). Managers may react negatively to frivolous or malicious complaints that are pursued with little regard for respecting the rights of others or complaints that use unfair tactics (Miceli & Near, 1997). But managers may recognize that whistle-blowers with valid reports can improve long-term organizational effectiveness, because they may suggest solutions to previously undetected but important organizational problems (Brief & Motowidlo, 1986). Therefore, how the observer of perceived wrongdoing expects these players to react may well influence whether and how the observer acts. These expectations may be influenced by the observer's characteristics.

A REVISED MODEL OF WHISTLE-BLOWING
AS PROSOCIAL BEHAVIOR

Research suggests that many acts of whistle-blowing are prosocial organizational behaviors (Dozier & Miceli, 1985). Prosocial organizational behavior has been defined as behavior that is:

(a) performed by a member of an organization; (b) directed toward an individual, group, or organization with whom he or she interacts while carrying out his or her organizational role; and (c) performed with the intention of promoting the welfare of the individual, group, or organization toward which it is directed. (Brief & Motowidlo, 1986, p. 711)

After demonstrating that whistle-blowing generally meets these criteria, Dozier and Miceli (1985) proposed a model of the decision steps that may precede whistle-blowing. Their model drew heavily from research on bystander intervention (e.g., Darley & Bateson, 1973; Latané & Darley, 1968, 1970). Generally, as shown in Fig. 8.1, the model proposes that organization members who encounter questionable activity or omissions consider several questions before deciding whether to blow the whistle.

We have modified the model slightly, in three ways. First, the questions have been refined. The revised model proposes that, when faced with questionable activity or omissions, an individual asks:

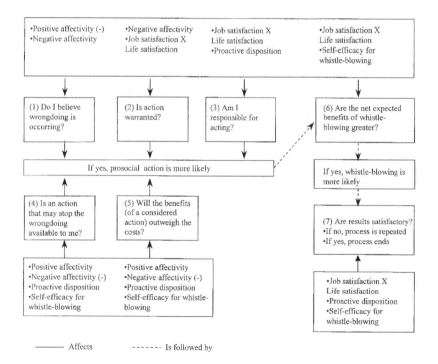

FIG. 8.1. A model predicting responses to perceived wrongdoing.

1. Do I believe wrongdoing is occurring?

2. Is action warranted?

3. Am I responsible for acting?

4. Is an action that may stop the wrongdoing available to me (i.e., is there something that I could do that might stop it)?

5. Will the benefits (of a considered action) outweigh the costs?

These questions, answered affirmatively, would tend to lead to intervention as opposed to other coping strategies, such as ignoring, redefining, or justifying the wrongdoing. In the case of Questions 4 and 5, the observer could believe that alternatives to whistle-blowing are potentially effective in stopping wrongdoing. For example, the observer may consider confronting the wrongdoer(s) or refusing a request to participate, in the hope that others will follow suit.

A sixth question might occur only after one has decided to act but is considering alternative courses of action: Are the net expected benefits of whistle-blowing greater than those for other interventions? If this question is answered affirmatively, whistle-blowing would be more likely to occur than other actions. Finally, in Question 7, the whistle-blower asks whether the results are satisfactory and may persist if they are not.

A second proposed modification is the clarification that organization members make action choices that are not dichotomous, for example, to blow the whistle or not. There may be different ways of blowing the whistle—to certain persons, with others or not, anonymously or not, and so forth. Furthermore, most questions in the revised model suggest conditions supportive of some action; only Question 6 differentiates whistle-blowing from other types of intervention, such as confronting the perceived wrongdoer. We view intervention as including a wide range of behaviors that a person might undertake that are aimed at halting wrongdoing. Thus we speak throughout much of the remainder of this chapter about intervention in general (rather than whistle-blowing specifically). We propose that variables that affect each of these decisions ultimately will determine the incidence and nature of intervention or the action in response to perceived wrongdoing. These variables also may determine whether the individual persists in taking further action if the outcome of the initial action is unsatisfactory.

A third proposed modification is that, despite the rational, logical approach implied by the numbering of these questions, we do not propose that all questions must be answered or that they must be answered in sequence. In fact, it is unlikely that a potential whistle-blower would consider the first five questions in sequence. For example, an employee may believe that no possible action can be taken that will stop the wrongdoer and therefore may rationalize that perhaps the perceived wrongdoing is not so wrong after all. Cognitive dissonance, or some other mechanism, might well explain such rationalization. In essence, then, the first five questions are a package, not a series of questions answered in sequence. Furthermore, deciding to blow the whistle, like some other organizational decision processes, may be influenced heavily by emotions (Bies & Tripp, 1998; Goldman, 1998). For example, moral outrage, anger, or a sense of betrayal may propel some people to act even though indicators of change do not look promising. Though we cannot yet account for these emotions and how and when they may have impact, we propose that the decision process is unlikely to be purely rational.

Finally, we wish to make explicit an implicit domain condition in the original model. Some incidents of whistle-blowing are more antisocial than prosocial, to the extent that whistle-blowers intend to harm others, actually do harm others, or use tactics that violate norms of procedural justice (Miceli & Near, 1997). Thus, whistle-blowers can intend to stop activity that they honestly believe to be immoral, illegitimate, or illegal while also intending to harm others. For example, some whistle-blowers also may be motivated to take revenge on another member whom they perceive to have harmed them (Bies, Tripp, & Kramer, 1997). The decision-making process that leads to antisocial whistle-blowing may be quite different from the prosocial model outlined here. As a case in point, if one believes that action is warranted, one may be more likely to engage in prosocial whistle-blowing because one intends to help someone or the organization. But whether action is believed to be warranted may be irrelevant to antisocial whistle-blowing. Simply observing any perceived wrongdoing may be enough to stimulate antisocial whistle-blowing. We now turn our attention to identifying predictors of prosocial intervention and, in some cases, whistle-blowing.

PROPOSED PREDICTORS OF PROSOCIAL INTERVENTION

The model suggests a number of individual variables that seem likely to predict prosocial intervention, one type of which is whistle-blowing. The relations between whistle-blowing and some individual variables, such as moral judgment development, have been reviewed elsewhere (e.g., Street, 1995). Yet some puzzling findings in whistle-blowing research suggest that exploration of new individual variables may be helpful. For example, threatened retaliation has been shown consistently to be unrelated to whistle-blowing, and experienced retaliation (as perceived by the whistle-blower) after one episode of whistle-blowing is unrelated to whistle-blowing regarding wrongdoing observed later (Miceli & Near, 1992). (However, perceived threat is related to where the wrongdoing is reported, once the individual has decided to blow the whistle; threatened whistle-blowers tend to go outside the organization; Miceli & Near, 1992.) With respect to the decision to report or not, there may be an "intervening personality" that is undaunted by situational variables, such as retaliation, that would discourage others.

It is unclear which dispositional characteristics are most important in predicting an observer's response to organizational wrongdoing, because there has been so little research on this topic. Furthermore, the dispositions probably are interrelated, so that all need to be examined at once, in a multivariate model, so that their separate effects can be evaluated. In most cases, variables discussed in this chapter have not been examined before in relation to whistle-blowing, but they seem to us to represent variables that might well play a predictive role, for theoretical reasons that this chapter spells out. Thus, we make no attempt to differentiate the more important from the less important predictors, because doing so would be premature.

Dispositional Affect

Positive affectivity (PA) and negative affectivity (NA) are two underlying dimensions of emotionality (Watson & Clark, 1992). Research suggests that PA and NA are distinct (Diener & Emmons, 1985) and enduring dispositions (Watson & Walker, 1996) that are associated with the way people experience their environment and react to it (Brief, Burke, George, Robinson, & Webster, 1988; Cropanzano, James, & Konovsky, 1993; Judge & Locke, 1993; Parkes, 1990). PA and NA act as filters that influence the way employees perceive and react to objects and events in the work environment. Thus, PA and NA are expected to be related to intervention in different ways and for different reasons.

PA is a general predisposition to experience positive mood states (Watson, Clark, & Tellegen, 1988). High-PA individuals view the world through rose-colored glasses. They experience events as more pleasant and positive than people with lower levels of the trait and tend to perceive neutral events favorably. Compared with low-PA individuals, high-PA individuals should be less likely to perceive activities as improper or potentially harmful to themselves or others. Higher levels of PA are expected to reduce the likelihood that an observer will judge an activity to be wrongdoing when it is not (i.e., fewer false positives) and to increase the likelihood that a wrongful activity will not be judged to be wrongdoing when it should be (i.e., more false negatives). Therefore, observers with higher PA will be less likely to perceive questionable activities as wrongdoing; that is, Question 1 in our model (Fig. 8.1) will more likely be answered "no." Thus, we predict the following:

> **Proposition 1:** Organization members with higher levels of PA will be less likely than those with lower levels of PA to say they observed wrongdoing.

High-PAs are described as active, alert, enthusiastic, strong, and outgoing, whereas low-PAs tend to be sad, lethargic, and inactive. High-PAs also have a generalized sense of personal well-being and competence and tend to be optimistic about their chances of success (Watson et al., 1988). Moreover, they have a greater tendency to try to control aspects of the environment that impact them (Judge, 1993). High-PAs also are more socially oriented than people low on the trait, are more likely to engage in social interaction, and report higher levels of coworker support (Iverson & Erwin, 1997). Research shows that people with higher levels of PA are more likely to perform prosocial acts (Isen & Baron, 1991; Van Scotter & Motowidlo, 1996). This suggests they are probably more likely than other people to use direct, problem-focused coping strategies (e.g., Parkes, 1990) and engage in cooperative efforts with others to stop perceived wrongdoing. Thus, people with higher levels of PA may be more likely to believe that a (prosocial) action is available (Question 4). Furthermore, this propensity along with their greater activity level and self-confidence (Question 5) suggests that high-PAs are more likely to believe that their intervention will stop the perceived wrongdoing. If so, then among those who have perceived wrongdoing, higher levels of PA will lead to increasing intervention. This leads to our next proposition:

> **Proposition 2:** Among observers of perceived organizational wrongdoing, there will be a positive relationship between PA and the likelihood the observer will intervene.

NA is expected to be related to intervention in a different way, and for different reasons. NA is described as a general disposition to experience subjective distress. High-NAs are more critical of themselves and others, and they experience more stress, anxiety, nervousness, anger, fear, and guilt (Watson & Clark, 1984). There is considerable agreement that NA influences the way people perceive their work environment (Brief et al., 1988; Judge, 1993; Parkes, 1990; Staw, Bell, & Clausen, 1986; Watson & Clark, 1984). High-NAs interpret ambiguous situations more negatively than other people and experience more work-related stress (Parkes, 1990). Higher levels of NA are expected to increase the likelihood that an observer will judge an activity to be more wrongful than will others (Question 1) and to feel that someone ought to do something about it (Question 2). This leads to our next proposition:

> **Proposition 3:** Organization members with higher levels of NA will be more likely to say they observed wrongdoing warranting action than those with lower levels of NA.

People with low levels of NA are dependable, willing to conform to job or social requirements, and pleasant to be around. In comparison, high-NAs are less concerned with fitting in than they are with the need to express the frustration and anxiety they experience. People with high levels of NA are more demanding, more hostile, and less willing to cooperate with others. It has been suggested that their persistent negative outlook and complaints may lead coworkers to avoid them (Brief et al., 1988). There is evidence that high-NAs are less likely to trust others (Watson & Clark, 1984) and that they experience more interpersonal conflict (Chen & Spector, 1994; Spector & O'Connell, 1994) and less social support (Moyle, 1995; Parkes, 1990). Thus, high-NAs seem less likely to go to their supervisors or other members of the organization for help when they encounter wrong-doing.

In addition, high-NAs tend to be less confident in their own abilities (Watson & Clark, 1984). Research also suggests that higher levels of NA are associated with lower job performance and less effective coping behavior (Cropanzano et al., 1993; Judge, 1993; Parkes, 1990). Studies suggest high-NAs feel they have less control over their work environment (Moyle, 1995) and are less likely to seek such control (Iverson & Erwin, 1997). Thus, they would probably be more likely to feel that no available course of action would stop the perceived wrongdoing (Question 4 in our model). Because high NA employees are more likely to use indirect coping techniques such as avoidance or suppression rather than confronting problems directly (Judge & Locke, 1993; Parkes, 1990), they will be unlikely to confront the perceived wrongdoer directly or take other action (i.e., the potential costs in Question 5 seem high). This brings us to our next proposition.

Proposition 4: Among observers of perceived organizational wrongdo-ing, there will be a negative relationship between NA and the likelihood the observer will intervene.

Job and Life Satisfaction

The extent to which job satisfaction is determined dispositionally has been the sub-ject of much debate in the last decade, with conflicting results (Arvey, Abraham, Bouchard, & Segal, 1989; Staw & Ross, 1985). The research also raises the ques-tion whether other types of satisfaction, such as life satisfaction, are dispositional. Because the cited research provides evidence that both types of satisfaction are dispositional to a point, we consider them further here.

Previous research examining the relation between job satisfaction and whis-tle-blowing has produced conflicting results (Miceli & Near, 1988; Sims & Keenan, 1998). However, at least some of the conflict may be explained by differ-ent methodologies. In a study showing a relation between satisfaction and whis-tle-blowing (Miceli & Near, 1988), employees were asked retrospectively about their own satisfaction and whistle-blowing. In a study showing no such relation (Sims & Keenan, 1998), business undergraduate and graduate students were asked about their own satisfaction and to react to scenarios describing hypothetical ethi-cal dilemmas. Obviously, further investigation is needed.

Among individuals for whom there is a high correlation between job and life satisfaction, the work ethic may be particularly strong (Rice, Near, & Hunt, 1980). The correlation for the average American worker is .31 (Near, Rice, & Hunt, 1978) or .44 when corrected for attenuation (Tait, Padgett, & Baldwin, 1989). But it is much higher (.62) among workers whose jobs seem to be a larger component of life, such as university faculty (Near & Sorcinelli, 1986) and small business owners (Daily & Near, 1995). For people in this category, work goals and life goals are interwoven tightly, in part because many of their interests and values may be work-related. In short, work seems to be a more important domain of life for some people than for others, which suggests that job satisfaction explains more variance in life satisfaction for this subgroup of American workers than for others.

People who find their jobs to be a relatively important part of their lives are likely to view negative events in the workplace, such as wrongdoing, as more critical than people whose job satisfaction and life satisfaction are not as closely tied together. Observing wrongdoing might be more troubling to the first group, and they also may be more likely than others to believe the wrongdoing warrants action (Question 2 of the model). Thus, we predict an interaction effect of job and life satisfaction, as in the next proposition:

Proposition 5: Among observers of perceived organizational wrongdoing, those with higher levels of both job and life satisfaction will be more likely than other organization members to say that the wrongdoing deserves action.

To the extent that employees are satisfied with their jobs and view satisfaction as an inducement to show loyalty to the organization by reporting wrongdoing, they may view whistle-blowing as a quid pro quo when they observe wrongdoing. However, this prediction may be stronger still for employees whose jobs are a very important part of their lives. Thus, "high–high" employees might feel they are personally responsible for acting (Question 3). Because of the centrality of work, they may care more about terminating wrongdoing and thus may view the expected benefits of whistle-blowing to be greater than do other employees (Question 6) and ultimately may be more likely to persist if necessary (Question 7).

Proposition 6: Among observers of perceived organizational wrongdoing, those with high levels of both job and life satisfaction will be more likely to take action.

Proposition 7: Among whistle-blowers and others who have intervened, there will be a positive relation between the interaction of job and life satisfaction and further action, if the initial action does not resolve the problem.

Proactive Disposition

We propose that intervention will be more likely when the observer of wrongdoing that warrants action has a proactive disposition. Proactive disposition differentiates the extent to which individuals take action to influence their environments (Bateman & Crant, 1993). Proactivity stems from people's needs to manipulate and control their environments (Bateman & Crant, 1993; Langer, 1983). Similarly, other authors have suggested that individuals with high needs for personal control may be more likely to blow the whistle (Greenberger, Porter, Miceli, & Strasser, 1991).

The "prototypic proactive personality" is "one who is relatively unconstrained by situational forces, and who effects environmental change" (Bateman & Crant, 1993, p. 105); as change agents, whistle-blowers may be more proactive than other organizational members (Bateman & Crant, 1993). Thus, high proactives may feel greater responsibility for acting (Question 3).

Being relatively unconstrained by the situation, high proactives are likely to be less sensitive to a threatening environment than are low proactives. In fact, the presence of a potentially retaliatory situation may provide yet another reason for high proactives to act: to change their environments. In terms of the model (Fig. 8.1), proactive disposition will affect the perception of whether any action could be effective (less proactive people may not think they can effect change) and perhaps that the benefits of acting (because the high proactive believes she or he will succeed) will outweigh the costs. Or, the proactive individual may feel more powerful, that she or he can stop the wrongdoing directly, without involving others besides the wrongdoer. For these same reasons, we expect proactive individuals to be more likely to take further action after judging the initial resolution to be unsatisfactory (Question 7). Thus we propose the following:

> **Proposition 8:** Among observers of perceived organizational wrongdoing, there will be a positive relation between proactive disposition and the likelihood that an observer will take action to stop wrongdoing.

> **Proposition 9:** Among whistle-blowers and others who have intervened, there will be a positive relation between proactive disposition and further action, if the initial action does not resolve the problem.

Self-Efficacy for Whistle-Blowing

Self-efficacy is concerned with individuals' judgments about their ability to perform effectively in specific situations, if called on to do so. It is an individual's estimate of the knowledge, skills, abilities, and motivational force that he or she can bring to bear on a specific situation (Bandura, 1989). Self-efficacy also influences an individual's decision to engage in various types of activities or to refrain from doing so (Brockner, 1988). People are more likely to engage in activities they feel they can perform successfully and they are more likely to persist in those activities. In a summary of recent research examining the relations among self-efficacy, anxiety arousal, and avoidant behavior, Bandura (1989) noted that "people avoid threatening situations and activities, not because they are beset with anxiety, but because they believe they will be unable to cope with situations they regard as risky" (p. 1178). Self-efficacy is much narrower than the more general disposition of self-esteem, which involves a person's overall evaluation of his or her ability to solve problems and overcome obstacles across situations (Bandura, 1989). Here we are concerned with self-efficacy with respect to one's ability to report a case of wrongdoing successfully; that is, can all the pieces be put together so that the wrongdoing is stopped? Thus, self-efficacy differs from self-esteem in two key ways: It is narrower, and it has a greater situational component, though we view it as partially dispositional.

Research on self-efficacy suggests that it may affect evaluation of potential actions and their outcomes (Question 4 onward). We do not expect self-efficacy for whistle-blowing to affect judgments about whether wrongdoing has occurred or whether the individual feels responsible for acting, except to the extent that rationalization of inaction might occur (i.e., "I didn't act because I didn't really think what I observed was wrongful"). Instead, observers with high self-efficacy for whistle-blowing would see whistle-blowing as an available action (Question 4), whereas others may not think of it. Those with high self-efficacy for whistle-blowing would see payoffs to be more likely (Question 5) and that the benefits of whistle-blowing would be greater than actions for which they had lower self-efficacy (Question 6).

Self-efficacy is not entirely dispositional. A recent study showed that self-efficacy training increased the percentage of recruits who volunteered for special forces training in the Israeli Defense Forces by boosting expectations of success (Eden & Kinnar, 1991). If self-efficacy also affects the likelihood that employees will choose to blow the whistle, it may be possible to increase organizationally beneficial whistle-blowing by developing training programs to increase employees' whistle-blowing self-efficacy. Thus, we expect the following:

Proposition 10: Among observers of perceived organizational wrongdoing, there will be a positive relation between self-efficacy for whistle-blowing and whistle-blowing.

There is evidence that people with higher levels of self-efficacy work harder and persist longer on difficult tasks than do other people (Bandura & Wood, 1989; Wood & Bandura, 1989). This suggests that individual differences in self-efficacy are likely to predict the extent to which an employee will persist in attempting to bring attention to wrongdoing or take other action when the initial attempt is not successful. Here, the determination of self-efficacy would be with respect to other action alternatives, for example, whistle-blowing to other parties. We expect the following:

Proposition 11: Among whistle-blowers and others who have intervened, there will be a positive relation between self-efficacy and further action, if the initial action does not resolve the problem.

SUMMARY

Whistle-blowing is a critical behavior that supports the social values of individual responsibility and accountability. Whistle-blowers play an important role in safeguarding their fellow employees, organizational customers, and the general public from improper, illegal, and potentially dangerous activities. They perform a function that cannot be provided by regulatory agencies, legislation, or the marketplace.

Most whistle-blowing research to date has focused on situational factors involved with whistle-blowing and on a limited set of individual characteristics of organizational members as predictors of whistle-blowing. Differences in individual disposition or other characteristics largely have been unexplored. Yet, when whistle-blowing is viewed as prosocial organizational behavior (Brief & Motowidlo, 1986), there is good reason to expect that individual differences also would influence whistle-blowing. One mechanism by which individual difference variables affect whistle-blowing activity may be through their impact on organization members' expectations that whistle-blowing will halt the perceived wrongdoing. To the extent that dispositional variables affect the likelihood that an employee who observes wrongdoing takes action—including the possibility of whistle-blowing—then such variables must be included in our models to understand such behavior.

Much remains unknown about whistle-blowing in organizations. We hope that this chapter will stimulate additional theoretical and empirical development. We hope to gain a better understanding of why whistle-blowing occurs, how effective whistle-blowing can be encouraged, and how to reduce the need for whistle-blowing by preventing wrongdoing. We hope ultimately that this research will help us better understand how individuals who do not hold top management positions can influence organizational change processes in general.

ACKNOWLEDGMENTS

Funding for the research in this chapter was jointly provided by Ohio State University (the first author's prior affiliation), the U.S. government, and the Coleman Chair Fund at Indiana University.

REFERENCES

Arvey, R. D., Abraham, L. M., Bouchard, T. J., & Segal, N. L. (1989). Job satisfaction: Environmental and genetic components. *Journal of Applied Psychology, 74,* 187–192.

Bandura, A. (1989). Human agency in social cognitive theory. *American Psychologist, 44,* 1175–1184.

Bandura, A., & Wood, R. E. (1989). Effect of perceived controllability and performance standards on self-regulation of complex decision making. *Journal of Personality and Social Psychology, 56,* 805–814.

Bateman, T. S., & Crant, J. M. (1993). The proactive component of organizational behavior: A measure and correlates. *Journal of Organizational Behavior, 14,* 103–118.

Bies, R. J., & Tripp, T. M. (1998). The many faces of revenge: The good, the bad, and the ugly. In R. W. Griffin, A. O'Leary-Kelly, & J. Collins (Eds.), *Dysfunctional behavior in organizations, Vol 1: Violent behaviors in organizations* (Part B, pp. 49–67). Greenwich, CT: JAI.

Bies, R. J., Tripp, T. M., & Kramer, R. M. (1997). At the breaking point: Cognitive and social dynamics of revenge in organizations. In R. A. Giacalone & J. Greenberg (Eds.), *Antisocial behavior in organizations* (pp. 18–36). Thousand Oaks, CA: Sage.

Brewer, G. A. (1995). *Incidence of whistleblowing in the public and private sectors* (working paper). Athens: The University of Georgia.

Brief, A. P., Burke, M. J., George, J. M., Robinson, B. S., & Webster, J. (1988). Should negative affectivity remain an unmeasured variable in the study of job stress? *Journal of Applied Psychology, 73,* 710–725.

Brief, A. P., & Motowidlo, S. (1986). Prosocial organizational behaviors. *Academy of Management Review, 4,* 710–725.

Brockner, J. (1988). *Self-esteem at work.* Lexington, MA: Lexington.

Callahan, E. S., & Dworkin, T. M. (1994). Who blows the whistle to the media, and why: Organizational characteristics of media whistleblowers. *American Business Law Journal, 32,* 151–184.

Chen, P. Y., & Spector, P. E. (1991). Negative affectivity as the underlying cause of correlations between stressors and strains. *Journal of Applied Psychology, 76,* 398–407.

Cropanzano, R., James, K., & Konovsky, M. (1993). Dispositional affectivity as a predictor of work attitudes and job performance. *Journal of Organizational Behavior, 14,* 595–606.

Daily, C. M., & Near, J. P. (1995, August). *Job and life satisfaction in family businesses: Spillover among automobile dealers.* Paper presented at the Academy of Management, Cincinnati, OH.

Darley, J., & Bateson, D. (1973). "From Jerusalem to Jericho": A study of situational and dispositional variables in helping behavior. *Journal of Personality and Social Psychology, 27,* 100–108.

Diener, E., & Emmons, R. A. (1985). The independence of positive and negative affect. *Journal of Personality and Social Psychology, 47,* 1105–1117.

Dozier, J. B., & Miceli, M. P. (1985). Potential predictors of whistle-blowing: A prosocial behavior perspective. *Academy of Management Review, 10,* 823–836.

Eden, D., & Kinnar, J. (1991). Modeling galatea: Boosting self-efficacy to increase volunteering. *Journal of Applied Psychology 76,* 770–780.

Elliston, F. A. (1982). Anonymity and whistle blowing. *Journal of Business Ethics, 1,* 167–177.

Fisher, B. D. (1991). The Whistleblower Protection Act of 1989: A false hope for whistleblowers. *Rutgers Law Review, 43,* 355–416.

Goldman, B. M. (1998). *Employment discrimination-claiming behavior: Test of a model of organizational justice.* Unpublished doctoral dissertation, University of Maryland, College Park.

Greenberger, D. B., Porter, G., Miceli, M. P., & Strasser, S. (1991). Dispositional factors and responses to inadequate personal control in organizations. *Journal of Social Issues, 47,* 111–128.

Isen, A. M., & Baron, R. A. (1991). Positive affect as a factor in organizational behavior. In L. L. Cummings & B. M. Staw (Eds.), *Research in organizational behavior* (Vol. 13, pp. 1–53). Greenwich, CT: JAI.

Iverson, R. D., & Erwin, P. J. (1997). Predicting occupational injury: The role of affectivity. *Journal of Occupational and Organizational Psychology, 70,* 113–128.

Judge, T. A. (1993). Does affective disposition moderate the relationship between job satisfaction and voluntary turnover? *Journal of Applied Psychology, 78,* 395–401.

Judge, T. A., & Locke, E. A. (1993). Effect of dysfunctional thought processes on subjective well-being and job satisfaction. *Journal of Applied Psychology, 78,* 475–490.

King, G. III (1997). The effects of interpersonal closeness and issue seriousness on blowing the whistle. *Journal of Business Communication, 34*(4), 419–436.

Langer, E. (1983). *The psychology of control.* Beverly Hills, CA: Sage.

Latané, B., & Darley, J. M. (1968). Group inhibition of bystander intervention. *Journal of Personality and Social Psychology, 10,* 215–221.

Latané, B., & Darley, J. M. (1970). *The unresponsive bystander: Why doesn't he help?* New York: Appleton-Century-Crofts.

Miceli, M. P., & Near, J. P. (1984). The relationship among beliefs, organizational position, and whistle-blowing status: A discriminant analysis. *Academy of Management Journal, 27,* 687–705.

Miceli, M. P., & Near, J. P. (1988). Individual and situational correlates of whistle-blowing. *Personnel Psychology, 41,* 267–282.

Miceli, M. P., & Near, J. P. (1992). *Blowing the whistle: The organizational and legal implications for companies and employees.* New York: Lexington Books.

Miceli, M. P., & Near, J. P. (1997). Whistle-blowing as antisocial behavior. In R. Giacalone & J. Greenberg (Eds.), *Antisocial behavior in organizations* (pp. 130–149). Thousand Oaks, CA: Sage.

Michel, J. G., & Hambrick, D. C. (1992). Diversification posture and top management team characteristics. *Academy of Management Journal, 35,* 9–37.

Moyle, P. (1995). The role of negative affectivity in the stress process: Tests of alternate models. *Journal of Organizational Behavior, 16,* 647–668.

Near, J. P., Baucus, M. S., & Miceli, M. P. (1993). The relationship between values and practice: Organizational climates for wrongdoing. *Administration and Society, 25,* 204–226.

Near, J. P., & Miceli, M. P. (1985). Organizational dissidence: The case of whistle-blowing. *Journal of Business Ethics, 4,* 1–16.

Near, J. P., & Miceli, M. P. (1996). Whistle-blowing: Myth and reality. *Journal of Management, 22*(3), 507–526.

Near, J. P., Rice, R. W., & Hunt, R. G. (1978). Work and extra-work correlates of life and job satisfaction. *Academy of Management Journal, 21,* 248–264.

Near, J. P., & Sorcinelli, M. D. (1986). Work and life away from work: Predictors of faculty satisfaction. *Research in Higher Education, 25,* 377–394.

Parkes, K. R. (1990). Coping, negative affectivity, and the work environment: Additive and interactive predictors of mental health. *Journal of Applied Psychology, 75,* 399–409.

Priest, D. (1997, September 12). Army finds wide abuse of women: Panel report faults leaders' commitment. *Washington Post,* pp. A1, A18.

Rice, R. W., Near, J. P., & Hunt, R. G. (1980). The job satisfaction–life satisfaction relationship: A review of empirical research. *Basic and Applied Social Psychology, 1,* 37–64.

Sims, R. L., & Keenan, J. P. (1998). Predictors of external whistleblowing: Organizational and intrapersonal variables. *Journal of Business Ethics, 17,* 411–421.

Spector, P. E., & O'Connell, B. J. (1994). The contribution of personality traits, negative affectivity, locus of control, and Type A to the subsequent reports of job stressors and strains. *Journal of Occupational and Organizational Psychology, 67,* 1–11.

Staw, B. M., Bell, B. E., & Clausen, J. A. (1986). The dispositional approach to job attitudes: A lifetime longitudinal test. *Administrative Science Quarterly, 38,* 304–331.

Staw, B. M., & Ross, J. (1985). Stability in the midst of change: A dispositional approach to job attitudes. *Journal of Applied Psychology, 70,* 469–480.

Street, M. (1995). Cognitive moral development and organizational commitment: Two potential predictors of whistle-blowing. *Journal of Applied Business Research, 11*(4), 104–113.

Tait, M., Padgett, M. Y., & Baldwin, T. T. (1989). Job and life satisfaction: A reexamination of the strength of the relationship and gender effects as a function of the date of the study. *Journal of Applied Psychology, 74,* 502–507.

Thompson, J. D. (1967). *Organizations in action.* New York: McGraw-Hill.

Van Scotter, J. R., & Motowidlo, S. J. (1996). Interpersonal facilitation and job dedication as separate facets of contextual performance. *Journal of Applied Psychology, 81,* 525–531.

Watson, D., & Clark, L. A. (1984). Negative affectivity: The disposition to experience aversive emotional states. *Psychological Bulletin, 96,* 465–490.

Watson, D., & Clark, L. A. (1992). On traits and temperament: General and specific factors of emotional experience and their relation to the five-factor model. *Journal of Personality, 60,* 441–476.

Watson, D., Clark, L. A., & Tellegen, A. (1988). Development and validation of brief measures of positive and negative affect: The PANAS scales. *Journal of Personality and Social Psychology, 54,* 1063–1070.

Watson, D., & Walker, L. M. (1996). The long-term stability and predictive validity of trait measures of affect. *Journal of Personality and Social Psychology, 70,* 567–577.

Weinstein, D. (1979). *Bureaucratic opposition.* New York: Pergamon.

Wood, R. E., & Bandura, A. (1989). Impact of conceptions of ability on self-regulatory mechanisms and complex decision making. *Journal of Personality and Social Psychology, 56,* 407–415.

9 Training in Ethical Influence

Robert B. Cialdini
Arizona State University

Brad J. Sagarin
Northern Illinois University

William E. Rice
Texas A&M University

A while ago, one of us wrote a general readership book on the social influence process (Cialdini, 1993). The book's purpose was twofold: to inform consumers of the most powerful psychological principles that lead people to say yes to requests, and to show them how to recognize and resist these pressures when they are used in an undue or unwelcome fashion. It is perhaps ironic that besides being purchased by defensively minded consumers—its intended audience—the book has been purchased by a large number of marketers, advertisers, attorneys, fund-raisers, and managers wishing to learn how to use these principles to move people in their directions.

Of course, there is nothing necessarily objectionable about using social influence principles to move people. But, in the process, issues of ethical practice arise. That is, if we grant that identifiable principles are effective in changing compliance decisions, we must ask when it is acceptable versus objectionable to use them. Just because a given principle is successful does not mean we are ethically entitled to commission its persuasive power to create change. However, social influence researchers have focused almost entirely on the issue of effectiveness—often asking whether a tactic would work, but rarely questioning whether it should be employed in the first place.

THE ETHICS OF INFLUENCE

After an extensive review of the social influence literature and an extended period of participant observation of the most prevalent influence practices of practitioners, Cialdini (1987a, 2000) specified a set of psychological principles that normally steer people correctly as to when to comply with a request for action: social proof (consensus), expert authority, commitment/consistency, reciprocity, scarcity, and liking.

Cialdini labeled these principles "universals of influence" and argued that they are employed regularly by influence professionals precisely because they are regularly employed by their influence targets as shortcuts to good decisions. That is, typically, it is adaptive to follow the lead of many similar others or the recommendations of an expert or the implications of one's commitments, and so on. Cialdini also argued that, because these principles usually counsel correctly, they may be used ethically to generate influence to the extent that they exist as a natural (inherent) and representative feature of the influence situation (Cialdini, 1987b, 1996, 2000).[1] It is objectionable, however, for an influence agent to counterfeit or import one of these principles into a situation where it does not reside (or to exaggerate its presence there).

A pair of classic television commercials illustrates this distinction. The old Trident commercial, which stated that, "four out of five dentists surveyed recommend sugarless gum for their patients who chew gum," used authority appropriately because the experts cited (dentists) could speak with true authority about the advantages of the product (sugarless gum). In contrast, the Sanka commercial in which Robert Young educated a coffee drinker about the dangers of caffeine and the advantages of caffeine-free Sanka used authority objectionably. The actor was no expert on caffeine, but he, nevertheless, dispensed medical advice—advice that may have misled viewers familiar with his well-known television role as Marcus Welby, MD.

Cialdini (1996) argued that an organization that employs the principles of influence unethically will bear hidden costs that can outweigh the short-term profits garnered through the unethical tactics. Despite this, many business organizations use such tactics (Grimsley, 2000). Thus, the present research focuses on the other side of the influence relationship: the target.

EMPOWERING TARGETS TO RESIST UNETHICAL INFLUENCE

In trying to empower targets to resist unethical influence, it would be of limited help to instill stubbornness or a blanket rejection of new information. Cynicism can be as costly as gullibility. A useful program should, instead, afford recipients a rule for discriminating between messages likely to steer them right versus wrong.

---

[1]This ethical distinction does not attempt to assert what is ethical in a general sense. Numerous additional factors go into that determination.

As McGuire (1964) put it, "Anyone can be made impervious to the most skillful propaganda if we reduce him to a catatonic schizophrenia … [but] the best of both worlds would be to discover pretreatments that would make the person receptive to the true and resistant to the false" (p. 192).

Following McGuire's recommendation, we developed a brief (12- to 15-minute) tutorial designed to teach college students to resist one kind of unethical use of expert authority in advertising. The tutorial showed students a variety of authority-based advertisements and taught them to determine their acceptability by asking, Is the authority depicted in this ad genuinely an authority on the product he or she is promoting? A comparable sample of control students examined the ads and was asked to consider the ways in which the advertisers used tone and color.

We anticipated that students who received the tutorial would (a) be able to discriminate between ethical versus unethical uses of expert authority and (b) be likely to discriminate against the latter. If, on the other hand, the tutorial merely reminded or inspired participants to perceive that advertisers attempt to limit their choices and freedoms, such participants might demonstrate reactance against subsequent ads (Brehm, 1966). This reactance would produce a less desirable outcome: reduced persuasion for all advertising, both unethical and ethical.

If the tutorial does generate the desired effect of mobilizing resistance only against the unethical ads, an important conceptual question must be addressed: By what mechanism did this effect appear? Our favored hypothesis is that participants who received the tutorial would subsequently perceive ads containing false authorities as unduly manipulative (i.e., unfair, improper, or deceptive), and this perception of undue manipulative intent then would lead to resistance.

EXPERIMENT 1

Two hundred forty-one Arizona State University (ASU) undergraduates participated in our first experiment. The participants were assigned randomly to either the tutorial or control conditions. After reading the six-page tutorial or corresponding control text, participants rated six authority-based ads, three ethical and three unethical, on two scales adapted from Campbell (1995). The first scale assessed the persuasiveness of the ad by using items such as, "If you were to use this type of product in the future, how likely are you to choose this brand?" The second scale assessed the perception of undue manipulative intent, asking participants to indicate how closely they agreed with statements such as, "The advertiser seemed to be trying to inappropriately manage or control the consumer audience."

As predicted, presence of the tutorial interacted significantly with type of authority with respect to ad persuasiveness, $F(1, 224) = 24.99, p < .001$ (see Table 9.1 and Fig. 9.1). Control participants rated the ads containing false authorities as more persuasive than those containing true authorities. In contrast, participants who received the tutorial found the false authorities less convincing and the true authorities more so. These results suggest that the tutorial made participants not more generally resistant to advertising but rather more discriminating about it.

TABLE 9.1

Cell Means and (Standard Deviations) Within Each Condition

Condition	Undue manipulative intent		Ad persuasiveness	
	True authority	False authority	True authority	False authority
Experiment 1				
Control (n = 121)	2.38 (1.07)	2.23 (0.99)	3.24 (0.88)	3.56 (0.74)
Tutorial (n = 120)	1.90 (0.97)	2.56 (0.93)	3.69 (0.89)	3.36 (0.77)
Experiment 2				
Control (n = 65)	2.28 (1.05)	2.61 (1.02)	3.25 (0.79)	3.36 (0.80)
Tutorial (n = 65)	1.98 (0.96)	2.71 (0.98)	3.67 (0.79)	3.23 (0.75)
Delayed control (n = 29)			2.68 (0.61)	2.91 (0.67)
Delayed tutorial (n = 26)			2.99 (0.77)	2.78 (0.54)
Experiment 3				
Tone/Color (n = 80)	2.42 (1.56)	2.61 (1.35)	3.31 (1.27)	3.31 (1.19)
No commentary (n = 80)	2.20 (1.19)	2.84 (1.42)	3.25 (0.92)	3.18 (0.91)
Asserted vulnerability (n = 2.11 (1.43)	3.47 (1.33)	3.58 (1.06)	3.00 (1.02)	
Demonstrated vulnerability (n = 80)	2.14 (1.24)	3.73 (1.42)	3.66 (1.12)	2.54 (1.36)

Note. Manipulative intent and ad persuasiveness were scored on 7-point scales from 0 to 6, with larger scores indicating more of the quality. The delayed measures of ad persuasiveness were scored on a 5-point scale from 1 to 5.

This finding stands in contrast to a reactance effect and to a reactance explanation of our findings. That is, according to reactance theory, resistance occurs when something is perceived as directing or controlling one's choices, thereby limiting one's freedoms to decide. Clearly, this is as much the intent of honest as dishonest ad content. Our results indicate that the tutorial did not stimulate resistance to attempts to direct and limit choices but rather attempts to do so unduly.

The measure of perception of undue manipulative intent also displayed an interaction that paralleled ad persuasiveness, $F(1, 230) = 36.29, p < .001$. These results are compatible with our hypothesis that the observed resistance stems from an increased perception that unethical ads inappropriately attempt to manipulate consumers.

Interestingly, the tutorial had an unanticipated, but fortunate, side effect: Honest ads were seen as more persuasive! Thus, participants learned not only to devalue inappropriate heuristic information but also to enhance the value of appropriate messages.

Although encouraged by the initial success of our brief training program in instilling resistance to persuasion, we were concerned that the observed resistance might have stemmed not from true resistance but rather from demand characteristics. We had, after all, just told participants how to identify "good" versus "bad" ads and then asked them to rate a series of examples that fit into our criteria for

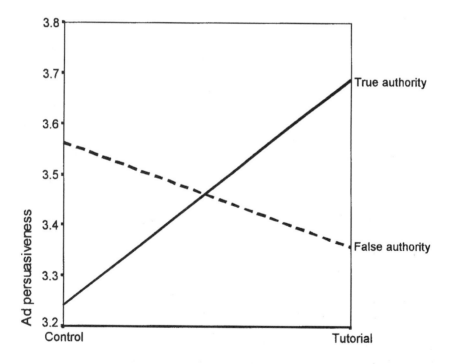

FIG. 9.1. The effects of the tutorial on the perceived persuasiveness of deceptive and nondeceptive advertisements in Experiment 1.

"good" and "bad" advertisements. In addition, for such a tutorial to be truly useful, its lessons must persevere over time and outside the context of the laboratory.

Experiment 2

In our next experiment, participants rated ads both immediately and after a 1- to 4-day delay, in a separate setting unrelated to the laboratory context. The separation of the training and measurement contexts allowed us to assess the viability of demand characteristics as an alternative explanation for the finding of the previous experiment. The delay between the tutorial and the test of its effectiveness offered a second benefit of more applied interest: an assessment of the perseverance of the training impact. If we are to develop a useful program for instilling resistance to improper persuasive messages, the lessons of that program must be retained and accessible to participants at later times when they are likely to encounter such messages in other settings. Without evidence of the durability and cross-situational robustness of our program, it would represent little more than an academic exercise of dubious practical value.

Participating in Experiment 2 were 130 undergraduates. As with the previous experiment, participants were assigned randomly to either the tutorial or control conditions and rated the same series of ethical and unethical ads. Then, 1 to 4 days later, a research assistant, posing as a representative from the campus daily newspaper, administered a delayed questionnaire in the participants' psychology classes. This questionnaire asked respondents to evaluate the articles and advertisements in a new newspaper insert. Two of these advertisements were authority-based, one ethical and one unethical. Respondents rated the ads on a four-question scale including items such as "How did you like the ad?" with answers "I hated it; I disliked it; It was OK; I liked it; It was great!" and "Do you think that seeing this ad will make you more likely to use this product or service?" with answers "Definitely not; Possibly; Maybe; Probably; Definitely."

The impact of the tutorial on immediate responses that we found in Experiment 1 was replicated in Experiment 2. Presence of the tutorial interacted with type of authority on both the perception of undue manipulative intent, $F(1, 123) = 3.58$, $p = .061$, and perceived persuasiveness of the ads, $F(1, 118) = 11.22$, $p = .001$ (see Table 9.1).

The effects of the tutorial also persevered 1 to 4 days after the experiment. As predicted, presence of the tutorial interacted significantly with type of authority in the delayed measure, $F(1, 47) = 4.51$, $p = .039$ (see Table 9.1).[2] An examination of the results for each day separately revealed that, if anything, the tutorial produced more prediction-consistent results on days 2, 3, and 4.

---

[2]One participant was removed from this latter analysis due to his or her statistical outlier status (the Studentized deleted residual for this data point was –3.22, outside the conventional range of –3 to 3).

Thus, participants maintained the benefits of the tutorial well after the end of the laboratory experiment, and these benefits did not appear to drop off, at least within the time period measured. The continued efficacy of the tutorial outside of the laboratory context increases confidence that demand characteristics cannot account for the results and suggests the practical value of tutorials of this type. If the present tutorial, using only a brief, written format, demonstrated significant effects days after its administration, an interactive, longer term program administered in schools could have profound and long-lasting results.

Experiment 2 did contain one worrisome finding. Although participants receiving the tutorial rated the ethical ads as significantly more persuasive than did controls, they did not resist the unethical ads significantly more effectively than controls. These results suggest that participants may agree with the distinction presented, but they may not internalize the lesson because they "wouldn't have fallen for the unethical ads anyway." Taylor and Brown (1988) suggested that such illusions are common and can be adaptive. However, in the present context, this self-enhancement bias (Fiske & Taylor, 1991) may leave targets less able to fend off inappropriate persuasive attacks. Indeed, as Fiske and Taylor put it, "Unrealistic optimism may lead people to ignore legitimate risks in their environment and fail to take measures to offset those risks" (p. 216).

These concerns were compounded by a common reaction obtained from nonpsychologists who heard about this research informally. "I think it's great that you're studying resistance to persuasion. TV ads are a real problem. Of course, they don't work on me ..."

To test our hypothesis that participants may have felt themselves to be uniquely resistant to the persuasive tactics that work on everyone else, we asked 888 undergraduates how much they believe television advertisements affect them, and we asked a separate 900 undergraduates how much they believe television advertisements affect the average ASU undergraduate. Participants responded on 0 to 6 Likert-type scales for which 0 indicated *very strongly,* 3 indicated *somewhat,* and 6 indicated *hardly at all.* As we suspected, participants rated themselves significantly less affected ($M = 3.56$) by television ads as compared with their peers ($M = 2.88$), $F(1, 1786)= 124.69, p < .0001$.

The results of this pilot study confirmed our concerns that participants maintained perceptions of personal invulnerability to advertising. These perceptions of invulnerability parallel those that frustrate educators seeking to convince youth of the dangers of drugs, alcohol, and sexually transmitted diseases. In each of these instances, as well as in the present research, illusions of invulnerability prevent people from perceiving their personal susceptibility to very real hazards.

Research in health psychology has uncovered a similar phenomenon, the optimistic bias (Weinstein, 1980). This bias appears as a discrepancy between perceptions of others' susceptibility to a disease and perceptions of one's own personal susceptibility to the illness. Unfortunately, this bias can lead to dire health outcomes, because low levels of perceived personal susceptibility are associated with poor compliance with preventive health behaviors (Aiken, Gerend, & Jackson, 2000).

EXPERIMENT 3

In Experiment 3, we sought to dispel these illusions of invulnerability by *demonstrating* in an undeniable fashion that participants can be fooled by deceptive ads. We predicted that participants "stung" by a deceptive advertisement would demonstrate increased resistance against such ads in the future. In contrast, we anticipated that simply asserting participants' vulnerability, as is done in many school-based programs on drug, alcohol, and sexually transmitted diseases, would prove less effective in motivating resistance.

The relative ineffectiveness of merely asserting vulnerability has been illustrated vividly in the area of health behaviors. For example, according to Aiken et al. (2000), "The public is inundated with information about cancer and with recommendations for cancer screening and prevention." Nevertheless, the National Health Interview Survey of 1994 reported that 44% of women over 50 had failed to have a mammogram within the previous 2 years (American Cancer Society, 1997; National Center for Health Statistics, 1996).

Aiken et al. (2000) listed three stages of perceived susceptibility: "First, an individual is assumed to become aware of a health hazard (awareness), then to believe in the likelihood of the hazard for others (general susceptibility), and finally to acknowledge his or her own personal vulnerability (personal susceptibility)." Researchers attempting to increase compliance with health behaviors have sought to move people from Stage 2 to Stage 3. For example, Curry, Taplin, Anderman, Barlow, and McBride (1993) increased cancer screening in higher risk women through the use of tailored personal objective risk information.

Our pilot study demonstrated that many of our participants fell squarely into stage 2. They perceived that others were vulnerable to advertising but that they, themselves, were relatively immune. We anticipated that asserting participants' vulnerability would leave many with their illusions intact. We predicted, however, that participants could be moved to Stage 3 by forcing them to acknowledge their own personal vulnerability.

Experiment 3 also enabled us to examine the mechanisms of the instilled resistance. We predicted that the observed resistance would be mediated by perceptions of undue manipulative intent. Furthermore, drawing on the cognitive response model of persuasion (Eagly & Chaiken, 1993; Greenwald, 1968; Petty, Ostrom, & Brock, 1981), we anticipated that resistance would manifest, at least in part, as an altered cognitive reaction to deceptive advertisements. We expected that these altered cognitive responses would mediate resistance, as well. To assess cognitive response, participants listed the thoughts they had in reaction to the ads. Subsequently, participants categorized these thoughts (as positive, negative, neutral, or irrelevant) in terms of their relation to the ad. Participants then completed a short content quiz to determine how well they remembered various features and characteristics of the ads.

Finally, we noted the possibility that our results could have stemmed not from the efficacy of the tutorial but rather from the inhibiting nature of our tone and color control condition. Specifically, though designed to be innocuous, the tone and color essay may have inadvertently focused participants away from the ethical distinction, on which they might otherwise have focused. To test this possibility, we added a second control condition that asked participants to look through the example ads but provided no commentary.

Three hundred twenty ASU undergraduates were randomly assigned to one of four conditions: tone and color control, no commentary control, tutorial plus asserted vulnerability, and tutorial plus demonstrated vulnerability.

Tone and Color Control

As in Experiments 1 and 2, participants in the tone and color control condition received a treatment packet that discussed cosmetic aspects of the accompanying ads.

No Commentary Control

Participants in the no commentary control condition received a treatment packet that asked them to examine the accompanying ads but did not discuss any particular aspects of the ads.

Tutorial Plus Asserted Vulnerability

Participants in the tutorial plus asserted vulnerability condition received a slightly modified version of the tutorial treatment packet of Experiments 1 and 2. Besides receiving a set of sample ads and a working definition of ethical (vs. unethical) authority-based advertisements as in the earlier experiments, participants were asked to consider whether they had been fooled by the deceptive ads of manipulative advertisers:

> Take a look at ad #1. Did you find the ad to be even somewhat convincing? If so, then you got fooled. Unethical ads like this fool most people. But if we want to protect ourselves from being manipulated, we need to know what makes an ad ethical or unethical.

> Many ads, such as ad #1, use authority figures to help sell the product. But not all ads use authority figures ethically. For an authority to be used ethically it must pass two tests. First, the authority must be a real authority, and not just someone dressed up to look like one. Second, the authority must be an expert on the product he or she is trying to sell.

Let's use these tests to examine ad #1. What about that guy selling the Wall Street Journal Interactive Edition? He sure looks like a stockbroker. But where are his name and credentials? The ad doesn't give us any. For all we know this guy is just a model. This ad is unethical because it fails the first test. This guy is just dressed up to look like an authority.

When you looked at this ad, did you notice that this "stockbroker" was a fake? Did you ask yourself whether you should listen to this so-called "expert"? If you didn't, then you left yourself vulnerable to the advertisers that are trying to manipulate you.

Tutorial Plus Demonstrated Vulnerability

Participants in the tutorial plus demonstrated vulnerability condition received a treatment packet that did more than simply assert their vulnerability to deceptive ads. It demonstrated that vulnerability by first instructing participants to examine a sample deceptive ad and to respond to a pair of questions concerning it. The initial question asked them to indicate how convincing they found it on a 7-point scale where $0 = $ *not at all convincing,* $1 = $ *somewhat convincing,* $2 = $ *fairly convincing,* $3 = $ *convincing,* $4 = $ *quite convincing,* $5 = $ *very convincing,* and $6 = $ *extremely convincing.* Results indicated that the great majority of participants rated the ad as at least somewhat convincing. The second question asked participants which two aspects of the ad they found most important in making this decision and to write these reasons down in spaces provided. At this point, the treatment packet was identical to that of the tutorial plus asserted vulnerability condition except in two places. Rather than merely instructing participants ,"Take a look at ad #1. Did you find the ad to be even somewhat convincing? If so, then you got fooled … ," the packet referred participants to their earlier committed response to the ad: "Take a look at your response to the first question . Did you find the ad to be even somewhat convincing? If so, then you got fooled …" Similarly, rather than merely being asked, "When you looked at this ad, did you notice that this 'stockbroker' was a fake?" participants were first referred to their earlier responses to the question regarding the most important aspects of the ads that contributed to its convincingness: "Take a look at your answer to the second question. Did you notice that this 'stockbroker' was a fake?"

Participants in Experiment 3 rated two new ads. After rating each ad, participants were instructed to list the thoughts they had while examining the ad. Then, after rating and listing thoughts for both ads, participants were asked to categorize each thought as (a) positive toward the ad, (b) negative to the ad, (c) neutral to the ad, or (d) irrelevant to the ad. Finally, participants answered an eight-question content quiz concerning the content and features of the ads. These questions included, "What type of product was shown in the ad?" "Who was the person pictured in the ad?" and "What was the last feature listed at the bottom of the ad?"

The two control conditions did not differ significantly on any measured variable; consequently, we were assured that the control condition used in the previous studies had not served as an active treatment.

The tutorial once again interacted with type of authority significantly with respect to both perception of undue manipulative intent, $F(3, 283) = 11.04, p < .001$, and persuasiveness of the ads, $F(3, 269) = 10.41, p < .001$ (see Table 9.1 and Fig. 9.2). Of particular note is the fact that the "tutorial plus asserted vulnerability" and "tutorial plus demonstrated vulnerability" conditions differed significantly in their interaction with type of authority with respect to ad persuasiveness, $t(269) = 2.61, p = .010$. An examination of the simple effects revealed that participants in these two treatment conditions did not differ in their perceptions of the nondeceptive ad, $t(269) = -.65, p = .514$, but they did differ significantly in their perceptions of the deceptive ad, $t(269) = 2.71, p = .007$. These results suggest that

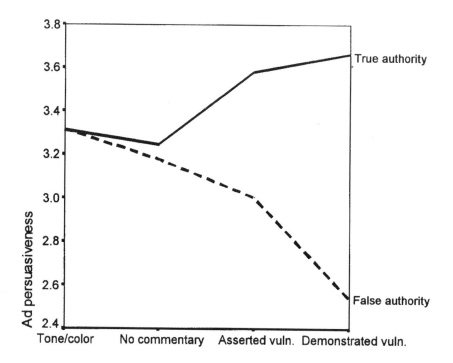

FIG. 9.2. The effects of the tutorial and the perception of vulnerability on the perceived persuasiveness of deceptive and nondeceptive advertisements in Experiment 3.

demonstrating participants' personal vulnerability to deceptive advertising significantly increased resistance to subsequent deceptive ads.

As suggested by our previous findings, the "tutorial plus asserted vulnerability" did not confer significant resistance to subsequent unethical ads, as compared with the control conditions, $t(269) = 1.38$, $p = .169$. In contrast, the "tutorial plus demonstrated vulnerability" produced significant resistance to subsequent unethical ads, $t(269) = 4.53$, $p < .001$. Thus, instilling resistance required more than merely asserting participants' vulnerability. Effective resistance required demonstrating this vulnerability.

MEDIATION

A test of our mediational hypotheses revealed that the resistance conferred by the tutorials, as compared with the control conditions, could be mediated entirely through perceptions of manipulative intent. Furthermore, the effect of perceptions of manipulative intent on ad persuasiveness could be mediated partially by cognitive response, although a significant direct effect remained (see Fig. 9.3). This

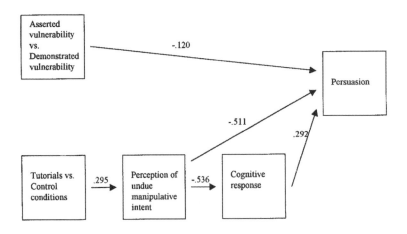

FIG. 9.3. The mediation of resistance by perception of undue manipulative intent and cognitive response in Experiment 3. All included paths have $ps < .01$. All excluded paths have $ps > .20$.

model fit the data well according to a chi-square goodness-of-fit test, $C^2(4, N = 300) = 4.989, p = .288$.

Interestingly, the additional resistance conferred by the demonstration of vulnerability was not mediated by perceptions of manipulative intent or cognitive response. Exploratory analyses suggest that this additional resistance may manifest as a result of these participants employing an alternative resistance strategy. Instead of closely examining and refuting unethical ads, participants faced with their vulnerability may have avoided the negative feelings now associated with unethical persuasive techniques by quickly dismissing unethical ads, resulting in decreased memory and intensity of thoughts regarding the ads.

One additional exploratory analysis revealed that a number of participants in the control condition reported thoughts of the type characteristic of those who received the tutorial. For example, these thoughts often questioned the ability or appropriateness of the spokesperson to give advice about the product advertised. However, many of these participants labeled such thoughts as neutral or irrelevant with respect to the ad. The greater proportion of controls who characterized such thoughts as neutral or irrelevant (21%) compared with participants who received the tutorial (13%) suggests that a portion of persuasive targets may already recognize the inappropriateness of unethical techniques, but they may not weigh the deceptiveness negatively in their assessment of the ad.

CONCLUSIONS

Aaker and Myers (1987) estimated that marketers target us with more than 300 persuasive messages every day. Many of these messages attempt to engage heuristic scripts to elicit the desired level of compliance or attitude change. Our ability to critically distinguish between messages that employ heuristics appropriately and those that misuse them has become increasingly important, given the expanding prevalence and pervasiveness of advertising.

Even schools, traditionally a haven from this barrage, have become a medium for advertising. Through the adept marketing of Channel One, 8 million students now are required to watch commercials in school each day along with a news broadcast ("Reading, Writing ... and Buying?" 1998). In addition, many schools, desperate for funds, now allow advertising in hallways and on the sides of school buses.

Historically, social psychologists have had little to offer to those hoping to instill resistance to deceptive persuasion. The present research offers a remedial first step. In three experiments, participants learned one distinction between ethical versus unethical uses of authority in advertising. Compared with control groups, participants who were taught this distinction demonstrated resistance against subsequent advertisements that employed authority deceptively. Furthermore, compared with controls, these participants perceived nondeceptive advertisements as less manipulative and more persuasive.

These results suggest that the observed resistance stemmed not from stubbornness, cynicism, or reactance but rather from the newly acquired ability to critically appraise persuasive messages. In this way, the tutorial manifested McGuire's (1964) goal of making participants "receptive to the true and resistant to the false" (p. 192).

Experiment 2 demonstrated that the instilled resistance persevered 1 to 4 days after the tutorial, generalized to novel exemplars, and appeared outside of the program context. These results offer evidence that the observed resistance stemmed from an effective and lasting new skill and not from demand characteristics.

In Experiment 3, we sought to enhance the efficacy of the tutorial by demonstrating participants' vulnerability to deceptive advertising. We feared that without dispelling the illusion of invulnerability, participants might ignore the training, considering it personally irrelevant. Participants in this study first rated the persuasiveness of a deceptive ad, only then to discover that they had been manipulated successfully by the advertiser. Compared with participants who received the standard tutorial, those who had been demonstrably "stung" by the deceptive ad showed significantly greater resistance to subsequent deceptive advertisements.

The ability to dispel the illusion of invulnerability has applications that extend far beyond resistance to persuasion. Perceived personal vulnerability has been shown to be a critical predictor of compliance with health behaviors (Aiken et al., 2000). In a dramatic illustration of the danger of the illusion of invulnerability, Apanovitch, Salovey, and Merson (2000) discovered that only 2% to 16% (depending on ethnicity) of college students considered themselves vulnerable to AIDS, despite 85% understanding HIV transmission and 25% personally knowing someone with AIDS. Educational interventions that ignore this crucial element seem doomed to miss the vast majority of those at risk. The present research suggests, however, that an intervention need not be particularly elaborate to pierce this illusion and motivate the recipient to accept the preventative message offered.

Experiment 3 also offered insights into the mechanisms of the conferred resistance. Our data were consistent with the hypothesis that the resistance instilled by the tutorial was mediated by perceptions of undue manipulative intent. In addition, by adopting a cognitive response perspective, we predicted that resistance would manifest as an altered set of cognitions produced in response to ethical and unethical ads. The data were somewhat consistent with this mediational prediction. The effect of perception of undue manipulative intent on persuasion could be mediated partially by cognitive response, but a significant direct path remained.

It was more difficult to find evidence for the mechanisms involved in the greater resistance conferred by dispelling the illusion of invulnerability. Exploratory analyses allow us to offer a cautious interpretation that different resistance strategies may operate in the tutorial plus asserted vulnerability and the tutorial plus demonstrated vulnerability conditions. Specifically, these latter participants demonstrated worse memory for both ethical and unethical ads and reported less intense thoughts in response to the unethical ad compared with those in the asserted vulnerability condition. This suggests that participants in the demonstrated vulnerability condition, after determining that an ad was deceptive, may have quickly turned their attention elsewhere to avoid being influenced or to avoid spending time on material that they thought would not influence them. It is possible that forced exposure to deceptive ads might engender more intense, negative thoughts in such participants, but that, given the opportunity to selectively avoid these ads, these participants actually experience less intense thoughts.

Results from Experiment 3 also suggest that a portion of the population already possesses the ability to detect deceptive techniques. However, detection does not always lead to resistance: a number of control participants who noted the inappropriateness of the spokesperson in the unethical ad nevertheless categorized the thought as neutral or irrelevant. For these participants, the tutorial might not provide a novel distinction but might, instead, suggest that the distinction should be taken into account when assessing future advertising.

As research psychologists continue to discover and develop the techniques of social influence, questions regarding the ethical use of such techniques become increasingly important. The present research suggests that such questions need not be pondered exclusively by influence agents. By learning to distinguish between the ethical and unethical uses of influence techniques, influence targets can build resistance to the deceptive while remaining receptive to the honest. These targets hardly are limited to prospective consumers exposed to advertising. Issues of ethical versus unethical communication exist in the organization as well (Neuliep, 1987, 1996). Indeed, Redding (1991) asserted that, owing to inherent power and authority differentials, the organizational environment is especially susceptible to ethical violations in the presentation of information. According to Redding (1991), one prominent category of unethical communications, labeled manipulative–exploitive, contains messages that are quite similar to those we examined in that they involve persuasive appeals presented under false pretenses. Because the dimension of expert authority is crucial to good decision making in any organization, our results easily could be generalized to the organizational domain, where individuals are regularly confronted with communications generated by purported authorities on the topic. Future research extending our findings and analysis to organizational communication settings would be welcome.

It is important to recognize that our purpose in this research is not to assert the superiority or validity of the particular ethical scheme we have chosen to employ. Instead, it is to investigate the extent to which reasonable ethical distinctions can be instilled readily in communication targets and can render these targets more resistant to messages that violate ethical criteria. A concomitant purpose is to identify the psychological mechanisms that are (and that are not) responsible for learned resistance to persuasive appeals. If both of these goals can be achieved, the outcomes stand to contribute to important applied and theoretical areas of concern.

REFERENCES

Aaker, D. A., & Myers, J. G. (1987). *Advertising management*. Englewood Cliffs, NJ: Prentice-Hall.

Aiken, L. S., Gerend, M. A., & Jackson, K. M. (2000). Perceived risk and health protective behavior: Cancer screening and cancer prevention. In A. Baum, T. Revenson, & J. Singer (Eds.), *Handbook of health psychology* (pp. 727–746). Mahwah, NJ: Lawrence Erlbaum Associates.

American Cancer Society (1997). *Cancer risk report: Prevention and control, 1997*. Atlanta, GA: American Cancer Society.

Apanovitch, A. M., Salovey, P., & Merson, M. (2000). *The Yale–MTV study of attitudes of American youth*. Unpublished manuscript.

Brehm, J. W. (1966). *A theory of psychological reactance*. New York: Academic Press.

Campbell, M. C. (1995). When attention-getting advertising tactics elicit consumer inferences of manipulative intent: The importance of balancing benefits and investments. *Journal of Consumer Psychology, 4,* 225–254.

Cialdini, R. B. (1987). Compliance principles of compliance professionals: Psychologists of necessity. In M. P. Zanna, J. M. Olson, & C. P. Herman (Eds.), *Social influence: The Ontario symposium* (Vol. 5, pp. 165–184). Hillsdale, NJ: Lawrence Erlbaum Associates.

Cialdini, R. B. (1987b). Personal influence: Being ethical and effective. In S. Oskamp & S. Spacapan (Eds.), *Interpersonal processes: The Claremont Symposium on Applied Social Psychology* (pp. 95–107). Newbury Park, CA: Sage.

Cialdini, R. B. (1993). *Influence: Science and practice* (3rd ed.). New York: Addison-Wesley Longman.

Cialdini, R. B. (1996). Social influence and the triple tumor structure of organizational dishonesty. In D. M. Messick & A. E. Tenbrunsel (Eds.), *Codes of conduct* (pp. 44–58). New York: Russell Sage Foundation.

Cialdini, R. B. (2001). *Influence: Science and practice* (4th ed.). Boston: Allyn and Bacon.

Curry, S. J., Taplin, S. H., Anderman, C., Barlow, W. E., & McBride, C. (1993). A randomized trial of the impact of risk assessment and feedback on participation in mammography screening. *Preventative Medicine, 22,* 350–360.

Eagly, A. H. & Chaiken, S. (1993). *The psychology of attitudes*. Fort Worth, TX: Harcourt Brace.

Fiske, S. T., & Taylor, S. E. (1991). *Social cognition*. New York: McGraw-Hill.

Greenwald, A. G. (1968). Cognitive learning, cognitive response to persuasion, and attitude change. In A. G. Greenwald, T. C. Brock, & T. M. Ostrom (Eds.), *Psychological foundations of attitudes* (pp 147–170). New York: Academic Press.

Grimsley, K. D. (2000, June 14). Office wrongdoing common. *The Washington Post,* p. E2.

McGuire, W. J. (1964). Inducing resistance to persuasion: Some contemporary approaches. In L. Berkowitz (Ed.), *Advances in experimental social psychology* (Vol. 1, pp. 191–229). New York: Academic Press.

National Center for Health Statistics (1996). *Healthy people 2000 review, 1995–1996*. Hyattsville, MD: Public Health Service.

Neuliep, J. W. (1987). The influence of Theory X and Theory Y management styles on the selection of compliance-gaining strategies. *Communication Research Reports, 4,* 14–19.

Neuliep, J. W. (1996). The influence of Theory X and Theory Y management styles on the perception of ethical behavior in organizations. *Journal of Social Behavior and Personality, 11,* 301–311.

Petty, R. E., Ostrom, T. M., & Brock, Y. C. (1981). Historical foundations of the cognitive response approach to attitudes and persuasion. In R. E. Petty, T. M. Ostrom, & T. C. Brock (Eds.), *Cognitive responses in persuasion* (pp. 5–29). Hillsdale, NJ: Lawrence Erlbaum Associates.

Reading, writing, and … buying? (1998, September). *Consumer Reports, 63,* 45–48.

Redding, W. C. (1991, June). *Unethical messages in the organizational context.* Paper presented at the annual convention of the International Communication Association, Chicago.

Taylor, S. E., & Brown, J. D. (1988). Illusion and well-being: A social psychological perspective on mental health. *Psychological Bulletin, 103,* 193–210.

Weinstein, N. D. (1980). Unrealistic optimism about future life events. (1980). *Journal of Personality and Social Psychology, 39,* 806–820.

ACKNOWLEDGMENTS

This research was supported in part by a National Science Foundation Graduate Fellowship to the second author. Some of the findings reported here were presented initially at the April 1997 meeting of the Western Psychological Association in Seattle, Washington, the January 1998 Kellogg Graduate School of Business's Conference on Social Influence and Ethics in Organizations in Evanston, Illinois, and the August 1998 meeting of the American Psychological Association in San Francisco, California. We thank Matthew Bogue and Jeff Quinn for their help in conducting these experiments, Kelton Rhoads for his many insights during this research program, and the members of ASU's Social Psychology Research Institute and Social Influence Interest Group for their commentary and guidance during the development and analysis of these experiments.

10 Authority, Heuristics, and the Structure of Excuses

Alan Strudler
Danielle E. Warren
The Wharton School, University of Pennsylvania

Stanley Milgram's (1983) famous obedience experiments show that in some contexts, ordinary people obey authority even when doing so involves gross wrongdoing. In this chapter we ask what, if anything, these experiments reveal about individual moral responsibility for wrongful conduct and its consequences. We propose approaches for evaluating the conduct of Milgram's subjects, and we propose ways to generalize these approaches to assess the behavior of managers who respond to authority inside complex organizations. Our inquiry is not empirical: We do not try to expand the stock of psychological explanations of the behavior of Milgram's subjects or to adjudicate among rival explanations. Our inquiry is instead conceptual and normative: We analyze and propose norms for assessing some instances of wrongful conduct.

Our normative arguments build on arguments that Schoeman (1987) made in a fascinating but neglected article about attribution theory and the Milgram experiments. Schoeman argued that some psychologists exaggerate the relevance of the Milgram experiments for interpreting normative judgments about moral responsibility. We agree. But, drawing on the legal theory of entrapment, Schoeman also sought to identify some reason that the Milgram experiments provide a source of insight about the normative relevance of relying on authority for certain excuses. We argue that the entrapment model cannot explain the normative relevance of relying on authority in Milgram cases because entrapment victims and Milgram's subjects think in radically different ways about authority. We outline an alternative to Schoeman's view. Our alternative starts with some empirical conjectures that Messick and Bazerman (1996) made regarding the role of cognitive heuristics in explaining some wrongful behavior. Relying on the legal theory of culpable ignorance, we then draw some conclusions about what people deserve for engaging in wrongdoing caused by their reliance on heuristics.

BLAMING MILGRAM'S SUBJECTS

Suppose that you are one of Milgram's experimental subjects.[1] After debriefing, you reflect on the fact that you administered increasingly severe shocks to an innocent person who pleaded with you to stop, and that you persisted in administering these shocks even when it seemed clear that your victim was in agony. You gratuitously inflicted pain on a person who begged you not to do so, and you did so only because your superior asked you. Should you blame yourself? Doing so seems natural. After all, nobody forced you to try to administer shock. And you were in control of your normally adequate cognitive resources. You did something wrong, or at least tried to do something wrong, and you had no good excuse. Here is an argument—we call it "the hard-nosed argument"—that suggests you should blame yourself.

1. It is wrong to try to inflict nonconsensual harm on an innocent person.
2. You tried to inflict nonconsensual harm on an innocent person and thus did something wrong.
3. If you do something wrong without a good excuse (e.g., that you were coerced or suffered a cognitive defect), then you are morally blameworthy.
4. You had no good excuse for the wrong you did. Therefore you are morally blameworthy.

The hard-nosed argument corresponds to some fairly traditional conceptions in morality (Donagan, 1977). This tradition distinguishes between the wrongness of an action and the blameworthiness of a person for engaging in an action. Hence an action may be wrong even though a person deserves no blame for engaging in it and even though he or she is not responsible for it. In such a case, a person has an excuse for what he or she does. Traditionally, complete excuses come in two varieties: volitional and cognitive. If a person's action was forced or coerced, the person is not responsible for it; if a person's action is the result of a mistake rooted in his or her innocent ignorance, the person is not responsible for it. A "complete excuse," as we employ the phrase, wholly relieves a person from responsibility for wrongdoing; it defeats the charge that a person deserves moral censure. A "partial excuse," on the other hand, merely diminishes a person's responsibility for wrongdoing but does not wholly relieve a person of responsibility. A partial excuse may apply, for example, if a person's wrongful act is issued from ignorance but the person is not wholly blameless for the ignorance. We will suggest that the idea of a partial excuse is relevant in the Milgram case.

---

[1]We borrow from Schoeman (1987) the expository device of placing oneself in the position of Milgram's subjects.

We maintain that, at least according to traditional morality as exemplified in the hard-nosed argument, the fact that a person tries to administer shock in the Milgram experiments creates a presumption that the person is morally blameworthy. There can be no doubt that it is wrong to directly inflict harm on innocent and unwilling victims, but that is exactly what the Milgram subjects tried to do. Still, although their actions were certainly wrong, it remains an open question whether and to what extent the Milgram subjects should be blamed for what they did. If they had good excuses, it might remove the basis for blaming them for their actions. We turn to social psychology for some possible excuses.

THE ATTRIBUTIONIST ARGUMENT

Contemporary social psychology suggests that the hard-nosed argument may be flawed. To see this, return to your perspective as a subject in the Milgram experiments and suppose that you hear the rest of the story about what happened. You learn that many other people faced the same situation that you did, and that most of these people administered the shock exactly as you did. Although at first you thought that your action was aberrant and even evil, now you see that it was normal and that your misdeed was an expression of ordinary human limits. So how could it be wrong? If you committed a wrong, it was not from anything distinctive about yourself.

In fact, even blaming yourself seems to be an instance of a fallacy psychologists have identified and named the "fundamental attribution error." Ross and Anderson (1982) summarized this error as follows: "The Fundamental Attribution Error is the tendency for attributers to underestimate the impact of situational factors and to overestimate the role of dispositional factors in controlling behavior" (p. 135). In this passage Ross and Anderson identified the fundamental attribution error as occurring in the context of judgments about controlling behavior.

It is important to understand as clearly as possible why blaming subjects who administer shock in the Milgram experiments may be regarded as an instance of the fundamental attribution error. You think that your wrongdoing arose out of some idiosyncratic trait that you possess, something that psychologists would call an "individual difference" or a "dispositional factor," because it is a distinguishing trait of yours, or an expression of the idiosyncratic dispositions of your character.[2] But it turns out that virtually anybody in your position would have done the same thing, that you behaved as we should expect a randomly selected normal person to behave. So your wrong action reflects nothing distinctive about you or your choice but something about your situation: It is a response to a "situational factor" rather than the expression of a "dispositional factor."

Here is an argument—we call it "the attributionist argument"—through which we hope to capture why concern about the fundamental attribution error suggests

---

[2]In our discussion of the fundamental attribution error, we are much indebted to Sabini (1997).

that you should not, as a moral matter, blame yourself for doing something wrong when you administer shock in the Milgram experiments:

1. If most people in situation *S* tend to do action *A*, then the fact that person *P* does *A* is not attributable to some idiosyncratic feature of *P*.
2. If *A* is not attributable to some idiosyncratic feature of *P*, then *A* is not *P*'s fault.
3. Most people who were asked to administer shock in Milgram's experiments did so.
4. The fact that Milgram's subjects administered shock is not attributable to an idiosyncratic feature of these subjects.
5. It is a mistake to blame Milgram's subjects for administering shock, and therefore you should not be blamed for administering the shock.

If one accepts the attributionist argument, one need not deny that what most Milgram subjects did was wrong. The attributionist argument is not about whether actions are right but instead about whether people should be excused for their wrongdoing, or to what extent people should be blamed for those actions. The attributionist argument suggests that we should limit the blame we direct toward Milgram's subjects; it suggests that psychological facts ground an excuse, or at least a partial excuse, for Milgram's subjects.

How should one understand the excuse derived from the attributionist argument? As we noted, traditional conceptions of morality divide excuses into two sorts, cognitive and volitional. It is not obvious where to place the attributionist argument excuse. Is it a cognitive excuse, suggesting that Milgram's subjects did not really understand what they were doing? Or is it a volitional excuse, suggesting that Milgram's subjects did not act voluntarily? Neither interpretation of the excuse seems wholly appealing. Consider, first, the volitional interpretation. It does not seem obvious that Milgram's subjects suffered any duress or coercive threat. Nobody forced them to administer shocks, and they risked no punishment by resigning from the project. Should one, then, understand the attributionist excuse as a cognitive excuse? The Milgram subjects seemed to know the morally relevant facts: They were administering potentially lethal shock to apparently unwilling and innocent victims.

Still, the idea of an excuse derived from the attributionist argument, despite our inability to classify it as volitional or cognitive, may seem plausible. Milgram's subjects were apparently ordinary people, not different on average from the rest of us. This suggests that there must be some powerful explanation or excuse for why they did something so much worse than the rest of us ordinarily do. Something about the experimental situation overwhelmed their will, distorted their deliberative process, or confused them in ways that mitigate their blameworthiness, one might think. But what? In the remainder of this chapter, we explore the idea that recent work in cognitive psychology helps to answer this question. We suggest that Milgram's subjects may be viewed as operating according to a heuristic that confuses them about the morally relevant background and that therefore provides some excuse for their wrongdoing. To make our analysis plausible, we advert to discussion by psychologists about other wrongdoing that occurs in contexts where reliance on heuristics may play an important role.

HEURISTICS AND INNOCENCE

DES is a pill pregnant women once used to ward off nausea and other symptoms of "morning sickness." Although the purpose of the pill was to help these women, the pill affected their fetuses, who later suffered a significant incidence of birth defects. Managers at the pharmaceutical companies that manufactured and sold DES knew that there was some risk of causing these birth defects but apparently underestimated that risk. In their discussion of responsibility for harm caused by selling DES, Messick and Bazerman (1996) explored the possibility that a mental mistake, erroneous reliance on a heuristic, may play a crucial role in explaining the occurrence of managerial wrongdoing in organizational settings. They explained:

> DES's most disastrous effects did not befall the consumers of the drug, namely the women who took it; the catastrophe struck their daughters. When there is a tendency to restrict the analysis of a policy's consequences to one or two groups of visible stakeholders, the decision may be blindsided by unanticipated consequences to an altogether different group. (Messick & Bazerman, 1996, p. 9)

Messick and Bazerman seem to suggest that managers who chose to manufacture and sell DES may have fallen prey to the "availability heuristic," which inclines people to think that risks are more serious when they are more readily called to mind, or more "available." In assessing the consequences of making and selling the pharmaceutical, managers focus on consequences for people whose interests are most salient or psychologically available. Because of this focus, managers neglect and hence undervalue the adverse impact of their action on people whose interests are less salient. If Messick and Bazerman were correct in asserting that some managerial wrongdoing in the DES case was caused by innocent, yet inapt, reliance on heuristics rather than by bad intentions, blaming managers for wrongdoing is a candidate for the fundamental attribution error: Perhaps instead of blaming managers, one should blame heuristics. In any event, that is a possibility we explore.

Messick and Bazerman's explanation of managerial wrongdoing in terms of innocent reliance on the availability heuristic is provocative and ingenious. At best, however, their explanation is a conjecture: They offer no evidence about the decision processes in which managers actually engaged. In our discussion, we are interested not so much in the particular heuristic Messick and Bazerman postulated as in their idea that innocent reliance on heuristics, rather than bad intentions, may lead to managerial wrongdoing. Their idea contrasts sharply with a more pessimistic tradition that prevails in much social science research. According to this pessimistic approach, the best explanation for wrongful conduct is simply that humans

are selfish creatures willing to harm others when doing so is personally advantageous. Loewenstein (1996) bluntly stated the pessimistic view, and even maintained that it is confirmed by experimental evidence:

> Managers' trade-offs between their own and others' well being are likely to be skewed to
> the point where they put very little weight on the effect of their decisions on other parties,
> except insofar as those effects have repercussions for their own well-being. (p. 215)

On Loewenstein's account, managers care predominantly about themselves. If social scientists were to find a way for managers to improve the rationality of their
decisions, it would only mean that managers would be more efficient in the way
that they exploit their customers and their employees. On Messick and Bazerman's
account, however, managerial wrongdoing often results from a simple mental mistake. Hence, they should expect that more efficient decision making would lead to
morally better behavior.

Who is right, Loewenstein, or Messick and Bazerman? Although these social
scientists have access to the same set of information about experimental behavior,
they come to radically different conclusions. We have our own opinion about who
is right, but we cannot attempt to adjudicate the matter in this chapter. Instead, we
wish to explore what we take to be a genuine insight in Messick and Bazerman's
position. We wish to develop their idea by considering the possibility that
heuristics play a function in explaining wrongdoing that occurs in response to authority. We sketch a model explanation of the wrongful behavior that occurs when
a person acts in accordance with what we will call the "authority heuristic."

Reliance on the authority heuristic is one example of a possible cognitive cause
of wrongful behavior. We do not wish to assert that factors others than purely cognitive factors are unimportant in explaining wrongful responses to authority. People may wrongly obey authority because they are frozen by fear, because they
desire to please, or for any variety of reasons that cannot be given a purely cognitive interpretation. Indeed, we suspect that when people give cognitive accounts to
explain their own wrongdoing, they often engage in ex post facto rationalization.
We nonetheless focus on a cognitive account that explains wrongful obedience to
authority because we need simplicity. Simplifying the content of psychological
explanations of wrongful obedience allows us to move directly to a discussion of
purely normative issues and paves the way for more interesting generalizations
about responsibility.

HEURISTICS, AUTHORITY, AND WRONGDOING

To make progress on issues about the moral significance of reliance on heuristics,
one must be clear about the idea of a heuristic. Tversky and Kahneman (1974) clarified this idea through an example taken from the psychology of perception:

> The apparent distance of an object is determined in part by its clarity. The more
> sharply an object is seen, the closer it appears to be. This rule has some validity,

because in any given scene the more distant objects are seen less sharply than nearer objects. However, reliance on this rule leads to systematic errors in the estimation of distance. Specifically, distances are often overestimated when visibility is poor because the contours of the objects are blurred. On the other hand, distances are often underestimated when visibility is good because the objects are seen sharply. Thus, the reliance on clarity as an indication of distance leads to common biases. (Tversky & Kahneman, 1974, p. 1124)

Tversky and Kahneman identified what might be called a "distance heuristic." Even though a person, if he chooses to invest the resources, can get a fairly accurate measurement of distance by using a mechanical device like a tape measure, in ordinary cases it is not worth the effort to do so. Hence people approximate distance by appeal to the rule, however implicit, that the more obscure an object appears, the farther away one should take it to be. Even though the distance heuristic is generally reliable, it is imperfect, and sometimes relying on it leads to inaccuracy. Of course, heuristics in visual perception are not the object of Tversky and Kahneman's research. Instead they focused on errors, which they regarded as instances of irrationality, that arise from relying on heuristics when making judgments about risk and probability.

In recent years, psychologists have postulated many different heuristics, extending the study of heuristics far beyond those employed in probabilistic or statistical reasoning. Messick (1993), for example, developed a distinctively moral heuristic, which he called the equality heuristic; it allows people to make judgments about fair allocation decisions without engaging in complex reasoning. We suggest that heuristics may play a role in explaining the moral attitudes that managers hold toward authority, and that the occurrence of inapt reliance on the authority heuristic may explain some managerial wrongdoing. We try to make this suggestion credible in several steps. First, we argue what we take to be the easiest case: establishing the reasonability of an authority heuristic in less morally charged situations. Second, we argue for the reasonability of relying on an authority heuristic when responding to some morally charged issues in which an individual who holds a position of authority issues an order; the Milgram experiments provide an example. Third, we extend the argument so that it covers cases in which managers rely on an authority heuristic in complex organizational settings in which a person does not respond to direct orders of a superior.

Relying on the judgment of an authority is utterly ordinary. This seems particularly true in technical matters concerning medicine, law, or technology. If your dentist insists that you need a root canal, for example, at some point you may reasonably defer to his or her judgment, even though doing so will cause considerable pain. Hence, if your dentist assures you that you have terribly deep tooth decay and shows you the x-ray, but you see nothing abnormal in it, you may question the dentist about it for a while. If you eventually agree to the procedure, it will not be because you think that you have developed an independent judgment that you need a root canal, but instead because you have decided to trust your dentist's judgment. Because the cognitive cost of developing a reliable independent judgment is prohibitive, relying on authority is sometimes a good way to make decisions. Thus we suggest that, in the simplest case, people reasonably employ an authority heuristic when, because they lack either the time or inclination to think a matter through for themselves, they defer to the judgment of someone who presumably knows more about the issue than they do.[3]

Now suppose, arguendo, the intelligibility of a heuristic that leads one to trust authority in technical matters such as endodontal medicine. Is it ever reasonable to rely on an authority heuristic in morally charged matters which are, after all, quite different from endodontal matters? We think so. Consider an example. Suppose that you arrive late to a meeting where a vote is to be taken on some issue of moral significance. You do not want to squander your vote, but you have not had time to study the issue, and you learn that a person whose judgment you ordinarily respect is going to vote in a certain way. Trusting his or her judgment is acting on a heuristic that prescribes deferring to authority. In this case, although you are perfectly competent to form your own judgment about how to vote, you lack time to do so. Your colleague has become an expert on this particular issue. You trust your colleague, who is an authority, as we are using the term.

In response to the time pressure you face, you trust someone who seems to have superior knowledge of the relevant moral issue than you do; you employ an authority heuristic on a moral matter.

There are good reasons to suppose that the subjects in Milgram's experiment may have used an authority heuristic. To see this, imagine again being one of Milgram's subject. You confront what seems, on the surface, a difficult decision; you are given little time to opt out of it but hardly are given the resources with which to fully evaluate the consequences of all alternative courses of action open to you. Furthermore, you have access to an apparently reliable authority, the experimenter, someone who seems to be in a good position to assess the matter. If you back out, you risk undermining what may be a valuable experiment. Facing a choice between trusting a reliable authority and backing out, you may find that it makes sense to trust the authority. Although it may seem morally wrong to shock your experimental subject, it also may seem plausible to suppose that the moral issue has been considered by the experimenter. The experimenter realizes that the victim suffers a cost in pain, but after careful reflection, concludes that the costs outweigh the benefits. The experimenter has more information and more time to reflect on it than you do, so why not defer? Unfortunately, you cannot know quite how the experimenter concluded that the experiment should be carried out despite the protests of the subjects. Perhaps the test results are so beneficial to society that it would be bad to jeopardize them by not carrying through the test. You do not know what the test is supposed to achieve, there seems to be no time to ask, and you

---

[3]Many writers use the idea of relying on a heuristic in a different way than we do. They use the idea to indicate an instantaneous mental reaction rather than something that occurs as part of a deliberative or reflective process. A reader put off by our use of the heuristic terminology might substitute the idea of satisficing found in March and Simon (1958) for our idea of a heuristic.

are unsure that you would be in a good position to evaluate an answer. You follow the heuristic: Defer to the judgment of a person who has better information than you and who is in a superior position to process that information.

We have argued that one plausible way to make sense of Milgram's subjects' behavior is to suppose that they employ an authority heuristic. We do not wish to argue that, as a matter of fact, all, most, or even some of the subjects employed the authority heuristic. Our point is conceptual, not empirical. We merely argue for the intelligibility and plausibility of the idea that reliance on an authority heuristic explains the behavior of some of Milgram's subjects. But our conceptual ambitions go beyond the Milgram case. We wish to urge the intelligibility of the authority heuristic as at least a partial explanation for much ordinary managerial wrongdoing, so that we may then explore the normative significance of relying on such a heuristic.

Situations that closely resemble the Milgram experiments are not common in the business world. Executives do not commonly stand over their subordinates and order them to directly harm identifiable and unwilling victims. How might an authority heuristic function in more ordinary cases of managerial decision making, in which wrongful choices are not responses to direct orders from a person in authority? Although we concede that there are significant differences between the decision facing Milgram's subjects and the decisions facing managers in more ordinary organizational settings, we also think that there are significant similarities. These similarities are tied to facts about the importance of compartmentalization in a person's own understanding of the decisions that he or she confronts. Why did Milgram's subjects administer shock? Because that was their job; that was the role they accepted. Why administer shock even though it seems morally problematic? Because they trusted the person running the experiment to have made the right moral decision. We argue that a similar rationale may be at play in the ordinary business case: One may trust authority as it is expressed through a person and one may trust authority as it is expressed in a role. To put matters more simply, when asked why they followed a wrongful order, people can say, "Because it was my job." And when asked why they administered some task that we regard as morally dubious, we suggest, employees in an organization can coherently say the same thing, even if nobody specifically ordered them to engage in that task. In both cases, we suggest, the authority heuristic may be operative.[4]

In a challenging critique of our view, Luban (2000) argued that the evidence Milgram adduced is not consistent with our idea that experimental subjects may have relied on an authority heuristic. Luban said:

> In one experiment, Milgram places the naive subject who draws the role of teacher with two experimenters. One experimenter announces that a second volunteer, who

---

[4]We use the word "authority" to denote a person with superior knowledge or expertise. The word may be used to describe very different phenomena. For instance, it may be used to denote a person with special power, for example, a judge. For a full description of authority, see Benn (1967).

would have been the learner, has canceled his appointment. After some discussion of how they are going to meet their experimental quota, one of the experimenters decides that he himself will take the learner's place. Like the learner in the basic set-up, he soon begins complaining about the pain, and at 150 volts he demands to be released. Indeed, he follows the entire schedule of complaints, screams, and ominous silence.

Surely, if subjects were relying on the ... [a]uthority heuristic, the fact that one of the authorities was demanding that the experiment stop should have brought about diminished compliance. Indeed, in another version of the experiment, in which two experimenters disagreed in the teacher's presence about whether the teacher should go on shocking the learner, all of the teachers stopped the experiment. Here, however, the usual two-thirds of the subjects complied to 450 volts. Apparently, it isn't deference to the experimenters' superior knowledge that promotes obedience. (Luban, 2000, p. 101)

The reason that we resist Luban's critique should now be plain. As we see it, authority commonly inheres in social and organizational roles, not merely in individuals. An order issued from an authoritative role may continue to have credibility even when there is a change in the person who occupies the role. In the Milgram experiment, a pronouncement is issued from an authoritative role that states the experimental subject must continue to administer shock. The evidence cited by Luban merely shows that an experimental subject did not follow the order issued by a person who once had occupied an authoritative role, but it casts no doubt that subjects continued to find credible the orders that issued from the role.

Applbaum (1995) offered a delightful account of the Executioner of Paris, who was official executioner for the French government both before and after the French revolution; a person who found authority in his job role. The Executioner of Paris did not just blindly carry out orders from a superior. To the contrary, his work was prized because his high professional standards compelled him to question orders when they were inconsistent with his professional role (e.g., when his equipment was not sharp enough, he demanded better). But he never questioned the propriety of the executions themselves. That fact should seem odd, because the Executioner of Paris seemed quite conscientious and killing for both the monarchy and the revolutionary government expresses a morally inconsistent set of commitments. He never doubted the moral legitimacy of his role or questioned the propriety of any acts consistent with that role, even when it meant killing royalty who once had been his employer. The Executioner of Paris regarded his professional role as setting demands for him that transcended any specific request made by any person occupying a role superior to his own. In an important and very realistic sense, he viewed his professional role as a source of authority even more demanding than the authority held by any person. For the Executioner of Paris, authority inhered not in a person but in a role. Instead of justifying his actions in terms of orders from individuals, he justified his actions in terms of the responsibilities of his job. And one reason, we propose, that the role came to have authority is that the Executioner of Paris adopted the authority heuristic. He supposed that when a person does a legitimate job well, he is doing a good thing. Rather than thinking through what he should do, he followed prescriptions inherent in his role.

In many ways, the Executioner of Paris is not so unusual. It is common for professionals to justify their actions in terms of the requirements of their professional roles. Lawyers, for example, sometimes justify presumptively wrong actions, including badgering innocent people (witnesses), unfairly tarnishing their reputations, and publicly bringing them to tears, by appealing to the requirements of the lawyers' roles as zealous representatives of their clients' interests. When lawyers do so, they can claim to be doing their jobs, just as Milgram's subjects could claim to be doing their jobs.

The authoritative prescriptions on which lawyers and other professionals, including the Executioner of Paris, rely may derive from their roles rather than from direct orders. To justify some particular action, for example, a beheading, the Executioner of Paris explained that he was doing his job. The presumption is that whatever is required to do a morally respectable job is a morally respectable action. Rather than rely on the authoritative prescriptions of a superior barking out an order, the Executioner relied on the authoritative prescriptions inherent in his job role. His action, we suggest, can be interpreted as reliance on the authority heuristic just as much as the actions of Milgram's subjects can be interpreted as reliance on the authority heuristic. If we are correct, his situation may resemble that of many people within organizations or broader professional institutions who rely on the norm of their job role to determine a proper course of action. And if we are correct, reliance on the authority heuristic should be a common feature of organizational and professional life. Yet when one relies on authority, either as expressed through the commands of an individual or as expressed in one's job role, one risks doing wrong because one risks following wrongful authoritative prescriptions. As humans, we all face that risk because it is an unavoidable consequence of our limited cognitive resources.

So far we have merely set out to establish the coherence of the idea that an authority heuristic helps explain some instances of wrongdoing. We have done nothing, of course, to establish that in fact an authority heuristic does explain the relevant behavior. Doing so raises issues of empirical confirmation outside the scope of this chapter. Nonetheless, suppose that the authority heuristic does in fact explain wrongdoing in the Milgram experiments. What is the normative relevance? Does it suggest that Milgram's subjects were not blameworthy for their actions? These questions remain surprisingly hard to answer.

NORMALITY AS INNOCENCE

What is the moral significance of the fact that wrongdoing occurs as the result of innocent reliance on a heuristic? Consider again the fundamental attribution error. Suppose that a person engages in wrongdoing (e.g., a Milgram subject administers shock) as a consequence of relying on a heuristic, but that in assessing the person's responsibility, one does not think about the fact that he or she relies on the heuristic. Then one might be inclined to blame the person, to suppose that he or she acts out of wrongful intentions or a character defect, or that the person's action expresses some morally problematic "dispositional factor." But, arguably, this would be fallacious. The person's action is perfectly normal. Most people in the same situation would have done the same. And hence, one might think, it is a mistake to blame the action on anything idiosyncratic in the person, or in effect to blame him or her. When one blames a person despite the fact that the cause of that person's wrongdoing is best seen as exogenous to dispositional factors in his or her character, it might be argued, one commits the fundamental attribution error.

Despite our language in the previous paragraph, our argument does not depend on expanding the notion of a situational factor so that it includes cognitive heuristics. We can construct an argument that borrows one underlying idea from past criticism of the fundamental attribution error, but that does not adopt the full linguistic framework of attribution theory. The relevant underlying idea of attribution theory, as we see it, is simply that it is a mistake to explain instances of conduct in terms of idiosyncratic personality traits when such conduct occurs as a normal response to certain situations irrespective of individual differences. Hence we call this the "argument from normality":

1. If it is normal for reliance on cognitive heuristics to cause specific wrongful conduct, then that conduct occurs as an innocent mental mistake, and the person who engages in it should not be blamed for it.
2. It is normal for reliance on cognitive heuristics to cause Milgram's subjects to administer shock.
3. Milgram's subjects should not be morally blamed for their wrongful conduct.

The argument from normality suggests that the best explanation for the wrongdoing that occurs when a person relies on a heuristic is nothing more diabolical than a simple mental mistake.

The argument from normality is easily generalizable, offering a way to understand the decision making of wrongdoers whose actions are caused by inapt reliance on a range of common cognitive heuristics. One may argue that not merely cognitive error but the occurrence of any sort of error is just a normal part of human decision making, that provides an excuse for wrongdoing. We believe that the argument from normality provides a charitable interpretation of Messick and Bazerman's (1996) position on whether those who produced and distributed DES should be regarded as wrongdoers, and that it provides a charitable account of why an attribution theorist may not wish to be harsh in judging Milgram's subjects. But we also believe that the argument from normality, even though it contains some insight, should not be accepted, at least in the form in which we have so far presented it.

What is wrong with the argument from normality? The mere fact that a reaction is normal or common does not by itself show that a person is not blameworthy for having that reaction. Schoeman (1987) nicely illustrated this point. He asked us to imagine that if you offer people money to speed in their cars and thus violate the traffic laws, and most people would accept the money and violate the laws, it would not follow that their actions were not blameworthy or that these speeders should be regarded as morally innocent. And, of course, the same holds true for worse wrongs. Suppose that most sons and daughters would beat their parents if offered 10 million dollars to do so. In some sense, their action would be normal. One might even say that, in some sense, their actions were caused by their being offered a large sum of money. Nonetheless, it hardly would follow that these people were not to blame for the actions. If all children behave in this way, it is a sad fact about the human race and perhaps demonstrates that we as a species are morally defective, but it hardly follows that any individual who has a normal response is thereby not blameworthy. The problem with the argument from normality, then, is that it seems to rely on the following controversial claim: If N is the normal human reaction to X, then P should not be blamed for doing N. But that claim is false. Still, we think that it would be a step backward to completely reject the argument from normality. The argument provides an attractive alternative to the view, quite popular in the social sciences and embraced by Loewenstein (1996), which explains wrongdoing as nothing more than simple selfishness.

Suppose that both the behavior of DES managers and the behavior of Milgram's subjects were in fact quite normal; suppose, furthermore, that we should expect most people, confronted with similar circumstances, to behave in the same way. To simplify the issue even more, suppose that the normal behavior in which we should expect people to engage is erroneous reliance on a heuristic. What moral attitude should we hold toward these wrongdoers? What attitude should they hold toward themselves?

HEURISTICS AND THE LIMITS OF BLAME

Heuristics may be relevant in thinking about blameworthiness, but the argument from normality is too crude to explain why. There are, however, other possibilities. Fortunately, once again, Schoeman (1987) made some helpful suggestions. He maintained that although people who commit wrongs while following the prescriptions of authority (or in our terms, adhering to the authority heuristic) should not be wholly excused for their actions, the facts sometimes warrant mitigation of the censure they deserve. Schoeman made his point by invoking an analogy with the traditional criminal law idea of entrapment, which precludes the state from prosecuting a person when state agents encourage a person to commit a crime:

> When an agent, including the state, has fallen below a certain level of rectitude, that agent has lost any standing to criticize. Analogously, if quasi-authoritative social forces have significantly contributed to wrongdoing by themselves falling below a

moral threshold, then these authoritative forces lack the standing to blame others for
misdeeds attributable to this failing. (Schoeman, 1987, p. 312)

Schoeman suggested that the grounds of mitigation for wrongly obeying authority
should be understood analogously to the grounds for not prosecuting a person who
commits a crime only because he was entrapped: Because we do not prosecute a
person whose wrongful action was caused by police agents, who in fact represent
authority, we also should be lenient on Milgram's experimental subjects, whose
wrongdoing also was caused by authority. We agree with Schoeman that reliance
on authority is morally relevant to assessing wrongful conduct. But we maintain
that it matters normatively how and why a wrongdoer relies on authority. For such
reliance to matter, it must at least be conscious reliance on authority, we maintain.
But we conclude that condition is not consistent with Schoeman's analysis of the
moral relevance of authority.

There are several problems with Schoeman's analogy between excuses for relying on authority in Milgram's cases and the entrapment defense. First, the
value of the entrapment defense seems to derive from considerations not relevant
to Milgram's cases. The purpose of the entrapment defense seems twofold: It
limits the temptation of police to cause people to commit crime, and it prevents
the state from hypocritically prosecuting people for crimes in which the state was
complicit. Neither of these considerations seems relevant to a judgment about
whether the criminal is morally blameworthy in entrapment cases. Instead these
considerations bear on the narrow issue of whether it is proper for the state to
prosecute such a person. But in this chapter, we are interested in questions about
blameworthiness and not whether it is appropriate to undertake punitive or other
adverse formal actions in Milgram cases. As Schoeman employed the entrapment analogy, its force depends on whether people who causally contribute to the
wrongdoing of others have moral "standing" to blame the wrongdoers. But
plainly this issue of standing is not relevant to many of the cases of interest to us
in this chapter. For example, we are interested in how one of Milgram's subjects
should morally assess himself or herself. It is absurd to suggest that a person may
lack standing to engage in self-criticism about his or her own choices. Moreover,
we doubt that any reader of this chapter causally contributed to wrongdoing in
the Milgram experiments or the DES injuries, for example. None of us is in any
sense complicit in these acts of wrongdoing in ways that may jeopardize our
standing for criticizing the involved parties.

More important, however, the decision-making processes of entrapment victims in law and the decision-making processes of Milgram's subjects differ in morally relevant ways. Milgram's subjects perceived themselves as responding to
authority. Although many subjects showed great strains of conflict, they nonetheless also seemed to believe that their actions were morally and rationally defensi-
ble, that they were doing the right thing because they were doing what legitimate
authority required. Entrapment victims, on the other hand, are victims precisely
because they do not perceive the presence of authority—they act only because they

think they are not dealing with police or other state representatives; they attempt to do something that they recognize as unequivocally wrong. The comparative wrongfulness of intentions thus presents a stark contrast between entrapment victims and Milgram's subjects. Because entrapment victims but not Milgram's subjects (or other dependents on the authority heuristic) unequivocally try to do wrong, the latter are more entitled to an excuse than are the former. That fact undermines Schoeman's analysis. We conclude, then, that contrary to Schoeman's suggestions, the reasons for not prosecuting entrapment victims cannot be analogous to reasons for mitigating blame of Milgram's subjects or of others who wrongly obey the varieties of authority. We still believe, however, that there is merit in Schoeman's suggestion that relying on authority provides an excuse for Milgram's subjects. It remains to explain why.

MORAL IGNORANCE

Many of Milgram's subjects administered shock under protest, while displaying physical symptoms of revulsion at their task. Nobody, of course, knows their exact thoughts and emotions; one can only speculate. Still, commentators agree that Milgram's subjects seemed torn by conflict (Miller, 1986). On the one hand, they understood the wrongness of inflicting pain on the unwilling. On the other hand, they presumed that their role was legitimate and felt a responsibility to perform that role conscientiously. But it was impossible to conscientiously execute their role while at the same time to avoid inflicting pain. Milgram's subjects had to make a choice, and most chose to administer shock. Thus, although Milgram's subjects seemed to have conflicted beliefs about what was right to do, most chose to follow the directions of authority.

If Milgram's subjects chose in accordance with the authority heuristic, then they made a good faith choice; they tried to do the right thing by assisting in what they concluded must somehow be a legitimate experiment but they made a mental mistake and did something wrong. How should one evaluate a person who tries to do the right thing but, because of mental error, does something wrong instead? Recall that traditional morality and jurisprudence countenance two varieties of excuse for wrongdoing: cognitive and volitional. One might think that if a person engages in wrongdoing because of false beliefs that derive from his or her reliance on a cognitive heuristic, that person makes an innocent mistake and hence is excused for any relevant wrongdoing.

The paradigm under which an excuse of ignorance falls involves mistake of fact. For example, if you offer someone a Coke, not knowing that it is laced with arsenic, and that person dies, you may be excused from any wrongdoing because of your ignorance. Might a similar excuse apply in the Milgram case? The Milgram case is distinguished from an ordinary case of ignorance because the Milgram case involves not merely mistake about fact but mistake about principle. Arguably the Milgram subjects knew the facts relevant to culpability. They knew that they were administering potentially lethal shock to an unwilling victim. But they were confused about the requirements of moral principle in their situation. They trusted the authority of the experimenter, who suggested that inflicting shock was the right thing to do.

Both traditional morality and law treat mistake about principle much less leniently than mistake about fact. If after serving a glass of arsenic-laced Coke, you say that you knew that there was arsenic in it but that you did not realize that it was wrong to poison somebody, it is problematic whether it gives you an excuse. Yet, if ignorance of principle provides no excuse, then it seems doubtful that reliance on the authority heuristic provides an excuse. We maintain that in some special cases, ignorance of principle provides some excuse. But first we wish to consider the contrary position.

In a broad-ranging defense of the idea that ignorance of principle should be no excuse in either law or morality, Leo Katz, a legal theorist, considered the case of the Milgram experiments.

> Think back on the infamous Milgram experiments, all those people who obliged the experimenter and continued pressing buttons which they thought would inflict severe electric shocks on the uncooperative learner, those concentration camp *manques*. Most of those people did not enjoy doing what they did. In fact, when the experimenter gave them half a chance to cheat and not inflict the required shocks, they did. They went through agonies. They only continued pressing the buttons because they felt that was what morality required of them. Yet we are willing to condemn them for their weakness, despite the fact that it seems to have been the product of moral ignorance. (Katz, 1998, p. 1477)

Katz thus asserted that mistake about moral principle, and the moral ignorance that corresponds to it, are no excuse generally, and no excuse for Milgram's subjects in particular. His position clearly resonates with established law, which is very stingy in recognizing excuses for ignorance of principle. For example, it is textbook law that one ordinarily cannot defend oneself against the charge that one has committed a crime by arguing that one did not know that the act was illegal, and this is so even if one was not negligent in determining the legal status of the act (Dressler, 1998). Law generally demands that people know the difference between right and wrong, and it denies the defense of negligence.

We agree with Katz that even outside of law, there are many cases in which ignorance of principle is no excuse. Indeed, the person serving arsenic-laced Coke because he or she does not know it is wrong seems such a case. Katz offered many others. He plausibly maintained that to whatever extent people like Hitler and Stalin were ignorant about the principles they were violating, then they were more guilty rather than less guilty for their actions. In many cases, one fairly presumes that people have moral knowledge, and to the extent they do not, it is their fault, and hence they are responsible for wrongdoing owing to absence of knowledge.

On the other hand, in some cases ignorance of the requirements of principle seems to provide some excuse, and we think that Milgram's subjects may be one such case. In fact, a well-respected jurisprudential tradition and a line of legal decisions support the idea that ignorance of principle is sometimes an excuse (Kahan, 1997). Consider the following hypothetical situation. There has been a terrible accident. A driver attempting to deliver organs for a transplant is involved in an accident, and both the driver and the truck are disabled. A nearby police officer must tend to the scene. The police officer orders and authorizes you to drive the organs to the hospital, at whatever speed it takes, to ensure timely delivery of the organs. On the way to the hospital, you have an accident, and you are charged with criminal recklessness. It turns out that it was illegal for you to speed to the hospital and that the police officer lacked authority to compel you to do so. Although you violated the law, it was an innocent mistake, and it would be a failure of imagination to judge you harshly. In this case, you did what you thought was required by law. But you were ignorant of the law. Your ignorance of the law mitigates your blameworthiness. If you break the law in ignorance and good faith, while trying to do the right thing, there is reason not to judge you harshly.

Why treat differently (a) cases in which a person does something wrong while acting in ignorance of the requirements of principle but in good faith and (b) cases in which a person does something wrong acting in ignorance of the requirements of principle but in bad faith or maliciously? Kahan (1997) offered a utilitarian argument in support of different treatment. He suggested that we need to punish those who act maliciously more than those who act in good faith because society will gain comparatively more advantages by deterring the former. Nonutilitarian arguments may provide other reasons why the cases should be treated differently. A nonutilitarian argument might focus on what people deserve for engaging in wrongful action rather than on the socially beneficial deterrence that might be achieved by punishing those who engage in wrongful action. For example, one might argue that the degree of blame or moral censure one deserves for wronging someone should be a function of the extent to which one's wrongful behavior is explained by vice. To the extent that Milgram's subjects and DES managers suffered mere mental lapses, it may be a mistake to judge them harshly, too.

A person who commits a wrong because of a reasoning miscue is in some important sense not doing what he or she really wants to do; one may complain that the person should not have allowed himself or herself to fall prey to this mistake and one may also complain about the wrong that the person commits, but it is a special sort of complaint that one makes; it makes little sense to say that such a person embraces warped or evil values. Other things equal, the evil expressed while doing wrong but trying to do right is of a lesser magnitude than the evil expressed while doing wrong and acting from a bad motive or evil intention. In the latter case, one embraces evil; in the former, one does not. That seems a morally relevant distinction. Katz's (1998) argument that ignorance of principle provides no excuse is most plausible for cases, like that of Hitler or Stalin, in which wrongdoers embrace values that are evil or warped. His argument is less plausible when wrongdoers embrace no defective values but make a faulty inference from acceptable values, as we suppose Milgram's subjects and DES managers did when they relied on the authority heuristic.

Should one conclude that Milgram's subjects and DES managers, on the assumption that their wrongful actions arose from mistaken reliance on something like the authority heuristic, are morally off the hook? Surely that would go too far. They have reason to feel guilty about their actions. Although, on our assumptions, their wrongdoing stems from a mental mistake of the sort that perhaps most people in their situations would have committed, it does not follow that they are innocent. They had a responsibility not to commit that mistake, and they failed in that responsibility even though it was in their power to avoid doing so. Because a moral breach was the cause of their wrongdoing and its consequences, they are responsible. But the censure they deserve, we suggest, is less than that which people deserve who commit the same acts from more reprehensible dispositions. Because their wrongdoing arises from a mistake, they have an excuse, but it is not a perfect or complete excuse. It is merely a partial excuse. It mitigates but does not eliminate blameworthiness.

Consider the different legal treatment given to a person who commits a grave criminal act while in a lucid frame of mind and a person who commits the same act while intoxicated. The latter gets a less harsh sentence. Even those who commit a crime while intoxicated may get different treatment depending on how they became intoxicated. Hence, a person who lucidly and coldly kills a person will get a longer sentence than a person who commits the same act while intoxicated. Most interestingly, however, whether a person is guilty for acts committed while intoxicated depends on his or her complicity in getting intoxicated. If someone slips the person a drug, he or she is wholly off the hook. If the person intentionally gets drunk to embolden himself or herself to commit a crime, that person is not much off the hook. We suggest that the case of heuristics is somewhere in between. A person does not intentionally adhere to a heuristic in the same way that he or she intentionally gets drunk. It is ordinarily not something that easily can be avoided. No person has the ability to avoid all heuristics all the time or even any single heuristic most of the time. To do so would be equivalent to never acting from mental habit, an impossibility. Because of the difficulty humans face in avoiding reliance on heuristics, it seems fair not to censure a person too harshly for relying on a heuristic.

ACKNOWLEDGMENTS

For helpful comments, we thank John Darley, Tom Dunfee, David Luban, David Wasserman, audiences at the Kellogg School, Jon Baron's lab group, and the 1999 Society for Business Ethics Conference. For financial support, we thank the Zicklin Center for Business Ethics Research.

REFERENCES

Applbaum, A. I. (1995). Professional detachment: The Executioner of Paris. *Harvard Law Review, 109,* 458–486.

Benn, S. I. (1967). Authority. In P. Edwards (Ed.), *The encyclopedia of philosophy* (pp. 215–217). New York: Macmillan and The Free Press.

Donagan, A. (1977). *The theory of morality.* Chicago: University of Chicago Press.

Dressler, J. (1998). *Understanding criminal law.* New York: Matthew Bender.

Kahan, D. H. (1997). Ignorance of the law is an excuse—But only for the virtuous. *Michigan Law Review, 96,* 127–154.

Katz, L. (1998). Incommensurable choices and the problem of moral ignorance. *University of Pennsylvania Law Review, 146,* 1465–1485.

Loewenstein, G. (1996). Behavioral decision theory and business ethics: Skewed trade-offs between self and other. In D. E. Messick & A. E. Tenbrunsel (Eds.), *Codes of conduct: Behavioral research into business ethics* (pp. 214–227). New York: Russell Sage Foundation.

Luban, D. (2000). Wrongful obedience, bad judgment, and warranted excuses. In D. Rhode (Ed.), *Ethics in practice* (pp. 94–120). New York: Oxford University Press..

Luban, D., Strudler, A., & Wasserman, D. (1992). Moral responsibility in the age of bureaucracy. *Michigan Law Review, 23,* 48–92.

March, J. G., & Simon, H. A. (1958). *Organizations.* New York: Wiley.

Messick, D. M. (1993). Equality as a decision heuristic. In B. A. Mellers & J. Baron (Eds.), *Psychological perspectives on justice: Theory and applications* (pp. 11–31). New York: Cambridge University Press.

Messick, D. M., & Bazerman, M. H. (1996). Ethical leadership and the psychology of decision making. *Sloan Management Review, 37,* 9–22.

Milgram, S. (1983). *Obedience to authority.* New York,: Harper & Row.

Miller, A. G. (1986). *The obedience experiments.* Westport, CT: Praeger.

Ross, L., & Anderson, C. (1982). Shortcomings in the attribution process: On the origins and maintenance of erroneous social assessments. In D. Kahneman, P. Slovic, & A. Tversky (Eds.), *Judgment under uncertainty: Heuristics and biases* (pp. 129–152). New York: Cambridge University Press.

Sabini, J. (1997). *The really fundamental attribution error.* Unpublished manuscript.

Schoeman, F. (1987). Statistical norms and moral attributions. In F. Schoeman (Ed.), *Responsibility, character, and the emotions* (pp. 287–315). New York: Cambridge University Press.

Tversky, A., & Kahneman, D. (1974). Judgment under uncertainty: Heuristics and biases. *Science, 185,* 1124–1131.

III

Social Influence in Groups, Networks, and Markets

11 Golden Rules and Leaden Worlds: Exploring the Limitations of Tit-for-Tat as a Social Decision Rule

Roderick M. Kramer
Jane Wei
Jonathan Bendor
Graduate School of Business, Stanford University

"Reciprocity is not only a social norm, but can also be an extremely successful operating rule for an individualistic pragmatist."

—Robert Axelrod, *The Evolution of Cooperation* (1984, p. 18)

Contemporary ethical theory and behavioral research on social influence enjoy at least one important point of conceptual convergence: Both lines of inquiry recognize the utility that human beings attach to general rules governing social conduct. In ethical theory, such rules often are justified on normative grounds and derived deductively from higher principles. For example, utilitarian perspectives on ethical behavior emphasize the central role that higher order rules play in individual conduct. In research on social influence, such rules more often are justified on empirical grounds and inferred from laboratory experiments or field studies (Cialdini, 1993).

Whether justified on a priori theoretical grounds or on the basis of evidence, however, both perspectives emphasize the constructive role that general prescriptive rules play in helping people decide how they ought to behave in a given situation in the light of some evaluative standard. In this respect, ethical theory and influence theory alike posit that individuals think about their social conduct in a consequentialist way. In ethical theory, consequentialism characteristically is "justified" in terms of consistency with higher order principles, such as "Do no harm" (Baron, 1996). In behavioral research, in contrast, consequentialism usually is operationalized along more pragmatic lines (e.g., a rule's efficacy in reliably producing a given outcome, such as a desired level of compliance; Cialdini, 1993).

In emphasizing the importance of prescriptive rules, contemporary ethical theorizing and behavioral research on social influence often have been driven by the search for powerful, generalized principles of effective conduct or guiding principles. Few rules have attracted as much attention in recent years as a very simple rule known as "tit-for-tat." Tit-for-tat dictates cooperating initially when dealing with other social actors and thereafter reciprocating whatever one's partner in an exchange relationship did in the previous encounter. As ethical theorists have noted, tit-for-tat has the attractive feature of seeming fair and just. It resonates with normative beliefs about the merits and universality of reciprocity, in terms of two important criteria: first, our sense of procedural fairness and, second, equality in the long-term outcomes generated in an exchange relationship (Wilson, 1993). For behavioral scientists, the allure of tit-for-tat has been, at least in part, its proven efficacy in eliciting and sustaining cooperative relations among interdependent decision makers (Axelrod, 1984).

In no small measure, the attention and acclaim accorded tit-for-tat can be attributed to Axelrod's important and provocative findings (Axelrod, 1980a, 1980b, 1984). His findings have been embraced by psychologists, moral philosophers, game theorists, organizational scholars, conflict theorists, and evolutionary biologists. Axelrod's findings have been enshrined as well in many popular treatments of the behavioral science literature. Bazerman (1994), for example, suggested that "while Axelrod's advice was built around a two-party problem, the logic of [his] advice can be applied when more than two parties are involved" (p. 190). Bazerman further proposed that "price wars (whether between airlines, oil-producing nations, or breakfast cereal manufacturers), promotional strategies, advertising wars, and military competition can all be fruitfully addressed using Axelrod's insights" (p. 190). Along similar lines, Thompson (1998) affirmed the power of tit-for-tat for inducing cooperation in negotiations, characterizing it as "an extremely effective stable strategy" (p. 221). Moreover, the merits of tit-for-tat are now widely and routinely touted in business and law schools throughout the United States, especially in courses on negotiation and conflict management. Tit-for-tat, in short, seems to represent a "golden rule" governing a broad class of exchange relationships.

When a behavioral prescription acquires the status of a golden rule, it is wise to scrutinize its virtues and flaws more fully. Is tit-for-tat a robust method for eliciting and sustaining cooperation across a wide range of situations, as many scholars and popularizers have concluded? Is it an extremely effective and stable strategy, as others have suggested? These are the primary questions we engage in this chapter. We pursue also the related question of how well people's intuitions regarding the strengths and weaknesses of tit-for-tat compare to its actual performance in different circumstances. The seemingly ubiquitous appeal of tit-for-tat can be understood, we suggest, at least in part by its resonance with people's intuitions about fair and efficacious rules.

In pursuing these questions and arguments, we focus first on empirical work on the efficacy of tit-for-tat when social uncertainty or "noise" (i.e., uncertainty about others' actions) is present (Bendor, Kramer, & Stout, 1991). Based on this evidence, we suggest that tit-for-tat suffers from several important limitations.[1] We then review more recent evidence suggesting that, in sharp contrast to empirical findings, people's intuitions often fail to appreciate the subtle and nontrivial effects of such noise on the efficacy of tit-for-tat.

From the perspective of the behavioral sciences, rules governing conduct in cooperation dilemmas can be viewed as a subset of a more general class of *social decision heuristics*. These heuristics typically do not lay out complete plans of action that say what to do in every possible contingency. (A complete plan is what game theorists mean by *strategy;* we will use the word in that technical sense.) Instead, social decision heuristics are behavioral "rules" that individuals use when deciding how they ought to act when they are interdependent with other actors (Allison & Messick, 1990). The heuristic of being "nice" (never be the first to defect in an iterated Prisoner's Dilemma; Axelrod, 1984), for example, is clearly not a strategy, because it is incomplete. (It doesn't tell one what to do if one's partner defects.) Nevertheless, it does serve as a guide to action, and when coupled with the heuristic of reciprocity (reciprocate today what your partner did yesterday) it does create a complete plan of action.

Because tit-for-tat embodies the social decision rules of reciprocity and niceness, it has a number of attractive features. It generally is perceived as a fair rule, and one that is consistent with social norms of reciprocity (Wilson, 1993). Its combination of niceness and reciprocity implies that it is honorable—it will never try to cheat a partner—and that it is forgiving (Axelrod, 1984) as well. The conjunction of such ethical and pragmatic virtues has proven a powerful lure to both the academic theorist and the social science popularizer.

Initial Evidence of Tit-for-Tat's Efficacy

Initial evidence of the efficacy of tit-for-tat for eliciting and sustaining cooperation was provided by Axelrod using the well-known and deceptively simple Prisoner's Dilemma (PD) game. Axelrod was interested in how cooperation could emerge among a group of self-interested actors involved in a repeated PD. At the heart of his inquiry was the fundamental question of which strategies and associated heuristics would be most effective at eliciting cooperation and which would be least effective).[2] To explore this general question, he conducted a computer tournament.

---

[1] Axelrod himself was careful to point out the limitations of his findings (see Wu & Axelrod, 1997, for a thorough discussion of analytic and empirical studies of the effects of noise on cooperation).

[2] In behavioral terms, we view these strategies as general decision rules.

In designing this tournament, Axelrod had a number of important insights about the limitations of previous empirical research using the PD. First, he recognized that much of the research on this game had used laboratory studies with relatively unsophisticated subjects, such as undergraduates encountering the dilemma for the first time. Such naive participants obviously do not resemble the strategically astute and experienced decision makers about whom researchers often hoped to generalize (e.g., the presumably savvy actors engaged in the real-world situations described by Bazerman, 1994). Consequently, questions could be raised about the external validity of these earlier laboratory studies. To remedy this problem, Axelrod decided to explore how more sophisticated decision makers would approach the dilemma. Accordingly, he invited game theorists, psychologists, and political scientists who were intimately familiar with the structure of the PD and the nuances of strategic choice in it to enter his tournament.

A second important insight Axelrod had was that much of the original work on the PD had focused on relatively simple, short-lived dyadic encounters between strangers. Axelrod was interested in how different strategies would perform in considerably more complex social ecologies, in which decision makers encountered each other repeatedly. Specifically, he organized his computer tournament as a round-robin, so that each participant's strategy was paired with (a) those submitted by all the other participants, (b) a twin (i.e., a copy of itself), and (c) random, a strategy that randomly cooperated or defected. The strategies then would be assessed by comparing their total tournament payoffs, which were simply the sum of their pairwise payoffs.

To provide a conservative test for evaluating the efficacy of a given strategy in generating cooperation, Axelrod deliberately made pessimistic assumptions about decision makers' social motivation. In particular, he assumed that decision makers were purely self-interested or egoistic actors, concerned only about their own outcomes.[3] If cooperation could gain a toehold and flourish even under such harsh conditions, he reasoned, the results arguably might be considered rather robust.

In response to his announcement of the upcoming tournament, Axelrod received 14 strategies. Given the sophistication of the people who designed these entries, it is not surprising that many strategies were quite clever and reflected subtle psychological intuitions about the dynamics (and dangers) of cooperation in iterated PDs. For example, one entry, called Downing, tried to develop a "model" of the other player and then acted to maximize its own payoff given that model. Thus, if the other party seemed vigilant and responsive to Downing's behavior, Downing cooperated. If, on the other hand, the other party seemed unresponsive, Downing defected. In other words, Downing tried to understand its partner and then act in accord with that understanding. Another submission, called Joss, tried to get away

---

[3]More precisely, although Axelrod allowed for social motives such as altruism, he required that these sentiments already be incorporated in the payoffs and that the payoffs satisfy the properties of a PD. Thus, the pessimism of his assumption was essentially that the egoistic motivations were sufficiently stronger than the nonegoistic ones so that cooperation remained problematic in the one-shot game.

with occasional defections. It thus tried to be a clever defector by posing as a cooperator. In addition to being clever, some of the strategies were quite complex.

From the standpoint of the present chapter, the most important result of Axelrod's tournament was that, counter to many entrants' intuitions about the importance of cleverness and complexity, the strategy that won the day (i.e., got the highest total payoff) was tit-for-tat, the simplest entry in the entire tournament.

Explaining Tit-for-Tat's Efficacy

Axelrod (1984) advanced several reasons for tit-for-tat's success in the tournament and for the performance of other strategies. First, he proposed, tit-for-tat encoded the important heuristic of being *nice* (i.e., it was never first to defect in its encounters with its partners). Strategies that used the nice heuristic performed well, Axelrod suggested, because they necessarily do well against each other and because there were enough entries with this property to ensure that niceness was rewarded over the long haul.

A second important feature of tit-for-tat that contributed to its success, Axelrod argued, was that it is *provocable*: It immediately retaliates whenever it sees that its cooperative gestures are abused (i.e., not reciprocated). In the language of reinforcement theory, tit-for-tat elicits cooperation from others by extinguishing noncooperative behavior through swift and unconditional punishment.

A third important property of tit-for-tat, however, was that it is also, in Axelrod's parlance, *forgiving*. Once punishment has been meted out—and tit-for-tat has, in a sense, communicated to its partner that defections will not be tolerated—it is willing to revert to a state of cooperation. Forgiveness is important, Axelrod noted, because it disrupts costly cycles of punishment and recrimination.

A fourth reason that tit-for-tat performed well, Axelrod asserted, was that it is a relatively clear strategy. Tit-for-tat's clarity, he noted, "makes it intelligible to the other player, thereby eliciting long-term cooperation" (Axelrod, 1984, p. 54). The importance of clarity is somewhat counterintuitive, because one might expect that opacity—the inability to be "read"—could confer some strategic advantages (consistent with disinformation theories and other more Machiavellian orientations toward such games, a la Schelling, 1960).

In sum, tit-for-tat seemed to possess a number of attributes that are quite laudable and made it an attractive candidate for golden rule status: it's nice, it's forgiving (willing to let bygones be bygones), and it's clear (not so clever that it got itself into unintended troubles). Furthermore, it seems fair, giving in kind what it receives, and it is efficacious.

In further elaborating on why tit-for-tat performed so well and why its attributes were useful social decision heuristics, Axelrod (1984) made an interesting observation about the intersection of the beliefs of the individuals who participated in his tournament and the strategies they generated: "Even expert strategists from political science, sociology, economics, psychology and mathematics," he suggested, "made the systematic errors of being too competitive for their own good, not being forgiving enough, and being too pessimistic about the responsiveness of the other side" (p. 40). We return to these points later when examining why people's general beliefs about human nature might influence their attraction toward a strategy such as tit-for-tat and their a priori beliefs about its general efficacy.

Armed with these findings, Axelrod conducted a second round-robin tournament. Based on the intense interest generated by the results of the first tournament, his second tournament attracted an even more impressive and diverse set of expert participants. Sixty-two strategies were submitted, including some designed by computer scientists, physicists, evolutionary biologists, social psychologists, and economists.

An important feature of this second tournament was that the first tournament's results were widely known and much analyzed. Consequently, entrants in this second tournament were in a good position to learn from the experience of participants in the original tournament. And, not surprisingly, many of the entrants to this second round did attempt to exploit insights they felt were gained from the first tournament. For example, one player submitted an interesting strategy named Tranquilizer that tried to take advantage of nice rules such as tit-for-tat. Tranquilizer's approach was to initially establish a mutually cooperative relationship, and then, after having lulled its partner into a false sense of security, it tried to sneak in a few defections, to see if it could get away with them.

Remarkably, tit-for-tat emerged as the winner of this second tournament as well. In interpreting the surprising ability of tit-for-tat to repeat its stunning first tournament performance, Axelrod (1984) cogently observed that the outcomes (payoffs) of strategies in this second tournament reflected an interesting interaction between conflicting lessons people drew from the original tournament. The first lesson was that it pays to be nice and forgiving. The second lesson was more exploitative: "If others are going to be nice and forgiving, then it pays to try to take advantage of them" (p. 47). Axelrod pointed out that those who drew the first lesson suffered at the hands of those who extracted the second: The latter were sometimes good at exploiting the former's niceness or forgivingness. However, these attempts to take advantage of other entrants backfired when the exploitive strategies encountered provocable partners. In such matchups, the would-be exploiter succeeded only in setting off bouts of retaliation from its provocable partner. In the end, therefore, exploiters would have been better off with more mutual cooperation.

As noted at the beginning of this chapter, the results of Axelrod's two computer tournaments excited enormous interest among behavioral scientists, and justifiably so. Moreover, the tournament methodology seemed to be a powerful approach for studying the evolution of cooperation. It was apparently a method that could yield fundamental insights about this evolutionary process and that could further generate useful prescriptions for developing and maintaining cooperative relationships among interdependent decision makers. On the basis of such tournaments, one could envision the emergence of a set of robust, empirically grounded rules for effective choice in dilemmalike situations. The results seemed to suggest, for example, that a number of effective behavioral heuristics, such as niceness, forgiveness, and provocability, are individually necessary and jointly sufficient for the emergence and survival of cooperation across a variety of ecologies. The results also seemed to strongly validate the presumption that reciprocity plays an important role in the emergence of cooperation, something evolutionary biologists, anthropologists, historians, political scientists, and sociologists had long argued. As Wilson (1993) concluded, "Axelrod's tournaments were a miniature version of how cooperative behavior probably evolved among people" (p. 68). And, as noted early, its insights were embraced widely and celebrated in many popular books, newspaper accounts, and university courses.

REVISITING AXELROD'S FINDINGS: EXPLORING THE LIMITS OF TIT-FOR-TAT

The insights that emerged from Axelrod's tournaments were enormously significant and fresh. They seemed, moreover, quite powerful and compelling. Almost single-handedly his provocative findings gave fresh impetus to research using the Prisoner's Dilemma game to study a host of issues on the evolution of cooperation in social systems. However, several features of the original methodology limited the generalizability of Axelrod's findings. The first problem was that in Axelrod's tournaments, the decision to cooperate was dichotomized: One could either cooperate fully or not at all. In most real-world decision dilemmas, the choices afforded to decision makers are seldom so stark. Instead, choice characteristically allows for varying degrees of cooperation. For example, a person decides not just whether to loan a friend money but how much money to loan him or her. People entering a new relationship must decide not only whether to pursue that relationship but how much time and attention to devote to it. Researchers embarking on a newly formed joint project must decide how much of one's theory or data to share with a potentially important but relatively unfamiliar collaborator. Nations motivated to reciprocally reduce their stockpiles of biological weapons must decide how much and over what time period. In short, decisions about cooperation more often come in shades of gray than in black or white. Hence the strategies that are needed must be able to handle degrees of cooperation and not simply decide whether to cooperate with someone (Kramer, Meyerson, & Davis 1990).

A second and more significant problem regarding the generalizability of Axelrod's results concerns the quality of social information. In his tournaments, decision makers learned with certainty whether their partner had cooperated or defected in the previous period. As a consequence, inferences about others' cooperativeness were, in a sense, flawless. In real-world encounters, people seldom possess such accurate information about the actions of the other parties on whom they depend. For example, two research collaborators may claim to be sharing all of the relevant data produced by their respective laboratories. However, it is often impossible for each to monitor the behavior of the other perfectly. One researcher may be holding back crucial findings or misleading the other in order to publish independently and preempt the other. The prospects for such strategic concealments and deceptive communications were captured vividly in Watson's (1980) popular book *The Double Helix,* which chronicled competing researchers' adventures and misadventures on the road to discovering the structure of the DNA molecule. As another example, a professor may tell a student that she wrote a great letter of recommendation for the student. However, it is hard for the student to know with certainty just how glowing the reference really was. The professor may have fully intended to write such a letter when the promise was made. However, subsequent situational pressures on her may have made her unable or unwilling to carry out that intention. Consequently, the intended long and laudatory letter may have become more perfunctory and restrained.

Because of such social uncertainty, we typically experience some measure of doubt about others' actions, making it harder to draw inferences regarding their cooperativeness. Such uncertainty introduces noise in the communication between interdependent parties, clouding their inferences and impeding learning about each other's cooperativeness. A fundamental issue in evaluating the efficacy of tit-for-tat, accordingly, is to assess its performance in such noisy worlds.

Study Rationale and Methodology

We turn now to discussing the results of a computer tournament created to examine precisely these issues (see Bendor et al., 1991, for a detailed exposition). To enhance comparability, we designed the tournament to be similar to Axelrod's. Hence, we sought to recruit participants who would be intimately familiar with theory and research on the PD and also conversant with the findings and implications of Axelrod's tournaments. Participants were invited to submit strategies that would be translated into computer programs. The programs then would be pitted against each other, pairwise, in a round-robin tournament, as in Axelrod's study.

To address these concerns, however, the tournament methodology was modified in two important ways. First, to capture the continuous nature of cooperative choice characteristic of real-world decisions, participants had to decide not simply whether to cooperate but how much to cooperate. This was operationalized as how much effort they wanted to exert on their partner's behalf, with zero effort being the least cooperative choice and 100% effort being the most cooperative choice possible.

To introduce social uncertainty into the tournament, each participant's cooperation level was obscured by adding or subtracting a small random amount during each period of play. This noise term was a random variable, distributed normally, with a mean of zero and a standard deviation of eight. This error term was generated by a normal transformation of a uniform random variable, and the distribution of the error term was truncated to the interval $[-100, +100]$. The noise was independent across participants and over periods. Because of this noise factor, participants (or more precisely, the computer programs of the strategies they submitted) could receive feedback that their partners (strategies) had behaved either more or less cooperatively than they actually had.

A player's payoff or benefit per interaction, therefore, was equal to the other player's actual cooperation level minus a cost factor of one's own effort or cooperation plus a random error term. Stated more formally,

$$V_t(i/j) = C_t(j,i) - \alpha C_t(i,j) + e_t(j,i)$$

where $V_t(i/j)$ denotes i's payoff in period t in its pairing with j, $C_t(j,i)$ denotes j's cooperation level vis-à-vis i in period t, $C_t(i,j)$ refers to i's choice, a is the cost of cooperation associated with i's choice, and $e_t(j,i)$ symbolizes the disturbance added to j's choice. To ensure that the game meets the requirements of a PD, the cost-of-cooperation parameter α must be between zero and one; accordingly, it was fixed at .80. With this structure, the symmetric average maximum payoff per period was 20 and the symmetric average minimum payoff was 0. However, with noise, realized payoffs could fall outside the region of feasible expected payoffs.

In each round of play, the computer generated two normally distributed error terms to determine the values of $e_t(i,j)$ and $e_t(j,i)$. The computer also used a fixed random number that was used to determine whether a given sample path would end after the current period of play. Each strategy then played all other strategies, including itself, using the generated error terms for each period.

Entrants to the tournament were informed fully of all of these parameters, including details about payoffs, the distribution of the random disturbances, and the stopping probability of the game. However, they also were instructed that they (i.e., their strategies) would not be told the realized values of the disturbances, their partner's true cooperation level, or the rules defining their partner's strategy.

Overview of Major Findings

The results of this noisy tournament are quite interesting. Thirteen strategies were submitted, which embodied a variety of intuitions about how one should or might cope with social uncertainty. Many of the strategies were similar to tit-for-tat, but reflected players' intuitions about how to modify tit-for-tat to accommodate the presence of noise.

Table 11.1 reveals how well each of these strategies did in terms of their average payoffs per period. As the table shows, an entrant called Nice and Forgiving was the most successful performer, earning an average per trial payoff of 17.05 (85% of the possible symmetric maximum). Note that Nice and Forgiving beat Tit-for-Tat. In fact, Tit-for-Tat was beaten by six other strategies as well. A distant eighth in the rankings, it earned only 75% of the possible payout per trial.

What accounts for these results? First, Nice and Forgiving differed from Tit-for-Tat in several ways. Instead of reciprocating by returning an unbiased estimate of its partner O's actions in the previous period, Nice tended to be generous, returning more cooperation than it had received. Nice's generosity took the form

TABLE 11.1

Average Per Period Payoff for Strategies

Rank	Name	Average per period payoff
1	Nice and Forgiving	17.05
2	Drifting	16.55
3	Biased Tit-for-Tat	16.17
4	Mennonite	16.13
5	Weighted Average Reciprocator	16.00
6	Tit-for-Two-Tats	15.67
7	Staying Even	15.39
8	Tit-for-Tat	15.00
9	Normal	14.78
10	Running Average	14.06
11	Deviation w/Anchor	13.74
12	Cheating Tit-for-Tat	12.88
13	Viligant	8.99

of a benign indifference: As long as O's observed (realized) cooperation exceeded 80, Nice would continue to cooperate fully. Second, although Nice was provocable and would retaliate if O's cooperation dipped below 80, it reverted to maximal cooperation even before O did, as long as O satisfied the threshold of acceptable behavior (i.e., its observed cooperation level was at least 80). These features helped Nice counteract the potentially deleterious effects of unintended (i.e., noise-triggered) vendettas that plagued strict reciprocators like Tit-for-Tat.

The results of Axelrod's original tournaments had demonstrated the power of a strict reciprocator such as Tit-for-Tat in a deterministic game, where decision makers had perfect information about a partner's actions. Yet, we found it suffered a sharp decline—both absolutely and relative to other strategies—when noise was added. What accounts for this degraded performance in a world with social uncertainty? Why did strategies like Nice and Forgiving do better? Part of the answer to such questions can be gleaned by observing how a strict reciprocator such as Tit-for-Tat behaves when it plays itself in the presence of uncertainty. Because Tit-for-Tat is nice, it starts off by cooperating fully with its partner. Sooner or later, however, an unlucky ("bad") realization of the random error term occurs. Because Tit-for-Tat is provocable, it will retaliate in the next period. Its partner, being similarly provocable, returns the compliment, leading to cycles of counterproductive mutual punishment that steadily decrease cooperation. In contrast, more generous strategies such as Nice and Forgiving slow down this degradation by returning more than an unbiased estimate of their partner's cooperation level. This generosity tends to dampen these cycles of unintended and costly vendettas.

If this explanation is correct, then we would expect that the longer a series of exchanges lasts, the bigger the difference between the payoffs garnered by decision makers using these different strategies. Why? Because the longer the tournament, the more opportunities for unintended vendettas between the nice but provocable entries, thus degrading their scores.

Figure 11.1, which depicts the decline in Tit-for-Tat's average payoffs over time, tends to support this argument. Note that the longer Tit-for-Tat plays, the lower its average performance.

In sharp contrast to this deterioration, Nice and Forgiving maintains a high level of performance no matter how long the tournament (see Fig. 11.2). It is remarkably even or robust in its performance across a wide range of strategies and over a long period of time.

It is also informative to compare the performances of the winner of the tournament (Nice and Forgiving) and of the last-place finisher, a strategy called Vigilant. Vigilant was a nice strategy in Axelrod's sense; that is, it would not be the first to depart from maximal (perceived) cooperation. However, as its name suggests, it was extremely attentive and reactive to any signs that its partners were not cooper-

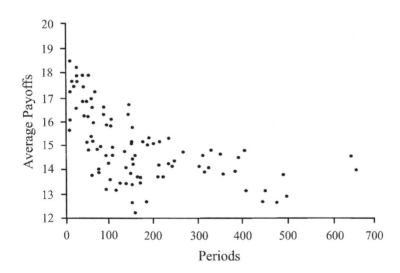

FIG. 11.1. Tit-for-Tat over time.

Nice and Forgiving over Time

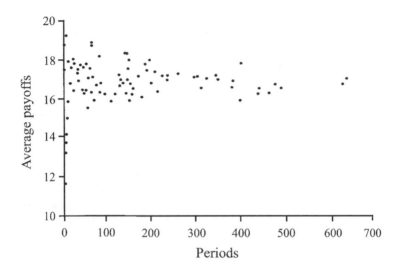

FIG. 11.2. Nice and Forgiving over time.

ating fully. Because Vigilant was determined not to be exploited, it "overassumed" the worst whenever it encountered a low return. In other words, it acted as if the partner were intentionally cheating; presuming this, Vigilant retaliated. As shown in Figure 11.3, this hair-trigger provocability helped to drive Vigilant's payoffs down sharply over time.

THE VIRTUES OF GENEROSITY IN AN UNCERTAIN WORLD

The surprising performance of Nice and Forgiving, especially when contrasted with Tit-for-Tat, merits more sustained analysis. Why does generosity tend to work better than strict reciprocity in a noisy setting? Stated differently, why does a heuristic of strict reciprocity work so poorly in an uncertain world, given its robust performance in the deterministic game?

Why Generosity Works

At first glance, the data in Table 11.2 seem to suggest a paradox. As is quite evident by comparing the row payoffs (Nice and Forgiving's payoffs from each of its partners) to the column payoffs (the payoffs its partners obtained), Nice and Forgiving

Vigilant over Time

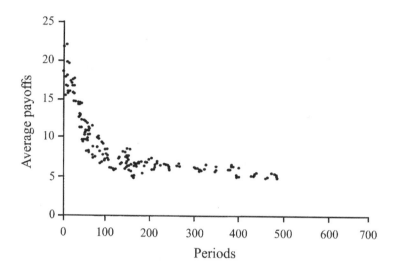

FIG. 11.3. Vigilant over time.

lost in pairwise play with every one of its partners. It thus seems to be a weak strategy that always walks away a bit bruised from its encounters. It hardly seems to be a good candidate for a survivor, let alone a winner, in this ecology. Apparently generosity is an expensive principle to live by!

In contrast, the performance of Vigilant is striking: In its pairwise encounters, it outscored every partner. Thus, it was never exploited. Given such data, one might infer that Vigilant is an effective strategy. After all, it not only avoided the sucker's payoff but even did consistently better than its partners. In terms of these local comparisons, it seems to be a hugely successful rule.

However, if we look instead at the absolute payoffs of these strategies, we read a very different story from the data—and one that explains the strong overall performance of Nice and Forgiving. As the low numbers in Vigilant's row reveal, this strategy may have never lost, but it never did very well either, compared to what both players could have obtained, on average. Vigilant's victories are pyrrhic: It may win in the limited sense of narrow interpersonal comparisons, but in a larger sense it walks away a loser. In contrast, although Nice and Forgiving always obtains less than its partners, its payoffs are high in absolute terms, as are its partners'. Both do well.

In Axelrod's parlance, Nice and Forgiving benefits by not being envious of what its partner gets; in contrast, Vigilant displays much concern about such com-

TABLE 11.2

Average Payoff of Strategy Against Other Strategies

	Nice	Drift	BTFT	Menn	WA	TF2T	Even	TFT	Norm	Run	Dev	CTFT	Vig
Nice	19.8	12.0	19.5	19.5	18.5	18.2	19.3	17.4	18.4	14.0	17.1	13.0	14.9
Drifting	26.0	16.8	23.7	18.1	20.5	17.6	17.5	19.2	12.3	12.4	6.7	0.7	3.1
BTFT	20.0	13.5	19.7	19.7	18.7	18.5	19.4	17.5	18.5	13.0	15.9	12.6	3.8
Mennonite	20.0	13.5	19.7	19.7	18.7	18.5	19.4	17.5	18.7	12.1	15.7	12.6	1.7
WA	20.8	15.7	20.4	20.4	17.9	19.3	18.4	17.0	18.7	12.5	18.0	7.3	-.02
TF2T	21.0	15.1	20.5	20.5	18.7	18.9	19.0	17.1	18.3	10.4	13.7	10.6	2.2
Even	20.2	16.2	19.9	19.9	18.3	19.0	19.3	15.4	18.0	13.4	12.1	6.2	1.0
TFT	21.7	16.2	21.1	21.1	17.7	19.1	15.9	14.2	15.9	13.1	11.5	6.6	-1.4
Norm	20.9	15.2	20.3	20.3	18.3	18.6	18.1	14.8	16.4	11.3	11.9	7.4	9.0
Run	17.0	11.5	18.0	19.1	14.8	18.3	14.3	14.4	17.0	12.8	6.2	10.4	9.0
Dev	21.9	11.6	20.0	20.4	17.8	16.5	12.8	12.4	15.0	7.4	14.4	7.2	1.2
Cheating TFT	25.1	7.8	22.7	22.7	12.3	17.4	8.7	9.4	11.4	13.7	10.9	5.8	-0.4
Vig	23.6	3.2	9.9	9.0	9.1	9.8	5.2	6.5	10.7	13.9	8.3	10.7	2.6

Note. Nice = Nice and Forgiving; Drift = Drifting; BTFT = Biased; Tit = Tit-for-Tat; Menn = Mennonite; WA = Weighted Average; TF2T = Tit-for-Two-Tat; Norm = Normal; Run = Running Average; Dev = Deviations; CTFT = Cheating Tit-for-Tat; Vig = Vigilant.

parisons. Over the long haul, it pays a steep price for its insistence on never getting the short end of the stick.

THE PRAGMATICS OF GENEROSITY: DIFFERENT PATHS TO THE SAME OUTCOME

Thus far, we have discussed what it means for a strategy to be generous, in terms of giving more than one has received.[4] However, we have said little about the different ways in which decision makers achieved or enacted generosity in our tournament. Seven different strategies in this tournament were generous. Inspection of these strategies reveals several different ways of implementing generosity. For purposes of illustration, we will focus attention on the four most generous strategies: Nice and Forgiving (Nice), Biased Tit-for-Tat (BTFT), Mennonite, and Tit-for-Two-Tats (TF2T).

The core of Nice's approach is an underreacting heuristic that gives the other party the benefit of the doubt. This part of the strategy can be characterized as a benignly insensitive social information processor, which says, in effect, "ignore your partner's observed levels of cooperation, and keep cooperating fully, as long as the observed level exceeds 80." Compared with Vigilant, Nice is a "Pollyannaish" strategy, benignly impervious to what its partner is doing (or not doing), as long as this threshold is not crossed.

Due to this benign insensitivity, Nice usually would choose 100 against strict reciprocators such as Tit-for-Tat. Meanwhile, Tit-for-Tat usually would fluctuate in the (84,100) range.[5] That in turn would result, more often than not, in an implemented level exceeding 80, satisfying Nice's threshold, and so Nice would continue to cooperate fully. Thus, because Nice allowed Tit-for-Tat to "fall off the wagon" when noise degraded the latter's performance below 100, while maintaining complete cooperation, it maintained a high score on the Tit-for-Tat-based index of generosity (see Table 11.3).

The other three strategies—BTFT, Mennonite, and TF2T—cooperated at levels that exceeded (by a fixed amount) the unbiased estimate of their partner's cooperation in the previous period, thereby also avoiding costly vendettas. For example, both BTFT and Mennonite gave their partners a "benefit of the doubt" compensatory response that exactly equaled the standard deviation of the noise.[6]

---

[4]More precisely, in Bendor et al. (1991), the generosity of any strategy i was measured as $V(TFT, i) - V(i, TFT)$. The rationale for this index is that Tit-for-Tat is designed to be pure reciprocator: to give exactly what it received. Hence the better Tit-for-Tat does with i, compared with i's payoff against Tit-for-Tat, the more generous i is.

[5]Because the normally distributed random disturbance had a mean of zero and a standard deviation of eight, whenever Nice choose 100, over 90% of the time it would actually implement between 84 and 116. Hence a choice of 100 by NICE would usually induce Tit-for-Tat to choose between 84 and 100 in response.

[6]That is, suppose in period t, strategy i chose $C_{i,t}$ and implemented $C_{i,t} + e_{i,t}$. Then BTFT, perceiving the implemented quantity, would choose $C_{i,t} + e_{i,t} + 8$, 8 being the standard deviation of e.

TABLE 11.3

Generosity Index of Strategies

Rank	Strategy	Generosity index
1	Nice and Forgiving	4.24
2	Drifting	−1.25
3	Biased Tit-for-Tat	3.57
4	Mennonite	3.57
5	Weighted Average Reciprocator	0.73
6	Tit-for-Two-Tats	1.97
7	Staying Even	0.54
8	Tit-for-tat	0.00
9	Normal	1.07
10	Running Average	−1.31
11	Deviations	−0.83
12	Cheating Tit–for–Tat	−2.84
13	Viglant	−5.58

Another important property of these four strategies, we should note, is that they are all, in Axelrod's terminology, *nice*. We extend this idea to our noisy tournament as follows: strategy i is categorized as nice if it chooses to cooperate fully at date t if its partner's observed level of cooperation in $1, \ldots, t-1$ was always at least 100. In our tournament, niceness and generosity were positively correlated: Most of the nice strategies were generous; most of the non-nice ones, stingy. We suspect that this correlation holds more generally.

ANALYZING THE OUTLIER

An impressive exception to the patterns connecting generosity and outcomes was the performance of a strategy called Drifting Maximum Likelihood Estimator. As shown by Table 11.4, Drifting was rather stingy, with a generosity index of −1.25. Despite this, it placed second in the tournament. This combination of solid performance and stinginess made Drifting the largest outlier in the regression of overall tournament scores on generosity.

Interestingly, Drifting's success was not based on exploiting the weakest entries in the tournament. We can see this by reinspecting the pairwise averages between strategies, reported in Table 11.2: Drifting did worse than average against the bottom two strategies but better than average against the strongest strategies. Suppose, then, we created a simple (and draconian) ecological dynamic by rerun-

TABLE 11.4

Regression Results for Strategies

Rank	Strategy	Generosity Index	Slope of time equation	R2 in time equation
1	Nice and Forgiving	4.24	.00052	.004
2	Drifting	−1.25	−.00445	.040
3	Biased Tit-for-Tat	3.57	−.00159	.042
4	Mennonite	3.57	−.00160	.043
5	Weighted Average Reciprocator	0.73	−.00403	.201
6	Tit-for-Two-Tats	1.97	−.00280	.108
7	Staying Even	0.54	−.00466	.256
8	Tit-for-Tat	0.00	−.00611	.314
9	Normal	1.07	−.00548	.236
10	Running Average	−1.31	−.01060	.456
11	Deviations	−0.83	−.01228	.510
12	Cheating Tit-for-Tat	−2.84	−.01312	.340
13	Vigilant	−5.58	−.01904	.454

ning the tournament several times, each time dropping the strategy that finished last. Vigilant would then disappear in Generation 2. Recomputing the average per period payoffs in Generation 2, we observe that Drifting has now moved from second into first place. Furthermore, the pairwise averages of Table 11.2 indicate that further ecological changes, such as the demise of the worst strategy in Generation 2 (Cheating TFT), would only strengthen Drifting's hold on first place.

The performance of Drifting is sufficiently good that the strategy warrants closer examination. In some ways Drifting is the most interesting entry in the tournament. It incorporates a pessimistic bias about the meaning of high observed values of its partner's cooperativeness, that is, of $C(j, \text{Drifting}) + e(j, \text{Drifting})$. In the words of Drifting's creator: "If [the] opponent appears to have been extremely cooperative, chances are that noise made him look more altruistic that [sic] he really is." And this statement is made despite the fact that the noise is neutral—$E(e)0$—which participants knew. For this reason most strategies used $C(j,i) = C(j,i) + e(j,i)$ as an (unbiased) estimator of their partner's true cooperative level, subject to the obvious truncations.

The quantitative implication of this pessimistic inference is that, against a nice opponent who plays maximal cooperation constantly, Drifting will settle down into playing 94 indefinitely. It therefore "cheats," although apparently its designer does not think it is doing so. This cheating is rather mild—a phenomenon that cannot be easily replicated in the classical (deterministic, binary choice) game—and generous strategies such as Mennonite, BTFT, and Nice usually let Drifting get away with it. Thus Drifting inadvertently "hides under the noise," getting the benefit of the doubt from strategies that are designed to avoid unintended cycles of noise-stimulated retaliation. Because the other top strategies are, within limits, generous, and because Drifting happens to stay within those limits, it does very well with/against them.

This however, is not the end of the story. Cheating TFT also scored well against Mennonite, BTFT, and Nice for similar reasons, but it did poorly overall. What accounts for this difference? The explanation is that Drifting's cheating is a pessimistic inference about the meaning of higher values of $c(j,$ Drifting$) + e(j,$ Drifting$)$; if this sum falls below 88, then Drifting turns into a reciprocator in the steady state. And in early rounds, when $c(j,$ Drifting$) + e(j,$ Drifting$)$ is below 88, Drifting is slightly generous. It is therefore less vulnerable to the downward spirals of vendettas that plague pure TFT.

In sum, the results of this noisy tournament led to conclusions quite different from those reached by Axelrod (see Footnote 3). These results could serve as a warning that people may have been overly enthusiastic about Tit-for-Tat and its heuristics (especially pure reciprocity). They also may suggest that some of Tit-for-Tat's strong appeal may reflect factors other than simple evidence of its effectiveness. (After all, presumably many natural ecologies suffer from noise, and one would not expect Tit-for-Tat to be particularly efficacious in these settings.) Perhaps some of Tit-for-Tat's attractiveness is belief-driven rather than data-driven. If so, it makes sense to consult people's intuition about different heuristics. We turn now to some results that explore this issue.

PITTING INTUITIONS AGAINST REALITIES: DECISION MAKERS' "NAIVE THEORIES" ABOUT THE FAIRNESS AND EFFICACY OF DIFFERENT SOCIAL RULES

People entertain a variety of beliefs regarding the fairness and efficacy of different rules for social conduct. Sometimes these beliefs reflect what they feel is normatively right (i.e., how they ought to conduct themselves in a given situation). In other instances, these beliefs focus on the efficacy of different rules (i.e., pragmatically, on what "works"). The particular rules or heuristics of a given person in a given situation are variable and idiosyncratic: "Never turn the other cheek," "Always give others the benefit of the doubt," and "Never give a sucker an even break" are just a few examples.

Most people articulate such rules quite readily. Moreover, they apparently have firm ideas about how others think about social conduct and how they are likely to behave as well. In short, people seem to easily assume the role of both philosopher and psychologist: They ponder both what is right (the social decision heuristics one ought to use in a given situation) and what is effective (the heuristic that is likely to produce the "best" outcome in that situation). But how well do such beliefs and intuitions correspond to the empirical conclusions suggested by our noisy tournament?

To explore decision makers' intuitions or "naive theories" about the fairness and efficacy of different heuristics, we investigated MBA students' beliefs about Tit-for-Tat and related strategies. We gave students enrolled in an elective course complete information about all of the parameters for our noisy computer tournament. In fact, their information was identical to the information given to the entrants in the original Bendor et al. (1991) study. We then asked them to predict how well the three strategies (Tit-for-Tat, Nice and Forgiving, and Vigilant) would do, that is, to predict the average payoff of each entry. We also asked students in a second class to predict the relative performance or ranking of the three strategies.

As shown in Table 11.5, the results suggest that students' intuitions about the comparative efficacy of these three strategies closely parallel the findings of Axelrod's original tournament. The students clearly expected Tit-for-Tat to be the most efficacious in terms of their expectations about both absolute and relative performance. Vigilant was also viewed as a fairly effective strategy. Significantly, Nice and Forgiving ran a distant third in student's expectations and predictions.

To probe further students' intuitions about these strategies, we explored their beliefs regarding the kinds of persons they thought would employ each one. Specifically, we were interested in the sorts of dispositional attributes (in a sense, the "personality") students associated with a given strategy. Such information would tell us something about people's lay theories about who is likely to be strong or weak, competent or inept, wise or foolish in the PD-like situations studied in these computer tournaments. Students thus were asked to try to visualize the sort of person who would be likely to embrace or adopt a given rule. Table 11.6 lists some of the attributes students most commonly associated with each strategy.

TABLE 11.5

Predicted Performance for Strategies

Heuristic	Predicted mean score[a]	Predicted rank[b]		
		1	2	3
Tit-for-Tat	18.35	42	17	7
Vigilant	17.64	18	44	4
Nice and Forgiving	15.66	6	5	55

Note.   Predicted scores and ranks provided by separate samples.

[a]$N = 63$. [b]$N = 66$.

TABLE 11.6

Positive and Negative Attributes Associated With Strategies

Tit-for-Tat	Vigilant	Nice and Forgiving
Positive Attributes		
Fair	Prudent	Nice
Smart	Intelligent	Good
Rational	Perceptive	Kind
Effective	Discerning	Altruistic
		Discriminating
Negative Attributes		
Rigid, inflexible	Untrusting	Too trusting, overly trusting
Mindless	Suspicious	Gullible
Too simple	Too risk averse	Naive, inexperienced
Naive		
Simple-minded		

Note. The rules were described to students in terms of their decision properties, that is, the labels Tit-for-Tat, Vigilant, or Nice and Forgiving were not used. However, a few students recognized Tit-for-Tat.

As a follow-up, participants in an executive program were asked to write short paragraphs describing their beliefs about how strategies would behave and perform. One participant noted about Nice and Forgiving that, "If you're generous, you probably will get screwed [out of your payoffs] too much. You'd be out of business in no time." In commenting on the attractiveness of Tit-for-Tat , another wrote, "The nice thing about Tit-for-Tat is that it keeps the playing field level—and that's important over the long term." Yet another wrote, "By far, Tit-for-Tat is the fairest strategy." In thinking about Vigilant, another participant stated, "In many situations, it's better to be safe than sorry. You've got to cover your back side."

IMPLICATIONS AND CONCLUSIONS

Based on the important and widely publicized findings from Axelrod's original computer tournaments, many people have embraced Tit-for-Tat as a powerful strategy for solving dilemmas of cooperation. The present chapter had two primary aims. The first was to explore some of the limitations of Tit-for-Tat's heuristics in noisy cooperation dilemmas. Our results suggest how readily Tit-for-Tat's performance degrades when social uncertainty exists. The second aim of our study was to examine some common intuitions about the efficacy of Tit-for-Tat and other social decision strategies. Here our findings suggest that people often underestimate the impact of uncertainty on the effectiveness of different behavioral rules.

Viewed together, the results from the noisy computer tournament and our examination of people's lay theories indicate a disparity between people's beliefs about Tit-for-Tat's efficacy and its actual performance (at least in some ecologies). People's intuitions regarding the virtues of generosity turn out to be no more accurate. In both instances, reality and intuition diverge sharply.

One reason why people's beliefs about Tit-for-Tat are at least partly wrong may be that players worry more about (and therefore overweight) the possibility of being exploited while underappreciating the mutual gains produced by generosity. Comparing the long-term performances of Nice and Forgiving and Vigilant illustrates how complex and sometimes counterintuitive are the trade-offs between short-term and long-term results. From the standpoint of social comparison, Vigilant virtually ensures that it is always safe and never sorry. But it leads a life of poverty. In contrast, to a myopic observer Nice and Forgiving looks like a perpetual loser, but it wins over the long haul.

An important question for future research is, "When is the heuristic of generosity more appealing and sustainable than the heuristic of strict reciprocity?" It seems reasonable to argue, on prima facie grounds, that a number of factors contribute to the attractiveness of generosity and lessen the perceived need for the strict auditing and balancing of accounts required by Tit-for-Tat. First, a shared identity among social actors may help. Decision makers are probably more willing to behave generously when interacting with others with whom they share a social tie or bond. For example, when decision makers from the same neighborhood meet face to face, they may trust each other more and cooperate more reliably than they would otherwise (cf. Ostrom, 1998). Furthermore, common identification with an ongoing partner along some salient dimension, such as a common group identity, may affect which strategy is viewed as most fair (Kramer, Pommerenke, & Newton 1993) and/or most effective (Rothbart & Hallmark, 1988). Research on moral exclusion (Opotow, 1990) suggests that individuals impute higher standards of fairness to those whose group identity they share. Consistent with Opotow's proposition, Kramer, Pommerenke, & Newton (1993) found that increasing the salience of shared identity enhanced concerns about equality of outcomes.

Taking the other party's perspective also may influence individuals' willingness to be generous in dilemmalike situations. Arriaga and Rusbult (1998) found that the experience of "standing in a partner's shoes" increases constructive responses to the accommodative dilemmas they jointly experience, at least in close personal relationships. In line with this hypothesis, it is interesting to note that students of the Cuban Missile Crisis have pointed out the restraint President Kennedy showed during that crisis. When choosing to underreact to some Soviet action that seemed to call for a Tit-for-Tat-like response, President Kennedy tried to put himself in Khrushchev's shoes. He sought to understand how the situation in Cuba might look to Khrushchev, to grasp the kinds of political pressures and institutional momentum driving his decisions (Garthoff, 1989).

Due to the actor–observer bias, individuals are likely to construe their partner's noisy realizations in dispositional terms while underestimating the impact of the noise as a situational factor. In contrast, they are likely to assume that their partner properly understands the situational constraints and liabilities under which they labor (cf. Jervis, 1976).

We have identified several significant ways in which our results diverge from Axelrod's. One common point, however, is that both stress the importance of not being envious. Vigilant was careful to avoid getting the short end of the stick in the short term, but ended up with a rather short stick overall.

A FINAL CAVEAT

Just as it is easy to overweight the virtues of tit-for-tat, it is also easy to embrace too uncritically the power of generosity. The virtues of generosity emerge only in a world in which there are enough other strategies to make generosity pay (and stinginess hurt). In nastier ecologies, where the costs of misplaced trust are steep, being very generous may put one on the path to peril. In nastier ecologies, never walking away the loser may be important for establishing reputational deterrence—leading to longer cumulative gains than nicer, more generous strategies that invite exploitation and attract predators. Thus, the wisdom of turning the other cheek depends ultimately on the distribution of dispositions in one's social world.

Indeed, this point can be stated more strongly. As Axelrod (1984) pointed out, in the noiseless repeated PD, no strategy—not even tit-for-tat—is optimal in all ecologies. In the wave of popular enthusiasm for the early tournament results, some people probably concluded that such a panacea exists; however, it does not. Moreover, this is not a mere practical difficulty that can be overcome with sufficient cleverness; one can prove that no such strategy exists. It is the game theoretical equivalent of perpetual motion machines: desirable but infeasible to design.

The addition of social uncertainty does not change this fundamental fact. It is not difficult to prove this. It is particularly easy to see why neither generosity nor niceness will always work. Consider a single nice and generous strategy (e.g., BTFT) in an ecology where everyone else plays Always Defect. (When there are more than two levels of cooperation in the game, as in our tournament, Always Defect means playing a cooperation level of zero in every period.) It is true that sometimes the generous strategy will observe its partners to be exerting some positive levels of effort. But this is a misperception caused by the noise. In fact, all of its partners are relentless cheaters; nothing can persuade them to alter their behavior. Clearly, to be generous in this kind of strategic environment is pointless. It merely invites exploitation.[7]

---

[7]More generally, if all of one's partners are playing unconditional strategies, such as Always Defect, then one's best (egoistic) response is to never cooperate. And this holds whether or not there is social uncertainty.

Accepting the contingent nature of optimal play in repeated dilemmas may be psychologically unpleasant. Moreover, it leads to practical advice that is less satisfying than simple, unconditional advice. (Be nice! Be retaliatory! Be generous!) However, it is the first step to wisdom in coping with these dilemmas.

ACKNOWLEDGMENTS

Earlier versions of this chapter were presented at the conference "Ethics and Social Influence," held at the Kellogg Graduate School of Management, Northwestern University; at the University of Michigan Interdisciplinary Colloquium on Organization Studies seminar series; and at colloquia held at Wharton School of Management, UCLA Anderson Graduate School of Management, and the University of California Berkeley Haas Business School. We gratefully acknowledge the constructive comments from participants at those conferences. We are also grateful for the helpful suggestions provided by Michael Cohen, Rick Price, and Robert Axelrod to earlier versions of these ideas.

REFERENCES

Allison, S., & Messick, D. (1990). Social decision heuristics in the use of shared resources. *Journal of Behavioral Decision Making, 3,* 195–204.

Arriaga, X. B., & Rusbult, C. E. (1998). Standing in my partner's shoes: Partner perspective taking and reactions to accommodative dilemmas. *Personality and Social Psychology Bulletin, 24,* 927–948.

Axelrod, R. (1980a). Effective choice in the prisoner's dilemma. *Journal of Conflict Resolution, 24,* 3–25.

Axelrod, R. (1980b). More effective choice in the prisoner's dilemma. *Journal of Conflict Resolution, 24,* 379–403.

Axelrod, R. (1984). *The evolution of cooperation.* New York: Basic Books.

Baron, J. (1996). Do no harm. In D. M. Messick & A. E. Tenburnsel (Eds.), *Codes of conduct: Behavioral research into business ethics* (pp. 197–214). New York: Russell Sage Foundation.

Bazerman, M. H. (1994). *Judgment in managerial decision making* (2nd ed.). New York: Wiley.

Bendor, J., Kramer, R. M., & Stout, S. (1991). When in doubt: Cooperation in the noisy prisoner's dilemma. *Journal of Conflict Resolution, 35,* 691–719.

Cialdini, R. (1993). *Influence: Science and practice.* New York: Harper-Collins.

Garthoff, R. (1989). *Reflections on the Cuban Missile Crisis.* Washington, DC: The Brookings Institution.

Jervis, R. (1976). *Perception and misperception in international politics.* Princeton, NJ: Princeton University Press.

Kramer, R., Meyerson, D., & Davis, G. (1990). How much is enough? Psychological components of "guns versus butter" decisions in a security dilemma. *Journal of Personality and Social Psychology, 58,* 984–993.

Kramer, R., Pommerenke, P., & Newton, E. (1993). The social context of negotiation: Effects of social identity and accountability on negotiator judgment and decision making. *Journal of Conflict Resolution, 37,* 633–654.

Opotow, S. (1990). Deterring moral exclusion. *Journal of Social Issues, 46,* 173–182.

Ostrom, E. (1998). A behavioral approach to the rational choice theory of collective action. Presidential address, American Political Science Association, 1997. *American Political Science Review, 92,* 1–22.

Rothbart, M., & Hallmark, W. (1988). Ingroup–outgroup differences in the perceived efficacy of coercion and conciliation in resolving social conflict. *Journal of Personality and Social Psychology, 55,* 248–257.

Schelling, T. C. (1960). *The strategy of conflict.* Cambridge, MA: Harvard University Press.

Thompson, L. (1998). *The mind and heart of the negotiator.* Upper Saddle River, NJ: Prentice-Hall.

Watson, J. (1980). *The double helix: A personal account of the discovery of the structure of DNA.* New York: Norton.

Wilson, J. Q. (1993). *The moral sense.* New York: The Free Press.

Wu, J., & Axelrod, R. (1997). Coping with noise: How to cope with noise in the iterated prisoner's dilemma. In R. Axelrod (Ed.), *The complexities of cooperation* (pp. 33–39). Princeton, NJ: Princeton University Press.

12 Power Asymmetries and the Ethical Atmosphere in Negotiations

Ann E. Tenbrunsel
University of Notre Dame

David M. Messick
Northwestern University

An individual faced with selling a used car must decide whether to tell a potential buyer that the car has been in an accident. House sellers must determine whether to reveal that the house has suffered water damage. At the corporate level, businesses must decide how much information should be revealed to potential acquisition partners. And at the country level, leaders must determine how honest they will be about defense inventories and technology.

At their core, all negotiations contain an ethical dilemma. Negotiators are always faced with a decision on how open and direct they will be about their preferences (Lewicki & Stark, 1996), their bottom lines, and their alternatives. The uncertainty surrounding ethically appropriate behavior makes negotiations particularly problematic (Bok, 1978) and prone to a variety of unethical actions, including selective disclosure, misrepresentation, false threats, deception, false promises, and falsification (Murnighan, 1992). An investigation of ethically questionable tactics revealed that although a few of these behaviors are deemed acceptable—gaining information by asking around, hiding your bottom line from your opponent, making a high opening demand, and pretending to be in no hurry to reach an agreement—many more are viewed as clearly unacceptable, including falsely demeaning the opponent's best alternative to a negotiated agreement (BATNA), intentionally misrepresenting facts, making false threats, and encouraging defection from the opponent's constituents (Lewicki & Stark, 1996).

Given the unacceptability of many of these actions, why might negotiators behave in an ethically inappropriate fashion? Profit and greed have been cited as causes (Lewicki & Litterer, 1985; Murnighan, 1992) and with good reason. Unethical behavior in negotiations has been found to be directly related to incentives, such that the higher the incentive to misrepresent information, the more likely one is to engage in misrepresentation (Hegarty & Sims, 1978; Tenbrunsel, 1998). Competition and justice-seeking motives also have been identified as causes of unethical tactics (Lewicki & Litterer, 1985; Murnighan, 1992).

We argue that an imbalance of power between two negotiators also may contribute to the ethical atmosphere within a negotiation. This chapter explores the ethical implications of such disparities. More specifically, we examine the role that power asymmetries play in influencing expectations of unethical behavior, the frequency of unethical behavior, and the obligation to behave ethically.

Power occupies a prominent role in the negotiations literature. Social conflicts, for example, are asserted to almost always revolve around power struggles (Ebenbach & Keltner, 1998). In a negotiation, power is important because it is directly linked to performance (Fisher & Ury, 1981; Pinkley, Neale, & Bennett, 1994). The sources of power that one has in a negotiation include having desirable alternatives, status, payoff matrices, reward structures, and influence strategies (Kipnis & Schmidt, 1983; Pinkley et al., 1994; Rubin & Brown; 1975). Although a significant portion of the research has operationalized power by status or reward structures, power in the format of attractiveness of a negotiator's alternative or BATNA has also been studied (Fisher & Ury, 1981; Lewicki & Litterer, 1985; Mannix & Neale, 1993; Pinkley et al., 1994; Raiffa, 1982). The link between these two is clear: The better a negotiator's alternative, the more powerful he or she is in the negotiation. Everyone can think about a situation where they fell in love with one item (a car, a painting) and just "had to have it." Chances are good that negotiating for that item was not successful if no alternative was perceived to exist. Conversely, in situations in which a buyer is indifferent between two items offered by two sellers, the buyer's power, and the likelihood of reaching a personally beneficial outcome, increases.

Desirable alternatives increase a negotiator's power because the negotiator does not have to reach an agreement. A negotiated deal must be more attractive than the alternative or the negotiator will walk away from the table (Pinkley et al., 1994). The ability to walk away from the negotiation affects the behavior of the powerful negotiator by reducing the sense of urgency and the need to make concessions (Mannix & Neale, 1993). In other words, attractive alternatives decrease the opportunity cost of failure to reach an agreement in a negotiation.

Although this chapter deals with negotiation, the point we are making is precisely the same one made by Thibaut and Kelley (1957) with regard to power in interpersonal relationships. They argued that the attractiveness of a relationship was related to the relative level of outcomes one could expect to achieve from it. One's power in a relationship, on the other hand, was related to the quality of outcomes one could obtain outside of the relationship. The party whose outside alternatives were better had the most power; it cost that party relatively less to leave the relationship.

While having resources, status, or the ability to walk away may provide the negotiator with power, many would argue that the difference in power between negotiators influences the process and outcomes (Fisher & Ury, 1981; Lewicki & Litterer, 1985; Mannix & Neale, 1993; Pinkley et al., 1994; Raiffa, 1982). In this sense, then, power is defined interdependently, as a function of the two negotiators. This definition resonates with more traditional definitions of power, in which power is defined as the inverse of dependence (Emerson, 1962). Similarly, in negotiations, the "question of power is argued to turn on who is less dependent" (Ury, Brett, & Goldberg, 1993, p. 8).

Differences, or asymmetries, in power between the two parties have been shown to affect the negotiation process. Many have found that in comparison with equal power negotiations, negotiations involving unequal power are characterized by lower joint gains and less effective outcomes, increased time to reach agreements, less concessionary behavior, and more competitive behavior (Mannix & Neale, 1993; McAlister, Bazerman, & Fader, 1986; McClintock, Messick, Kuhlman, & Campos, 1973; Rubin & Brown, 1975). Conversely, others have found the opposite, with unequal power resulting in more cooperative choices (Komorita, Sheposh, & Braver, 1968) and more integrative agreements (Sondak & Bazerman, 1991). Although many explanations have been offered concerning the effects of power asymmetry on outcomes—including the impact of symmetry in producing deadlock (Rubin & Zartman, 1995) and the relation between domination strategies and available cognitive energy (Mannix & Neale, 1993)—the results are clear: Asymmetries in power do impact the process and associated outcomes.

We propose that in addition to influencing outcomes, asymmetries of power also affect the ethical atmosphere of a negotiation. Power has been identified as one of the situational influences on ethics in negotiations (Lewicki & Litterer, 1985), and we suggest that asymmetry of power, in particular, increases the ethical tension in a negotiation. In this chapter we explore this tension by examining the relation between asymmetries of power and expectations of unethical behavior, unethical actions, and ethical obligations.

POWER ASYMMETRY AND EXPECTATIONS
OF UNETHICAL BEHAVIOR

Observations from a negotiations case used by the first author first hinted at the association between asymmetries of power and expectations of unethical behavior. The case, Federated Science Fund (Mannix, 1998), involves three pharmaceutical companies—Stockman, Turbo, and United—who have the potential to obtain research and development grants from the National Science Fund (NSF). The NSF has specified that to receive a grant, at least two of the firms must form a consortium to apply for the grant money. As indicated in Table 12.1, the value of the grant money varies depending on who is included in the consortium.

TABLE 12.1

Federated Science Fund: Coalition Outcomes

Coalition members			Total grant
Stockman	Turbo	United	
X	X	X	$480,000
X	X		$440,000
X		X	$380,000
	X	X	$300,000

Although all parties bring value to an agreement, most negotiators assume that Stockman, who brings the most value to the table, is the most powerful, followed by Turbo, followed by United. The case proceeds with parties forming coalitions, dissolving them, and then forming new ones. The resulting formations are varied, consisting of both two- and three-way coalitions.

What is interesting about this case is the expectation that Stockman is to be the least trusted, particularly by the person playing the role of United. Although both Turbo and Stockman are perceived to be more powerful than United, United's distrust of Stockman, who is seen as the most powerful, always appears to greatly overshadow any negative feelings toward Turbo. This distrust seems to stem from Stockman's position of power and United's position of weakness, independent of Stockman's reputation. Repeated instances of this observation over many cases thus hinted at a possible connection between power distance and expectations of undesirable behavior.

A search for supporting evidence provided preliminary support for this intuitive notion. A study of the influence of incentives and temptation on misrepresentation and expectations of misrepresentation revealed that asymmetry in incentives produced greater expectations of unethical behavior than incentive symmetry (Tenbrunsel, 1995). In this study, negotiators were asked to provide a third party with information on the estimated value of an item; this information then would be used by the third party to determine the allocation of the resources awarded to each of the two negotiators. Individuals were motivated to misrepresent the information that they provided, such that the more they inflated the estimated value, the more they would be awarded a high allocation of resources and, as a result, the more likely they would receive a reward. The size of these rewards, and hence the size of the incentive to misrepresent, varied across participants: Negotiators were faced with either a low incentive ($1) or a high incentive ($100) to misrepresent their information. Likewise, negotiators' opponents were faced with a low ($1) or high ($100) incentive to misrepresent their information, and the negotiator knew of the opponent's incentive. Expectations of misrepresentation were found to depend on the interaction between the focal negotiator's incentive and the opponent's incentive: When the two parties were in different incentive conditions ($1 and $100 or $100 and $1), there was a greater expectation of misrepresentation than when both parties were in the same incentive condition ($1 and $1 or $100 and $100). Particularly interesting is the $100/$100 condition, where, with both parties highly tempted to engage in misrepresentation, one might hypothesize that expectations of unethical behavior would be highest. Yet, expectations were higher in the $1/$100 and $100/$1 conditions.

Another study allowed for a more direct exploration of the relationship between power and expectations (Tenbrunsel & Messick, 2000). In this study, we asked individuals to judge the ethicality of tactics used in a negotiation. The scenario described a negotiation between the mayor of Crowley, a medium-sized, Midwestern town, and the CEO of Man-Tech, a firm that produced high-tech automation equipment. Man-Tech, which was interested in building a new plant in Crowley, had initiated negotiations with the mayor concerning tax concessions and wage structures. Individuals were given information about the relative power of the two parties as measured by their respective BATNAs. Individuals were told either that Crowley was in a poor economic position and had not been approached by any other firms that were interested in building a plant (low BATNA), or that Crowley was in a good economic position and had been approached by several firms that had expressed an interest in building a plant (high BATNA). Individuals also were told either that Man-Tech desperately needed to build a plant in Crowley and there were no other potential sites for Man-Tech in this area (low BATNA), or that several towns provided equal benefits and these towns had all expressed an interest in a Man-Tech facility (high BATNA).

Judgments of how much the mayor of Crowley could be trusted to provide accurate information (on the growth of the community, the skills and educational level of the employees, and the expected tax savings) depended on the interaction between the BATNAs of the two parties. Specifically, expectations that the mayor of Crowley could be trusted were lowest in one of the power asymmetry conditions (when Man-Tech had a strong alternative and Crowley had a weak alternative), whereas trust was highest in one of the power symmetry conditions (when both had strong alternatives). Thus, it appears that asymmetries do affect expectations of undesirable behavior.

Thompson and DeHarpport (1998) provided support and a potential explanation for this pattern of findings. Their research suggested that incongruencies in communal orientation (i.e., the extent to which individuals feel responsible or obligated to others' well-being) negatively impact negotiator effectiveness. They found that although friends can reach integrative agreements when both have high or both have low communal orientation, "the most detrimental combination occurs when friends are heterogeneous in communal orientation" (p. 43). Thompson and DeHarpport argued that congruence enables accurate expectations to be developed and, conversely, that incongruence produces confusion and frustration.

Asymmetries in power may produce a similar confusion in ascertaining the expected consequences of one's behavior. Putting oneself in one's opponent's shoes, argued to be critical for the development of cooperative behavior, may be difficult when two parties are experiencing a different situational context (Hofstadter, 1985; Tenbrunsel, 1995). Symmetry in power may allow for a more accurate and confident assessment about one's opponent's actions, whereas asymmetry may result in uncertainty and hence a default expectation of unethicality. As discussed next, these expectations may influence, or be influenced by, the actual behavior of the negotiators involved in negotiations characterized by power asymmetries.

POWER ASYMMETRY AND UNETHICAL BEHAVIOR

The connection between expectations and behavior has been well documented (Dawes, McTavish, & Shaklee, 1977; Tenbrunsel, 1998). On the one hand, expectations of unethical behavior may produce "defensive ethics" where individuals feel they must behave unethically to protect themselves (Carson, Wokutch, & Murrmann, 1982; Dees & Crampton, 1991; Tenbrunsel, 1998). Conversely, the desire to behave unethically may influence expectations of others' unethical behavior, such that individuals seek justification for their anticipated behavior (Bok, 1978; Lewicki & Litterer, 1985; Murnighan, 1992; Tenbrunsel, 1998). Although the causal direction between expectations and behavior is somewhat unclear, what is clear is the association between expectations and behavior. It therefore seems to make sense to extend the connection between power asymmetries and expectations of unethical behavior to actual behavior.

Power and unethical behavior have been linked in the literature. Crott, Kayser, and Lamm (1980) claimed that asymmetries in negotiations, measured by differences in potential payouts, influence the number of bluffs exchanged. Researchers differ, however, in whom they identify as the culprit. Crott et al. (1980) asserted that the increase in bluffs prevalent in asymmetrical negotiations comes from the person who is in the more advantageous condition. In comparison with power equality, which results in a focus on the fair distribution of resources, power inequality is believed to produce a game of dominance, in which the powerful player behaves in an exploitative manner (Rubin & Brown, 1975).

Other research, however, suggests that the less powerful may be suspect. Weaker parties are argued to be not silent opponents but rather aggressive in their quest for more power (Rubin & Zartman, 1995). These weaker parties adopt strategies to challenge, circumvent, upstage, or outmaneuver their more powerful opponent to reduce the initial asymmetry. The desire for justice, identified as one of the primary motives of unethical behavior, may prompt the weaker party to attempt to increase his or her power (Lewicki & Litterer, 1985). One strategy for increasing this power revolves around unethical tactics, the purpose of which may be to equalize power by changing the balance of accurate information between two negotiators (Lewicki & Litterer, 1985).

Thus, perhaps for very different reasons, power asymmetry may induce both parties to increase their use of unethical tactics. The study conducted by Tenbrunsel (1995), described previously, further supports this notion. In that study, negotiators had either a low ($1) or a high ($100) incentive, and their opponents a low or high incentive, to misrepresent information. In addition to increasing expectations of unethical behavior, asymmetries also enhanced assessments of one's own unethical behavior. Negotiators in the asymmetrical incentive conditions rated themselves as more unethical than individuals in the symmetrical conditions. Again, this result seems surprising—being faced with a different incentive than one's opponent, rather than the same, diminished self-perceptions of ethicality, even compared with the condition in which both parties had a large incentive to deceive.

Another study was conducted to directly test the relation between asymmetries in power and misrepresentation in negotiations (Tenbrunsel & Messick, 2000). In this study, individuals were asked to assume that they were representing a business student, Smith, who was graduating from a prestigious, Midwestern university. Individuals were told that Smith had been offered a job by Jones, a recruiter who worked for a prestigious consulting firm, and that as Smith, they were in the process of deciding whether to accept the job. Individuals in the role of Smith were told, however, that they knew they only planned on staying in the position for 1 year, after which they would enter a medical school program in which they had already been accepted. In preparation for a negotiation with Jones during which salary, benefits, moving expenses, and insurance were to be discussed, individuals were aware that they would have to decide whether to reveal that they only intended to work for a year before going to medical school. Individuals were then provided with information on the alternatives (BATNA) of both parties. Individuals were told either that as Smith, they had no other offers and this was the only offer they would receive (low BATNA), or that they had many offers and this was just one of the offers that they would receive (high BATNA). Individuals also were told that Jones, the recruiter, did not have any other potential candidates for this position (low BATNA) or that Jones had several other potential candidates (high BATNA).

On receiving this information, individuals playing the role of Smith were asked several questions, including how likely it would be that they would tell Jones that they only intended to stay in the position for a year. Results revealed that, contrary to those predicted by prior research, the disclosure of information was higher in situations of power asymmetry (Smith with a low BATNA and Jones with a high BATNA or vice versa) than in situations in which power was symmetrical (Smith and Jones both with low BATNAs or Smith and Jones both with high BATNAs).

Thus, although power asymmetries appear to influence the likelihood of unethical tactics, the direction of this influence is unclear. On the one hand, symmetry may promote a norm of moral behavior. Messick (1993) asserted that equality invokes norms of fairness that are not present in situations characterized by inequality. On the other hand, it has been argued that high–low power asymmetry in negotiations is similar to the child–parent relationship (Rubin & Zartman, 1995). In both cases, behavior is clearly defined such that "the parties know their roles and play them complementarily" (p. 358). In symmetrical situations, however, the roles may be more uncertain, resulting in individuals using a variety of tactics (including unethical behavior) to gain the power position.

One possible factor that may resolve these disparate findings is the history between the two parties and its influence on power salience. When individuals know each other, as in parent–child relationships or ongoing negotiations between the same two parties, power asymmetries may make it easy to establish rules of behavior, which actually may reduce the salience of these power symmetries. Without this history, however, differences in power may become paramount in influencing behavior. Furthermore, ongoing versus one-shot negotiations may change the economic rationality of an ethical act. This is particularly true for low-power players, who may be less likely to engage in unethical behavior in repeated negotiations because they could easily become targets for retaliative behavior on the part of the high-power players. More research aimed at identifying when symmetry versus asymmetry promotes norms of ethical behavior may explain these seemingly contradictory findings.

POWER ASYMMETRIES AND ETHICAL OBLIGATIONS

Federated Sciences, the case described earlier, highlighted another variable—obligation to behave ethically—that may be affected by the relative power of the two parties. As discussed, the case involves three parties—Stockman, Turbo, United—who participate in a negotiation in which coalitions form and dissolve over a period of time. A common observance is that Stockman is judged more harshly for violating a bond of trust than the other negotiators. For example, it is typical for two-way coalitions to form that exclude one of the players. Often, a private meeting with the excluded player and one of the coalition members will result in that coalition member leaving its previous partner to form a new coalition with the excluded member, an action that generally is not looked on favorably and usually is seen as a breach of trust. During debriefs of this case, however, it has become apparent that judgments of this action depend on the role that a party assumes. Negotiators in the role of Stockman, perceived to be the more powerful, are usually subject to more condemnation than Turbo or United, the less powerful negotiators, even though they made the same decision and engaged in the same action.

This observation led us to propose that power may influence the judgments of ethically questionable tactics and consequently to search for literature that might lend some insight into this relation. Lewicki and Litterer's (1985) discussion on the intersection between judgments of ethical behavior and utilitarianism theory suggests that the moral value of a given behavior may be judged on the consequences that are produced. An extension of this reasoning would imply that ethically questionable actions committed by a low-powered negotiator may be deemed more acceptable than those committed by a high-powered negotiator because the consequences or violations to the victim of the behavior are less. That is, if a low-powered player misrepresents his or her information to the other party, the damage to the high-powered player may be judged as relatively small and perhaps justified if equality of power is an acceptable "ends." Conversely, if a high-powered player misrepresents information, it may be seen as widening the power gap and having serious implications for the outcome of the low-powered player, which in turn would result in more negative judgments.

Rodin, Price, Bryson, and Sanchez's (1990) work on discriminatory behaviors supports this notion. They found robust support for an "asymmetry hypothesis," in which discriminatory behaviors committed by the strong toward the weak are seen as more indicative of prejudice than those same actions committed by the weak and directed by the strong. For example, individuals who excluded a Black, female, gay, or older person from a company softball team were viewed as more prejudiced than one who excluded a White, male, straight, or younger person. Similarly, if a Black person and a White person were each attempting to register for the only remaining hotel room, giving the room to the Black person was seen as less indicative of prejudicial behavior than giving the room to the White person. Rodin et al.'s (1990) explanations for this effect parallel the preceding discussion on perceived consequences: Questionable behaviors committed by the strong toward the weak signal more of an intent to harm and a violation of a norm of social responsibility, whereas the same action committed by the weak toward the strong are more forgivable because motives of self-protection and solidarity are seen as acceptable justifications.

Although this research provides interesting insight into judgments of behavior in asymmetrical conditions, it does not allow us to compare ethical obligations in situations characterized by power symmetry versus those characterized by power asymmetry. Our research (Tenbrunsel & Messick, 2000) on job negotiations described previously is of some assistance. In that study, the job candidate knew that he or she intended to stay for one year and needed to decide whether to reveal this information to the recruiter. As part of this study, individuals (in the role of the job candidate) were asked what duty they had to tell the recruiter that they planned on leaving the job within a year if the recruiter inquired about their expected tenure. The answer depended on the relative power of the two parties: Individuals felt a greater duty to reveal their intentions when power was asymmetrical, regardless of the direction of that asymmetry, than when power was symmetrical.

These results imply that individuals feel more of a sense of obligation to behave ethically when power asymmetries exist, independent of whether they are in a power-advantaged or power-disadvantaged position. Perhaps power asymmetries promote adoption of a "be careful" heuristic, which may be due to increased scrutiny in these situations. An interesting extension lends itself to the issue of whether the judgments of others, including those directly involved in the negotiation (i.e., the opponent) and those external to the negotiation (i.e., neutral third party), would be similar. In general, do others hold individuals to more stringent ethical standards when those individuals are in negotiations characterized by power asymmetries than negotiations characterized by power symmetries? As discussed subsequently, the answer to this question, independent of the direction of that answer, is important in understanding the links between obligations, expectations, and behavior.

FUTURE RESEARCH AGENDA

The purpose of this chapter was to explore possible connections between power and ethics in a negotiation setting. Doing so allowed for a more concrete examination of a relationship we have observed for several years in the classroom while teaching negotiations. The framework developed is sparse and the hypotheses and conclusions tentative. More than anything, however, we hope that this chapter sparks interest in this topic and a desire to understand more about it. Several potentially fruitful areas are listed next.

Connections Between Obligations, Expectations, and Behavior

Although the organization of this chapter lends itself to separate considerations of the role of power in influencing expectations of unethical behavior, unethical behavior, and ethical obligations, integrating these three factors poses some interesting questions. First, it is important to understand how expectations, behavior, and obligations are related causally so that efforts designed to alter the ethical atmosphere in these situations are directed toward the appropriate source. Do power asymmetries influence expectations, which in turn influence behaviors? Or do these asymmetries promote certain behaviors, which in turn influence expectations? Furthermore, do beliefs about ethical obligations drive behaviors and expectations, or are these obligations a post hoc derivation?

Second, questions of alignment between these variables should be raised. More specifically, are expectations, behavior, and obligations aligned, such that higher expectations of unethical behavior coincide with a greater frequency of unethical behavior that occurs because there is less obligation to behave ethically? Or are there some discrepancies among these three variables that may produce problems for the negotiator? The research reviewed suggests that the latter question may more accurately reflect the data. The data suggest that power asymmetries promote greater expectations of unethical behavior and a greater obligation to behave ethically and may either increase or decrease the frequency of actual unethical behavior. If power asymmetries increase unethical behavior, that would suggest that expectations and unethical behavior are congruent, with individuals accurately expecting more unethical behavior because it exists. However, the relation between behavior and judgments then would appear incongruous: Individuals behave more unethically in situations in which there is a greater obligation to behave ethically. Conversely, if power asymmetries result in a lower frequency of unethical behavior, then behavior and obligations are aligned—such that individuals engage in less unethical behavior because it is subject to more stringent evaluation—but behavior and expectations are misaligned, with individuals erroneously expecting an increase in unethical behavior. In this sense, then, power asymmetries may enhance the tendency for negotiators to "see" unethical behavior that isn't really there.

The first step in exploring the connection among expectations, behavior, and obligations and potential discrepancies in their alignment is additional research designed to more thoroughly examine the basic relations. This type of research will clarify the influence of power asymmetries on the ethical atmosphere of the negotiation and will provide a more rigorous assessment of possible incongruities between expectations, behavior, and obligations.

The Role of Justification

The ability to justify one's unethical behavior may be a critical determinant of unethical behavior and expectations of unethical behavior (Lewicki, 1983; Lewicki & Litterer, 1985; Tenbrunsel, 1995). The more justifiable an unethical action is, the more individuals feel that it is okay to engage in that action. An examination of the justification processes that occur in negotiations characterized by power asymmetries versus power symmetries may shed some light on the connection between power and the ethical atmosphere. Do individuals feel more justified in behaving unethically when they are faced with power asymmetries? What are the sources and theoretical foundations for these justifications? At least as important as identifying potential justifications is understanding whether these justifications are distorted. It has been argued that individuals faced with an ethical dilemma distort their perceptions and justifications to support a desire or decision to behave unethically (Bok, 1978; Tenbrunsel, 1995, 1998). The greater the incentive, for example, the more one is argued to distort potential justifications (Tenbrunsel, 1998). Negotiators faced with power asymmetries may have more motivation to behave unethically (i.e., the low-power player desires to increase his or her power, whereas the high-power player is motivated to maintain or exploit his or her power), which in turn may influence the types and accuracy of the justifications that are developed. Future research should examine how power, including the perceived legitimacy of this power, impacts the temptation to behave unethically and the role it plays in the justification process.

Consideration of Total Power

Although the focus of most research on power in negotiations has centered on Emerson's (1981) notion of dependence and the concept of relative power, others have proposed a non-zero-sum theory of power, which allows for a variation in the total amount of power (Bacharach & Lawler, 1981; Lawler & Yoon, 1995). Similar to relative power, absolute power (i.e., the sum of the value of both parties' alternatives) has been shown to positively influence the likelihood that an agreement will be reached (Bacharach & Lawler, 1981; Lawler, 1992). Absolute power is argued to give the dyadic pair more flexibility to negotiate, which in turn is seen as facilitating exchange and producing more relational cohesion (Lawler & Yoon, 1995). An extension of these ideas to the notion of negotiation ethics suggests that absolute power, because of its positive effects on the negotiation process, may result in a more positive ethical atmosphere: The greater the absolute power, the less negotiators may behave unethically, expect their opponent to behave unethically, and believe that they have a greater obligation to behave unethically. Empirical research examining total power in this context, and potential interactions between total and relative power, will provide a more complete understanding of the nature of the relation between power and negotiation ethics.

Schemas

Research that investigates negotiators' understanding and perception of the situation may lend the most insight into the connections between power and the ethical atmosphere. Several researchers have assisted in this exploration. Hofstadter's (1983) discussion of metamagical themas suggests that coordination and cooperation are enhanced if individuals can engage in deeper level thinking about their opponent. The ability to put oneself in one's opponent shoes results in a deeper level understanding of the situation, one that presumably accounts for a variety of perspectives. The balance of power in a negotiation may affect the ability to engage in this type of reasoning and hence affect actions and perceptions.

In cognitive psychology terms, then, power may influence the schemas that negotiators hold, and perhaps most important, the degree to which schemas are congruent across negotiators. Schemas or scripts are cognitive representations of social interactions that influence behavior, expectations of behavior, and the way that individuals think about an event (Abelson, 1976; Bower, Black, & Turner, 1979; Forgas, 1982). These schemas have been asserted to impact a variety of phenomena, the most relevant perhaps being crime perception and responsibility attribution (Forgas, 1982). Messick (1999) suggested that much of the research in social science, including negotiation research, can be understood by examining individuals' construal of a situation. He argued that individuals make judgments about what is appropriate in a situation, which then precede and mediate choice, perceptions, expectations, and attributions.

Larrick and Blount (1997) provided evidence that interpretation plays a critical role in determining behavior in social dilemmas. They demonstrated that subtle differences in the way in which an action is framed—that is, as a social dilemma or an ultimatum game—can substantially influence bargainers' actions and the degree of cooperativeness that is exhibited. More specifically, the authors suggested that in these two games, instructions provided to the subjects vary in terms of the way in which potential behaviors are described (i.e., "to claim" vs. "to accept or reject"). In turn, these differences are argued to influence actual behavior and the accuracy of expectations of one's opponent (Larrick & Blount, 1997; Messick, 1999).

Tenbrunsel and Messick's (1999) investigation of sanctioning systems and co-operation in dilemma situations also highlights the important role that individual interpretations play in influencing behavior. They find that weak sanctioning systems (i.e., those characterized by a low probability of detection and/or those with a low cost associated with defection) designed to increase cooperation, can actually have the adverse effect of decreasing cooperation. Results suggest that the type of decision that individuals perceive they are making can help explain these results: Individuals who are not faced with a sanctioning system perceive they are making an ethical decision, whereas individuals faced with a strong or weak sanctioning system perceive they are making a business decision. Tenbrunsel and Messick (1999) argue that situational influences, such as the presence of a sanctioning system, change individual's interpretation of the situation, which then drives perceptions, expectations, and behavior.

Applying this line of research to the topic of ethics and power asymmetries leads us to consider the types of scripts that individuals hold in situations characterized by power symmetries versus power asymmetries. What are the differences in the types of scripts held in these two situations? How do these scripts relate to ethical and unethical behavior? In addition to independently examining the individual scripts that each negotiator holds, it also would be useful to examine the degree of congruity between scripts. Do opponents in a negotiation hold more congruous scripts when power symmetries are present than when power asymmetries are present? Does congruity in scripts lead to more ethical behavior?

If there is an association between the types and/or congruity of scripts that are held and unethical behavior, the next step involves understanding mechanisms that impact this relationship. One factor may be the uncertainty that is characteristic of negotiations involving power asymmetries. Lawler and Yoon (1993) proposed that one reason equal power facilitates conflict resolution whereas unequal power impedes it is because power inequalities introduce uncertainty about linking power differences to outcomes, which in turn complicates the bargaining process. Those with power may prefer unequal outcomes that favor them, whereas less powerful parties may favor equal outcomes. Thus, when equality in power exists, outcomes are well defined, but when inequalities exist, solutions may be more vague and conflictful. Research by Wade-Benzoni, Tenbrunsel, and Bazerman (1996) suggests that uncertainty promotes self-interested behavior. In their discussion of asymmetric versus symmetric social dilemmas, they demonstrated that the uncertainty introduced by asymmetric social dilemmas, as compared with symmetric dilemmas, lends itself to more egocentrism, which in turn results in more detrimental outcomes for individuals and for the group. Negotiations characterized by power asymmetries similarly may increase uncertainty, producing more self-focused and therefore less congruent interpretations of the situation.

Two additional factors that may help explain the types of scripts that are developed are the experienced emotion between the negotiators and the future orientation that they hold. Lawler and Yoon (1993, 1995) argued that equal power between negotiators generates more interest and excitement than unequal power, which in turn leads to a greater degree of commitment behavior. Thus, the degree of power asymmetry may influence emotions and expectations of future interaction, impacting a negotiator's construal of the situation and the extent to which unethical behavior is seen as more or less appropriate.

The preceding ideas for future research are presented to do more than underscore the potential depth of this topic. We hope that they spark an interest in understanding why there is a connection between power and unethical behavior so that we can better inform negotiators of this relationship and perhaps restructure negotiations—that is, by reducing uncertainty, generating positive emotion, and influencing expectations of future interaction—to produce a more positive ethical atmosphere. Unethical behavior and expectations of unethical behavior create a vicious cycle in negotiations (Cohen & Czepiec, 1988; Zinkhan, Bisesi, & Saxton, 1989), leading to more and more unethical and detrimental behavior. We hope that a better understanding of the connection between power relations and ethical context of negotiations will help break this downward spiral.

REFERENCES

Abelson, R. P. (1976). Script processing in attitude formation and decision making. In J. Carroll & J. Payne (Eds.), *Cognition and social behavior* (pp. 33–45). Hillsdale, NJ: Lawrence Erlbaum Associates.

Bacharach, S. B., & Lawler, E. J. (1981). *Bargaining: Power, tactics, and outcomes.* San Francisco: Jossey-Bass.

Bok, S. (1978). *Lying: Moral choice in public and private life.* New York: Pantheon.

Bower, G. H., Black, J. B., & Turner, T. J. (1979). Scripts in memory for text. *Cognitive Psychology, 11,* 177–220.

Carson, T. L., Wokutch, R. E., & Murrmann, K. F. (1982). Bluffing in labor negotiations: Legal and ethical issues. *Journal of Business Ethics, 1,* 13–22.

Cohen, W., & Czepiec, H. (1988). The role of ethics in gathering corporate intelligence. *Journal of Business Ethics, 7,* 199–203.

Crott, H., Kayser, E., & Lamm, H. (1980). The effects of information exchange and communication in an asymmetrical negotiation situation. *European Journal of Social Psychology, 10,* 149–163.

Dawes, R. M., McTavish, J., & Shaklee, H. (1977). Behavior, communication and assumption about other people's behavior in a commons dilemma situation. *Journal of Personality and Social Psychology, 35,* 1–11.

Dees, J. G., & Crampton, P. C. (1991). Shrewd bargaining on the moral frontier: Toward a theory of morality in practice. *Business Ethics Quarterly, 1,* 135–167.

Ebenbach, D. H., & Keltner, D. (1998). Power, emotion, and judgmental accuracy in social conflict: Motivating the cognitive miser. *Basic and Applied Social Psychology, 20,* 7–22.

Emerson, R. M. (1962). Power-dependence relations. *American Sociological Review, 27,* 31–41.

Emerson, R. M. (1981). Social exchange theory. In M. Rosenberg & R. H. Turner (Eds.), *Social psychology: Sociological perspectives* (pp. 30–65). New York: Basic Books.

Fisher, R., & Ury, W. (1981). *Getting to yes: Negotiating agreement without giving in.* Boston: Houghton Mifflin.

Forgas, J. P. (1982). Episode cognition: Internal representations of interaction routines. *Advances in Experimental Social Psychology, 15,* 59–101.

Hegarty, W. H., & Sims, H. P. (1978). Some determinants of unethical behavior: An experiment. *Journal of Applied Psychology, 63,* 451–457.

Hofstadter, D. R. (1985). Metamagical themas. *Scientific American, 28,* 14–20.

Kipnis, D., & Schmidt, S. M. (1983). An influence perspective on bargaining within organizations. In M. H. Bazerman & R. Lewicki (Eds.), *Negotiation in organizations* (pp. 303–319). Beverly Hills, CA: Sage.

Komorita, S., Sheposh, J., & Braver, S. (1968). Power, the use of power, and cooperative choice in a two-person game. *Journal of Personality and Social Psychology, 8,* 134–142.

Larrick, R. P., & Blount, S. (1997). The claiming effect: Why players are more generous in social dilemmas than in ultimatum games. *Journal of Personality and Social Psychology, 72,* 810–825.

Lawler, E. J. (1992). Power processes in bargaining. *Sociological Quarterly, 33,* 17–34.

Lawler, E. J., & Yoon, J. (1993). Power and the emergence of commitment behavior in negotiated exchange. *American Sociological Review, 58,* 465–481.

Lawler, E. J., & Yoon, J. (1995). Structural power and emotional processes in negotiation. In R. M. Kramer & D. M. Messick (Eds.), *Negotiation as a social process* (pp. 143–165). Thousand Oaks, CA: Sage.

Lewicki, R. J. (1983). Lying and deception: A behavioral model. In M. H. Bazerman & R. J. Lewicki (Eds.), *Negotiating in organizations* (pp. 68–90). Beverly Hills, CA: Sage.

Lewicki, R. J., & Litterer, J. (1985). *Negotiation.* Homewood, IL: Irwin.

Lewicki, R. J., & Stark, N. (1996). What is ethically appropriate in negotiations: An empirical examination of bargaining tactics. *Social Justice Research, 9,* 69–95.

Mannix, E. A. (1998). *Federated science fund.* Case published by the Dispute Resolution Resource Center, Kellogg Graduate School of Management, Northwestern University, Evanston, IL.

Mannix, E. A., & Neale, M. A. (1993). Power imbalance and the pattern of exchange in dyadic negotiation. *Group Decision and Negotiation, 2,* 119–

McAlister, L., Bazerman, M. H., & Fader, P. (1986). Power and goal setting in channel negotiations. *Journal of Marketing Research, 23,* 238–

McClintock, C. G., Messick, D. M., Kuhlman, D., & Campos, F. (1973). Motivational bases of choice in three-choice decomposed games. *Journal of Experimental Social Psychology, 9,* 572–

Messick, D. (1993). Equality as a decision heuristic. In B. Mellers & J. Brown (Eds.), *Psychological issues on justice: Theory and application* (pp. 11–81). Cambridge, UK: Cambridge University Press.

Messick, D. (1999). Alternative logics for decision making in social settings. *Journal of Economic Behavior & Organization, 39,* 11–28.

Murnighan, J. K. (1992). *Bargaining games.* New York: Morrow.

Pinkley, R. J., Neale, M. A., & Bennett, R. J. (1994). The impact of alternatives to settlement in dyadic negotiation. *Organizational Behavior and Human Decision Processes, 57,* 97–116.

Raiffa, H. (1982). *The art and science of negotiation.* Cambridge, MA: Harvard University Press.

Rodin, M. J., Price, J. M., Bryson, J. F., & Sanchez, F. J. (1990). Asymmetry in prejudice attribution. *Journal of Experimental Social Psychology, 26,* 481–504.

Rubin, J. C., & Brown, B. R. (1975). *The social psychology of bargaining and negotiating.*
New York: Academic Press.

Rubin, J. C., & Zartman, I. W. (1995). Asymmetrical negotiations: Some survey results that
may surprise. *Negotiation Journal, 11,* 349–364.

Sondak, H., & Bazerman, M. H. (1991). Power balance and the rationality of outcomes in
matching markets. *Organizational Behavior and Human Decision Processes, 50,* 1–23.

Tenbrunsel, A. E. (1995). *Justifying unethical behavior: The role of expectations of others'
behavior and uncertainty.* Unpublished doctoral dissertation, Northwestern University,
Evanston, IL.

Tenbrunsel, A. E. (1998). Misrepresentation and expectations of misrepresentation in an
ethical dilemma: The role of incentives and temptation. *Academy of Management Journal, 41,* 330–339.

Tenbrunsel, A. E., & Messick, D. M. (2000). *Power and negotiation ethics.* Working paper,
University of Notre Dame, Notre Dame, IN.

Thibaut, J. W., & Kelley, H. H. (1959). *The social psychology of groups.* New York: Wiley.

Thompson, L., & DeHarpport, T. (1998). The role of social context on decisions: Integrating social cognition and behavioral decision research. *Basic and Applied Social
Psychology, 20,* 33–44.

Ury, W. L., Brett, J. M., & Goldberg, S. B. (1993). *Getting disputes resolved.* Cambridge,
MA: Harvard Law School Program on Negotiations.

Wade-Benzoni, K. A., Tenbrunsel, A. E., & Bazerman, M. H. (1996). Egocentric interpretations of fairness in asymmetric, environmental social dilemmas: Explaining harvest-
ing behavior and the role of communication. *Organizational Behavior and Human
Decision Processes, 67,* 111–126.

Zinkhan, G. M., Bisesi, M., & Saxton, M. J. (1989). MBAs' changing attitudes toward marketing dilemmas: 1981–1987. *Journal of Business Ethics, 8,* 963–974.

13 Marketlike Morality Within Organizations

Thomas W. Dunfee

The Wharton School, University of Pennsylvania

Moral desires are embedded in markets.[1] Individuals act on their moral desires as consumers, investors, and workers and in so doing sometimes create generally accepted and followed moral norms. What is true of markets generally is also true of organizations specifically. Moral desires are embodied in internal markets within organizations. When such desires produce organizational moral norms, do such norms become ethically legitimate? What insights, if any, can be gleaned by thinking about morality within organizations as a marketlike process in which competing moral desires may be "priced" into moral norms? For example, do certain types of organizational environments or policies influence the moral desires held by employees? More generally, how are organizational moral norms produced? How can organizational moral norms be identified? What about problematic organizational norms that impose harms on outsiders or are inconsistent with broader societal standards? This chapter discusses these important issues pertaining to morality within organizations.

---

[1]This chapter assumes that moral desires are embodied in general markets and, more specifically, within organizational environments as a foundation for a normative analysis. Moral desires, explained more fully herein, are desires pertaining to beliefs about ethically right and wrong behavior. Moral desires are equivalent to economic desires for preferred goods and services at favored prices in the sense that a person will somehow resolve competing desires into a specific decision. Thus, he or she may directly trade off moral and "economic" desires. It may be that the individual will require a lower price to buy goods that are inconsistent with a moral desire, for example, an animal lover deciding to buy a deeply discounted cosmetic that has been tested on animals. In that sense the individual "prices" his or her morality into the decision. In turn, the decisions of an aggregation of individuals will reflect the impact of their moral desires (some refusing to buy at all, some requiring a lower price, others indifferent to the particular moral issue). This will in turn affect the observable price and quantity of goods and services. Thus, moral desires become embedded in markets.

MORALITY IN MARKETS IN GENERAL

Individuals try to implement their desires in their interactions with others.[2] Desires may pertain to a wide variety of objectives including health, salvation, happiness, sex, and so on. Among the diverse and eclectic set of desires that humans seek to fulfill are what might be called moral desires. Moral desires[3] pertain to personal beliefs concerning right and wrong behavior for oneself and for others. Moral desires may be contrasted with purely economic desires to obtain desired goods and services at the lowest possible price. On the other hand, moral desires may be directly related to business decisions. For example, moral desires may be the basis for refusing to do business with someone deemed to be unfair, for boycotting firms on the basis of their identification with disfavored policies or practices, and for other similar actions.

Morality is assumed to be reflected in certain market outcomes. That is, the quantity and prices of certain goods may be influenced by moral desires. On the other hand, there is no specific expectation concerning the amplitude of any effect.[4] It is hard to imagine serious advocacy of either extreme position: Morality never matters in markets; only morality matters.[5] The claim that some, perhaps many, people trade off moral desires against desires for good quality and low price in their own decision making rings true. Many people seem to act, on occasion, under the influence of some moral preference concerning the environment or various "causes" such as concern for animals or the elimination of child labor. The nature and intensity of specific moral desires should, of course, vary among individuals.

To better understand this phenomenon, we need to consider how moral desires may be reflected in marketlike behavior by individuals. Familiar capital market

---

[2]This section tracks closely with a section of my article in *Law and Contemporary Problems* (Dunfee, 1999) exploring the normative implications of morality in markets for corporate governance and the stakeholder debate.

[3]Elsewhere I define moral desires as pertaining to personal beliefs concerning right and wrong. They "may be based in religious, ethical, or sociopolitical convictions. Examples include observance of religious dietary laws or a religious-based refusal to accept any form of medical assistance. [Moral desires] may reflect a belief that it is wrong to discriminate on the basis of gender or sexual preferences. [They] may be motivated by a hope for salvation, by an interest in leading a virtuous life, or by a more immediate need for approval by peers" (Dunfee, 1998, p. 129). The term *desires* is used to signal a broad set of personal utilities that go beyond traditional economic factors. The definition of preferences given by Bowles (1998), "preferences are reasons for behavior, that is, attributes of individuals that (along with their beliefs and capacities) account for the actions they take in a given situation" (p. 78), is fully consistent with the use of the term *desires* in this chapter. The term *moral preferences* is used to describe reasons for behavior resulting from the resolution of conflicting desires (including moral desires) in the context of a particular decision.

[4]Posner (1990) appears willing to recognize the existence of some morality in the market but refuses to believe that it would ever have much impact. "People seem to behave morally in situations in which the costs of behaving morally are small, but to respond to incentives in situations in which those costs are large" (p. 195).

[5]Messick's (1996) observation that ethics is not the only thing that matters is unquestionably true.

examples include buying mutual funds that engage in social screening, or screening personal investments. There are people who refuse to own tobacco or gambling stocks in their personal portfolios.[6] Some pension funds eschew certain securities, often on the basis of social criteria that presumably reflect the preferences of their beneficiaries. Although the total impact of all forms of screening is hard to measure, it is estimated that the amount invested in socially screened mutual funds increased from $639 billion in 1995 to $1.18 trillion in 1997 (Hutton, 1998).

Some critics of socially screened investing assume that there is (or should be) a single, universal definition of socially responsible investing. For example, Hylton (1992) noted a "persistent inability on the part of all participants in the debate to develop a simple, coherent definition of what is meant by socially responsible investing" (p. 2), while expressing some dismay that many funds purporting to engage in the practice have little in common. Hylton's dismay is consistent with the idea that there is a single exogenous definition of what constitutes socially responsible behavior. That is not the way in which this market works. With adequate disclosure, some investors will invest influenced by their own moral desires. Thus, one person might buy shares in a fund eschewing firms that violate the MacBride Principles in Northern Ireland, whereas a different investor might be totally indifferent to the MacBride issue while detesting firms catering to those with addictions. The latter investor might buy shares in a screened fund that excludes tobacco and gambling stocks yet holds securities of firms violating the MacBride principles.

Similar actions occur in consumer markets. The sales of StarKist tuna increased when it switched to suppliers that protected dolphin even though the switch required higher prices (Frank, 1996). Consumers supported their desires for a clean environment by paying more for pollution-reducing gasoline even though not required by law to purchase it.[7] Firms such as the Body Shop, Tom's of Maine, and Ben & Jerry's target potential customers by engaging in social cause marketing. Such firms seek to identify with particular social causes, such as saving whales, as a means of attracting consumers who want to support those causes. Consumers may choose to do business with these firms solely on the basis of an assumed alignment of moral preferences. Customers even may be willing to pay a higher price, or accept less desirable goods, to support a favored cause through their purchasing decisions.

Consumers also may boycott products to show disapproval of a firm's actions. Examples include negative consumer reaction to Shell's failure to intercede in the execution of Ken Saro Wiwa in Nigeria, to Nestlé's marketing practices for selling infant formula in developing countries, and to Exxon's handling of the Valdez oil spill. Kahneman, Knecht, and Thaler (1986) found that individuals are willing to

---

[6]Some, like the author, may refuse to own certain kinds of stocks directly in a personal portfolio yet, at the same time, own an index fund that owns the verboten securities.

[7]Kassarjian (1971): "Within six weeks after the introduction of the [pollution-reducing] gasoline, more than half of the population had paid an additional two to 12 cents per gallon to try the new brand" (p. 65).

incur additional costs, such as traveling a greater distance to deal with a competitor, to punish a retailer who in their opinion had acted unfairly by trying to take advantage of a condition of scarcity. The long-standing recognition that consumers may make trade-offs in their own purchasing to effectuate their social, moral, and political desires is also reflected in the use of the familiar "union made" and "made in the USA" labels.

Similarly, firms themselves may act on the basis of certain moral desires.[8] For example, a firm may choose to do business with a supplier in part on the basis of the perceived morality of the supplier's practices. Levi Strauss and Dillard's select suppliers operating in emerging economies on the basis of their compliance with child labor standards. The Ford Motor company pulled its ads from the *New Yorker* when the magazine, without warning to Ford, placed sexually explicit lyrics from the singing group Nine Inch Nails on a page adjacent to a Ford ad (Knecht, 1997).

Frank (1996) found similar effects in labor markets. Frank identified the existence of a compensating wage premium for less altruistic jobs reflected in large salary gaps between profit and nonprofit jobs, between corporate and public interest law, and between expert witnesses for the tobacco companies and those for the public interest groups in opposition.[9] Job searchers may select among competing employment offers on the basis of their perception of the moral environment at the prospective employers.

Given these examples, what are the implications of morality found in markets? What kind of outputs occur when individuals seek to achieve their diverse moral preference through market interactions? Is it possible to identify, at least in certain circumstances, an outcome in the nature of a "price term" constituting a community position on the underlying moral issue?[10] Is it possible to identify moral issues,

---

[8]A firm may act on the basis of its own morality or moral desires derived from its culture. This is likely the case when firm representatives refer to credos or ethics codes to explain behavior that appears inconsistent with economic objectives. On the other hand, a firm may take a moral position solely because it believes that it will profit from aligning itself with the moral desires of key stakeholders.

[9]Frank (1996) also contrasted attitudes toward being a lawyer for the National Rifle Association (NRA) and being a lawyer for the Sierra Club. This apparently is based on the assumption that most people would prefer to work for the Sierra Club than the NRA. But there may be people whose moral desires favor the right to own and use guns and who, consistent with the approach taken in this chapter, would be willing to work for the NRA for a lower salary than they would require to work for handgun control. Moral desires come in all hues and tones in the overall market, and within the overall market the effect may be to cancel out the impact of particular competing desires. Some "moral" desires in the market such as a preference for racial segregation may violate manifest universal moral principles, or hypernorms, as discussed infra. In many instances they will be canceled out by contrary preferences, as was the case in the example of civil rights in West Virginia (see Footnote 10). If they come to dominate and become a community norm, they are nonetheless illegitimate because they violate hypernorms.

[10]A personal example helps to demonstrate. When the civil rights movement reached West Virginia in the early 1960s, my parents, who had regularly patronized a segregated cafeteria in my home town, stopped eating there when it failed to follow the lead of other local eating places in integrating. Through their actions as consumers, my parents reflected their support for integration. Parents of a neighbor, who had rarely ever eaten at the cafeteria, starting eating there regularly while the cafeteria was under pressure to integrate. The overall effect of those boycotting, or supporting, all acting on the basis of their moral desires, was to decrease the business for the cafeteria.

such as the appropriateness of certain severance packages in downsizing, the use of animals in medical research, or even abortion, where the input of competing moral desires operates in a manner similar to, if not totally congruent with, a market? Some may prefer that animals never be killed or intentionally hurt, regardless of the context. Others may only prefer that animals not be killed or hurt for sport or for discretionary products. Some even may be totally indifferent to the treatment of animals. As the people who hold these differing viewpoints act in economic and political contexts, they produce outcomes that reflect an outcome among the competing moral inputs. The outcome or price-term equivalent would be the number and type of abortions, the typical size of severance packages, and the amount and manner of animal use in medical research or cosmetic testing. For most markets, price and quality considerations may dominate, but for certain markets moral desires may be dominant. Attitudes about morality may be a major influence in reference to such products and services as furs, certain types of drugs, prostitution, even the scalping of sports and entertainment tickets.

These moral prices would be expected to change constantly as the result of changing understandings concerning the nature of moral issues, variations in the way in which moral disputes are framed and argued, modifications in the background institutions, and similar factors. In this sense, moral prices would appear to be similar to economic prices, for example, the ever-changing prices of goods and services. One important question is the relation between the form of economic interaction and moral preferences. If it is true, as Bowles (1998) suggested, that the structure of markets affects the preferences of the participants, then choices concerning background laws and regulations may have a major influence on the resulting "moral price" in a given society.

The idea of a marketplace of morality is consistent with the phenomenon of changing societal "views" concerning certain types of moral issues. Attitudes have changed during the last several decades about the use of mind-altering drugs (less favorable) and the use of drug testing in the workplace (more favorable). Similarly, attitudes about smoking near others and indirectly marketing tobacco products to young people also apparently have changed during the last few decades.

Assuming, then, that specific moral norms representing the output of moral desires in markets can be discerned, what is their value? In an instrumental sense, one easily can argue that business organizations should pay close attention to extant morality for both offensive and defensive reasons. Offensively, paying attention to extant morality may produce opportunities to make profits, as in the case of social cause marketing. Defensively, firms can avoid costs by taking steps to avoid moral wrath. Perhaps the tobacco companies in the United States could have reduced the ultimate costs they bore had they acted in the early 1990s to bring their marketing practices more in tune with changing extant morality. The normative issues are more complex. What is the value of marketplace moral norms in deciding what constitutes right or wrong behavior? For example, should such norms be granted a prima facie status as moral obligations? Arguments in support of such status would include the following. A marketplace norm represents the output of competing moral desires and thus represents the community's view on the issue, particularly when it is clearly recognizable. In a sense, the moral norm is the winner in the marketplace of contesting moral viewpoints. Though not technically democratic, the norm can be assumed to constitute a representative output of community interactions. Second, marketplace moral norms capture changing circumstances and views. Third, norms of this sort are contextual in that they are the outcome of discrete processes focused on the specific exchanges in capital, consumer, and labor markets. As a consequence, they are grounded in reality and are likely to reflect dynamic compromises and trade-offs.

Various arguments may be advanced against granting prima facie obligatory status to marketplace moral norms. Marketplace moral norms may be inconsistent with fundamental tenets of major religions or philosophies. They may seem intuitively wrong to many people. The process by which marketplace moral norms are created may be tainted by coercion or misinformation.

Before seeking to resolve the normative status of marketplace moral norms, it is necessary to consider the special case of marketlike morality within organizations.

MORALITY WITHIN ORGANIZATIONS

Is there also marketlike morality within organizations? That is, do marketlike interactions reflecting individuals' moral desires occur within firms? If so, do they produce discernible organizational moral norms? These and related questions are discussed in this section.

Consider the following examples of organizational moral norms. One should not smoke within an office building even though the firm has not implemented a formal rule forbidding smoking. It is okay to follow a well-known departmental practice and use frequent flyer coupons for vacations even though the corporate employee handbook forbids personal use of coupons. It is okay to accept a cup of coffee from a potential supplier even though the organization's policy bans all gifts of any type. Employees of an airline generally support the idea that random drug testing is acceptable for pilots and maintenance personnel but not for counter attendants or bookkeepers. Or, more controversial norms may evolve. Partnoy (1997) detailed how derivatives traders within an investment bank developed a norm that it was proper behavior to "rip the face off" of clients by selling them securities from the bank's own account that "were about to explode" (p. 61).

Organizational moral norms may evolve in a wide variety of ways well known to social psychologists. Similar to the messy process by which norms emerge in broader markets, organizational norms are the outcome of interactions among individuals acting on the basis of their moral desires within the organization. Individuals are particularly likely to be influenced by social proof, a commitment to membership in the organization, and the attitudes and behaviors of significant others. The organizational environment may be expected to have a major influence on the development of individual moral preferences. Some organizations explicitly seek to change the moral preferences of employees through formal ethics codes, ethics programs, ubiquitous "help" (formerly "hot") lines and similar devices. More generally, the extensive literature on moral climate indicates that "organizational culture and climate are particularly influential determinants of moral conduct in the workplace" (Vidaver-Cohen, 1995, p. 318). Influential factors include the nature of leadership, organizational structure, policies, and incentive systems. Incentive systems may be significant in one environment (e.g., a new commission system in Sears Auto Centers produced questionable diagnoses by repair managers) and less so in another (e.g., Morgan Stanley follows procedures to ensure that its commission system doesn't harm clients, and thereby the firm). The role that one has in an organization also may strongly impact individual preferences, as for example when a floor worker is promoted to the job of foreman causing an expectation that the worker will "quite rapidly accept the opinions and values of other foremen" (Festinger, 1957, pp. 271–273.)

Organizational forces may be so forceful that they are seen as coercing individuals, particularly when power is used to produce group moral norms greatly at odds with an individual's initial moral desires. This in turn may produce responses such as individuals preserving strategic ignorance for themselves (Darley, 1996) as a means of coping with strong, dissonance-producing organizational norms. External factors influencing the evolution of organizational moral norms include law and other forms of social control. Thus, background rules concerning discrimination or sexual harassment may influence the development of compatible moral norms within an organization.

As a result of the messy, diverse process by which they are created, organizational moral norms are expected to vary extensively among industries and even between firms within the same industry. Norms supporting racial discrimination, sexual harassment, or, as in the case of the derivatives traders, systematic breaches of fiduciary obligations may evolve and, when they do, raise profound questions of legitimacy. Questions of legitimacy also may arise in less obvious contexts, as for example when the norms pertain to processes of procedural justice. An organization may develop a system of performance review and promotion that the members of the organization consider to be extremely just, fair, and appropriate. Yet, when viewed from a broader perspective, the system may seem problematic.

Consider the decision process by which Price Waterhouse (now Price Waterhouse Coopers) determined to defer promoting Ann Hopkins to partner status in 1982. Hopkins, a major producer as a senior manager in the firm's Office of Government Services, was the only woman among 87 candidates for partner that year. A majority of the candidates were offered partnerships. Price Waterhouse had an elaborate system for reviewing candidates for partnership. A booklet was prepared for each candidate containing evaluations from anyone who wished to comment along with data from prior evaluations and counseling. An admissions committee reviewed the file and interviewed partners who had had significant contact with the candidate. Ultimately names were placed on a ballot in which individuals could vote "yes," "no," or "hold." It may well be that the vast majority of members of the firm felt that the partnering process satisfied all requirements of procedural justice. After all, the process allowed for advocacy for the candidate from the candidate's own area or group, it was open to all members of the firm, and the process incorporated relevant information relating to prior performance evaluations and counseling. Yet, as a federal court later found, the process was open to sexual stereotyping (Barkan & Badaracco, 1991).

Before assessing the normative status of organizational moral norms such as these, we need to explore how they can be identified by an external observer.

READING ORGANIZATIONAL MORALITY

Tom Donaldson and I have proposed a normative social contracts–based theory emphasizing the role of legitimate ethical norms within organizations and other communities. Called integrative social contracts theory (ISCT) (Donaldson and Dunfee, 1999, 1995, 1994; see also Dunfee, 1991; Dunfee & Donaldson, 1995), it emphasizes microsocial "authentic" norms that represent a consensus pertaining to the propriety of particular actions based on aggregate attitudes and behaviors of individuals within a specific organization or other community. Organizations and other communities are recognized as having a substantial "moral free space" in which to develop their own internal moral rules. As described subsequently, this moral free space is circumscribed by manifest universal ethical norms and principles and also is subject to the influence of norms of other communities. Authentic norms that pass these screens are characterized as legitimate and become ethically obligatory.

The use of aggregate attitudes and behaviors in the definition of an authentic norm requires caution. Behavior may be coerced. Some organizations may have a pervasive atmosphere in which enormous pressure is placed on employees to go along with certain accepted practices. Such practices may range from the benign (give blood, or money to the United Way) to the venial (overbill the firm by a set amount for travel and entertainment expenses) to the outright criminal (dump toxic waste in the local river). Attitudes may be difficult to identify. Opportunists may hide or misrepresent their true attitudes in an attempt to convince others they are trustworthy. Messick (1991) described rational motives underlying a "tendency to endorse an ethical principle and to behave according to its opposite" (p. 321). By tricking others into believing she is altruistic, an opportunist may reap benefits from those who cooperate with or assist altruists. Similarly, reliance on attitudes may reflect the type of "false consciousness" that concern Tyler (chapter 6). Even though the attitudes at issue may be honestly and genuinely held, they may be the product of skillful playing on an individual's sense of justice, thereby producing a false consciousness in support of outcomes that objectively disadvantage her.

The correct reading of attitudes also is complicated by potential social desirability bias. Formal testing of attitudes through questionnaires may cause those tested to make assumptions concerning the answers expected by the researchers, leading those tested to give what they believe to be the "correct" answers. There may be a similar "public relations" bias at the level of the organization. A majority within an organization may think it desirable to project a positive image for the firm on issues such as protecting the natural environment or equal opportunity. They may express sentiments consistent with the positive image and in fact may come to hold the attitude, yet they may act inconsistently with the attitude in key decisions.

Both attitudes and behavior are emphasized in ISCT's definition of an authentic norm to help guarantee that a putative norm reflects a genuine consensus among the members of a community. Behavior alone is unsatisfactory because behavior can be coerced. If attitudes could be read scientifically, there would be little need to couple behavior into the test. But, as a practical matter, it may be necessary to rely on proxies for attitudes that may, on occasion, produce false readings. Insistence on complying behaviors helps to guard against the misreading of a community consensus.[11]

ISCT responds to these concerns through two devices. First, authentic norms may be invalidated on the basis of manifest universal principles called hypernorms. Hypernorms are defined in the context of ISCT as "principles so fundamental to human existence that we would expect them to be reflected in a convergence of religious, philosophical and cultural beliefs" (Donaldson & Dunfee, 1994, p. 265). Walzer (1992) expresses a similar idea in his recognition of a thin "set of standards to which all societies can be held—negative injunctions, most likely, rules against murder, deceit, torture, oppression and tyranny." (p. 9) Second, the communities or organizations themselves must satisfy certain minimal conditions to be perceived as capable of generating authentic norms. Because consent is the foundation of authentic norms within organizations, it is important that the organizational environment support informed consent. Among other things, organizations must not inappropriately constrain the right and ability of members to exit. Third World work camps that are the modern equivalent of the old company town often violate the right of exit, sometimes by the use of physical constraints. Shockingly, some of these practices have been found in New York and Los Angeles, where illegal aliens have been forcibly bridled to sewing sweatshops and similar enterprises. Beyond exit, organizations should allow for the appropriate exercise of voice in reference to moral norms. Political coercion used to stifle or completely eliminate voice, as has been alleged in reference to enterprise organizations within China, produces a community that is both de facto and de jure (under ISCT) incapable of generating authentic norms. ISCT thereby gives normative significance to Hirschman's (1970) identification of the importance of exit and voice in economic relationships.

Through its recognition of moral free space and its emphasis on authentic norms within communities, ISCT provides a framework recognizing organiza-

---

[11]Tyler's (1998) concerns about false consciousness remain. On the other hand, the problem for Tyler is justification of the criteria by which to determine that an individual's genuine attitude is not in his or her own self-interest.

tional moral norms produced by marketlike interactions among individuals. At the same time, ISCT provides a structure through which to deal with problematic organizational morality.

LEGITIMACY OF ORGANIZATIONAL MORALITY

The existence of morality within organizations raises a host of issues. Assuming we can "read" the morality within an organization, what are the implications for the organizational members? Are they always ethically bound to follow organizational moral norms? What, for example, should be the impact of a coercive organizational environment? Should all norms found in the environment be discounted? Or, suppose that most (or even all) people within an organization believe that a particular practice is just. Does that fact alone provide moral credibility, as some of the writings on organizational justice imply? These and similar questions are discussed in this section.

Even though organizational norms may be problematic in certain circumstances, they nonetheless have many positive attributes that should be considered in any analysis of their normative status. At the most basic level, an organizational moral norm represents a contextual, sui generis resolution of an ethical issue. Such a norm innately reflects the decision-making processes indigenous to the organization, the extant allocation of power therein, plus all other special characteristics of that organization's environment. As a consequence, organizational norms are unique to each organization and reflect a consensus within each organization concerning standards of proper behavior. For example, what is considered to be fair treatment of an employee on the intensely competitive trading floor at Goldman Sachs may differ greatly from what is considered to be fair treatment in the operating environment of Goodwill Enterprises or Ben & Jerry's. Organizational moral norms often may reflect a compromise worked out among the members of the organization, thereby reflecting a reasonable middle position. Such norms would be expected to reflect the diversity within an organizational environment and presumably would be open to changing societal and organizational values. Despite these and other good reasons for recognizing organizational morality, there are numerous ways in which organizational morality may be problematic.

Problematic Organizational Morality

Norms may be produced within a particular organization that strike many people as intuitively bad. Such norms may impose considerable harms on outsiders and even on society generally. Norms produced within an organization may be at odds with widely accepted ethical theories. Or organizational norms may conflict with the norms of other organizations or those of broader social and political groups. They may be the product of the coercive exercise of power within an organization. As Strudler and Warren (chap. 10, this volume) discuss, individuals may rely on authority as a heuristic in determining how they as individuals should act. Norms represent authority within the organizational environment.[12] Thus, problematic norms can be expected to translate into harmful organizational behavior. This section briefly considers some of the forms of problematic organizational morality and then discusses their implications for the use of organizational morality as a component of a normative analysis.

Organizations and other types of communities may produce specific authentic norms that appear to be problematic. Norms may emerge, such as using a legal technicality to take advantage of clients, that seem improper or counterintuitive to many people. For example, Amplicon, a computer leasing firm, became mired in litigation with hundreds of its former clients over the terms of Amplicon's form lease. As is common with such leases, there was a provision indicating the circumstances and terms by which the client could buy the equipment at the end of the lease. In the litigation that ensued, some former salespeople at Amplicon stated that they were urged by firm officials to mention verbally a low figure as a ballpark price for buying hardware and software at the end of the lease. The written contract did not contain a specific price and instead provided that any price had to be "mutually agreeable." Amplicon was accused of systematically demanding a price at the end of the lease much higher than the verbal price. Under the parole evidence rule, Amplicon was not bound by the verbal price and the term "mutually agreeable" essentially meant only that the price was open for negotiation. The owner of the firm was quoted as saying, "if those dummies don't read the lease document, it is more their problem than mine" (Emshwiller, 1998, p. 1). Many of the salespeople went along with this strategy of promising a low price, and this appeared to be a norm at the firm.

Nor is such behavior uncommon. Darley described socialization processes by which "corporations come to the perception of their customers as fools to whom no moral obligations are owed" (1996, p. 37). A norm based on taking advantage of relying customers may seem incoherent to many, particularly those who would advocate a fundamental ethical principal of consumer sovereignty for marketers (Smith, 1995). But we should not be surprised to discover that norms of this sort do in fact emerge within certain firms.

Darley (1996) described how mangers may harm others when they act to preserve strategic ignorance for themselves. He discussed as examples systemic willful blindness concerning defective brakes produced by Goodrich and the infection-causing Dalkon Shield produced by Robbins. Such incidents may be viewed as the product of an improper framing of the issue or the use of faulty reasoning by the decision makers (Messick & Bazerman, 1996). But in some organizations, the problem runs deeper. In these organizations, problematic authentic

---

[12]See Strudler and Warren (chap. 10, this volume) for an analysis of whether those who rely on such are morally blameworthy. They conclude that "because of the difficulty humans face avoiding reliance on heuristics, it seems fair not to censure a person too harshly for relying on a heuristic."

norms emerge that directly and significantly influence individual managers. For example, a strategy of strategic ignorance may be embedded in a broader norm reflecting an adversarial orientation toward legal requirements. The norm may be that the firm will act consistently with a legal requirement (e.g., rules concerning environmental hazards or product safety testing) only when the probability of getting caught and the likely sanction if caught, taken together, are enough to outweigh the likely benefits of noncompliance. Strategic ignorance may be purposefully employed to reduce the chances of detection and, if that fails, the size of any sanction imposed. Such a firm will follow a comprehensive strategy designed to limit detection of its legal malfeasance.

Norms that evolve within organizations may be inconsistent with prescriptions of multiple well-recognized moral theories. For years, organized baseball in the United States excluded players and segregated fans on the basis of race in violation of the tenets of many moral theories. Similarly, organizational norms may be inconsistent with broader societal norms, for example, those pertaining to sexual harassment, which were famously inconsistent with the practices occurring in the "Boom-Boom Room" at Smith Barney, or the strikingly hostile working environment at the Normal, Illinois, Mitsubishi plant.

Organizational moral norms often may run counter to norms found in other communities. A firm may develop a strong internal norm that justifies providing lavish entertainment and gifts for those responsible for making new business decisions for prospective clients. This norm may be at odds with those of other firms in the industry or particularly with some of the potential clients who do not want their purchasing agents to be influenced by the receipt of personal gifts. How conflicting legitimate norms should be sorted out is a complex matter beyond the scope of analysis in this chapter. Note, however, that ISCT specifies priority rules[13] designed to provide a basis for sorting among conflicting norms when all are compatible with manifest universal ethical norms or principles.

Organizational moral norms may be the product of an imbalance of power within an organization. Senior management may use its power coercively to forcibly create norms that run counter to the genuine personal values of the rank-and-file employees. The example given by Darley (1996) of the environment at Goodrich demonstrates how extreme pressure can be brought to bear on

---

[13]The rules are as follows: (1) Transactions solely within a single community that do not have significant adverse effects on other humans or communities should be governed by the host community's norms; (2) community norms indicating a preference for how conflict-of-norms situations should be resolved should be applied, so long as they do not have significant adverse effects on other humans or communities; (3) the more extensive or more global the community that is the source of the norm, the greater the priority that should be given to the norm; (4) norms essential to the maintenance of the economic environment in which the transaction occurs should have priority over norms potentially damaging to that environment; (5) where multiple conflicting norms are involved, patterns of consistency among the alternative norms provide a basis for prioritization; (6) well-defined norms ordinarily should have priority over more general, less precise norms.

individuals to cause them to conform to norms that are detrimental to broader societal interests.

As we have seen, organizational moral norms may be problematic in a variety of contexts. Should this result in organizational morality being completely excluded from normative judgments? Before answering this question, we also should consider whether there are strong theoretical grounds for excluding consideration of organizational moral norms. A generally accepted view among ethicists is that it is wrong to construct an "is" into an "ought." Otherwise, we are caught in the trap of relativism. Freeman and Gilbert (1988) are among those who would extend arguments against ethical and cultural relativism to condemn reliance on norms of accepted practice, a phenomenon they termed "social group relativism." They argue that social group relativism "is not a good theory or position to believe" because it provides no basis for selecting among competing norms and is "an inherently conservative idea" (p. 34) relying too much on accepted practice.

From the opposite side come theoretical challenges from those who believe in a thick set of universal values, which therefore would often run counter to a particular group's or organization's morality. Consider Pava's (1998) discussion of a Jewish perspective of business ethics:

> For example, from a Jewish perspective authentic norms need to fit with the historical understanding of what it means to be a good Jew. Regardless of whether or not a majority of contemporary Jews accept or reject a particular norm, it is difficult to suggest that such a norm—with no grounding in traditional Jewish sources—is an authentic Jewish norm. (pp. 78–79).

The mere fact that some organizational norms may be problematic, or that they may appear counter to the views of those who would advocate a particular set of universal ethical principles, does not justify their total exclusion from a normative analysis. The ultimate question for our purposes is whether organizational morality should play some role in a normative analysis. A major implication of ISCT is that actions taken within the "moral free space" of organizations do have normative significance. After all, organizational moral norms by definition reflect the consent and consensus of organizational members regarding a contextual resolution of a moral dilemma. The resolution often will be the product of a compromise among competing viewpoints that reflects the history, culture, and diversity of the organization. Thus, much valuable information may be contained in such norms. That is not to say that organizational norms should be considered to, ipso facto, represent valid moral positions. Freeman and Gilbert (1988) rightly criticized approaches that rely on local norms as the definitive end of the moral story. That is not the position of ISCT and that is not the position taken in this analysis. Instead, the issue is when and how organizational morality should play a role in a normative analysis.

Screening Organizational Morality

When, then, should organizational moral norms count? The following caveats point toward solutions for problematic organizational norms. Operationally the use of organizational moral norms might work as follows. Such norms would be considered prima facie to be ethically legitimate subject to two tests: (a) whether specific norms came about as the result of coercion or deception, and (b) whether the norms are inconsistent with manifest universal ethical principles (hypernorms).

The seminal issue is how one defines and then identifies an organizational moral norm. If an organizational moral norm is defined in a manner similar to an authentic norm under ISCT, then some of the issues concerning coercion and imbalance of power are resolved at this level. The attitudes necessary to recognize an organizational moral norm are defined as the attitudes one genuinely holds based on one's moral desires. The definition thus separates the attitude itself from the evidence supporting the existence of the attitude. One does not determine attitudes by having people signal their attitudes in a public forum. Coercion pertaining to the expression of an attitude thereby is avoided. The truly difficult task is to identify these genuine attitudes. Social psychology should be able to offer insights concerning how this might be done.

A related issue is whether the extent of consensus underlying an organizational norm is significant in assessing its moral value. Elsewhere (Dunfee, 1998) I proposed as a tentative (and awkwardly named) idea, a "test of greater preponderance": "The greater the consensus within the marketplace of morality that a particular practice is good/bad, the greater the burden of proof for those who claim a higher normative ground for rejecting that consensus" (p. 140). Consider Pava's argument. If every living Jew, except Pava, believes in and acts consistently with an organizational norm and also believes that the norm is consistent with traditional Jewish sources, we certainly can demand overwhelming proof from Pava before we are willing to abide by a principle that he might be right and everyone else wrong.

Operationally, such a test would suggest that when organizational morality represents a very strong consensus, there should be strong support for the counterposition before such norms are discounted. Particular organizational morality should stand against Kant when Kantians substantially disagree among themselves whether a given norm is problematic. Similarly, organizational morality should stand when utilitarians dispute among themselves concerning the likely consequence of a given norm. On the other hand, it should be sufficient to condemn an organizational norm when there is a convergence among respected ethical theories, and those applying them, that a particular norm is problematic.

One also could focus on the characteristics of the organization, requiring that the organizational environment meet certain minimal standards to enable its members to act consistently with their own moral desires. Thus, an organization might be held to certain minimal standards of fairness and justice to ensure that its members aren't coerced and that their basic rights of exit and voice are respected. An alternative would be to focus on the individual organizational norms and to exclude, for example, those that appear to be the result of deception or misunderstandings. This type of approach might be most responsive to Tyler's concerns about false consciousness (chapter 6).

The second test would discount organizational moral norms when they are found to be inconsistent with hypernorms. Under this idea, the process of discovering or identifying hypernorms becomes critical. Donaldson and I (1999) suggested the use of presumptions as a way of identifying hypernorms that may be relevant to a given decision. We recognized that the practical process of identifying hypernorms works more effectively when one considers the existence of possible hypernorms applying to a given practice or decision. The alternative of seeking to spell out a definitive list of hypernorms in the abstract is not likely to produce satisfactory results, at least not at the present. Instead, it is better to work on the basis of factors that create presumptions that one or more hypernorms apply to the case at hand. Factors triggering a presumption include evidence of widespread consensus, use in global industry standards, support from global nongovernmental organizations, consistency with precepts of major religions and/or philosophies, support in empirical studies of universal values (e.g., reciprocity), and so on.

CONCLUSION

Organizational morality may be viewed as the product of an internal marketlike process in which competing moral desires produce norms that most people follow. Organizational moral norms provide information about the resolution of moral dilemmas within the firm environment, and they should be given some weight in normative analysis. A plausible approach is to consider organizational moral norms as prima facie ethically legitimate, subject to tests relating to whether specific norms were tainted by coercion or deception and whether the norms are inconsistent with manifest universal ethical principles (hypernorms). Such an approach relies on and at the same time validates the long tradition of empirical research on the ethical attitudes and behaviors of members of organizations. It also validates the actions of individuals who provide inputs into the development of norms as part of their effort to realize their own moral desires. Recognizing a role for organizational moral norms helps to mitigate against the imposition of exogenous, potentially extreme views on the members of an organizational community. Giving weight to organizational moral norms reflects and respects the diversity of organizational environments while remaining open to changing societal values.

The policies, strategies, and structures of organizations can affect the moral preferences of their members. Organizations can hold great power over the moral beliefs of employees. Those responsible for establishing and operating policies that potentially affect moral preferences must be careful to avoid creating a coercive environment that may repress moral autonomy.

ACKNOWLEDGMENTS

The comments and suggestions of John Darley, David Hess, Elizabeth Scott, Alan Strudler, and Danielle Warren are gratefully acknowledged.

REFERENCES

Barkan, I., & Badaracco, J. L., Jr. (1991). *Ann Hopkins*. Cambridge, MA: Harvard Business School Publishing Division.

Bowles, S. (1998). Endogenous preferences: The cultural consequences of markets and other economic institutions. *Journal of Economic Literature, 36,* 1, 75–111.

Darley, J. M. (1996). How organizations socialize individuals into evildoing. In D. M. Messick. & A. E. Tenbrunsel (Eds.), *Codes of conduct: Behavioral research into business ethics* (pp.13–43). New York: Russell Sage Foundation.

Donaldson, T., & Dunfee, T. W. (1994). Towards a unified conception of business ethics: Integrative social contracts theory. *Academy of Management Review, 19*(2), 252–284.

Donaldson, T., & Dunfee, T. W. (1995). Integrative social contracts theory: A communitarian conception of economic ethics. *Economics and Philosophy, 11,* 1, 85–112.

Donaldson, T., & Dunfee, T. W. (1999). *Ties that bind: A social contracts approach to business ethics*. Cambridge, MA: Harvard Business School Press.

Dunfee, T. W. (1991). Business ethics and extant social contracts. *Business Ethics Quarterly, 1*(1), 23–51.

Dunfee, T. W. (1998). The marketplace of morality: First steps toward a theory of moral choice. *Business Ethics Quarterly, 8*(1), 127–145.

Dunfee, T. W. (1999, Summer). Corporate governance in a market with morality. *Law and Contemporary Problems, 62*(3), 129–158.

Dunfee, T. W., & Donaldson, T. (1995). Contractarian business ethics: Current status and next steps. *Business Ethics Quarterly, 5*(2), 173–186.

Emshwiller, J. R. (1998, June 11). What's in writing: Read the fine print is lesson of disputes with computer lessor. *Wall Street Journal*, p. 1.

Frank, R. H. (1996). Can socially responsible firms survive in a competitive environment? In D. M. Messick & A. E. Tenbrunsel (Eds.), *Codes of conduct: Behavioral research into business ethics* (pp. 86–103). New York: Russell Sage Foundation.

Festinger, L. (1957). *A theory of cognitive dissonance*. Stanford, CA: Stanford University Press.

Freeman, R.E., & Gilbert, D. R., Jr. (1988). *Corporate strategy and the search for ethics*. Englewood Cliffs, NJ: Prentice-Hall.

Hirschman, A. O. (1970). *Exit, voice, and loyalty*. Cambridge, MA: Harvard University Press.

Hutton, R. B. et al. (1998). Socially responsible investing: Growing issues and new opportunities. *Business and Society, 37,* 285–305.

Hylton, M. O. (1992). 'Socially responsible' investing: Doing good versus doing well in an inefficient market. *American University Law Review, 42,* 1.

Kahneman, D., Knetsch, J. L., & Thaler R. (1986). Fairness as a constraint on profit seeking: Entitlements in the market. *American Economic Review, 76*(4), 728–741.

Kassarjian, H. H. (1971). Incorporating ecology into marketing strategy: The case of air pollution. *Journal of Marketing, 35,* 61–65.

Knecht, G. B. (1997, April 30). Magazine advertisers demand prior notice of 'offensive' articles. *The Wall Street Journal,* p. A1.

Messick, D. M. (1991). On the evolution of group-based altruism. In R. Selten (Ed.), *Game equilibrium models.* Berlin: Springer-Verlag, 304–328.

Messick, D. M. (1996). Why ethics is not the only thing that matters. *Business Ethics Quarterly, 6*(2), 223–226.

Messick, D. M., & Bazerman, M. H. (1996). Ethical leadership and the psychology of decision making. *Sloan Management Review, 37*(2), 9–21.

Partnoy, F. (1997). *F.I.A.S.C.O.: Blood in the water on Wall Street.* New York: Norton.

Pava, M. L. (1998). Developing a religiously grounded business ethics: A Jewish perspective. *Business Ethics Quarterly, 8*(1), 65–83.

Posner, R. A. (1990). *The problems of jurisprudence.* Cambridge, MA: Harvard University Press.

Smith, N. C. (1995). Marketing strategies for the ethics era. *Sloan Management Review, 36*(4), 85–97.

Vidaver-Cohen, D. (1995). Creating ethical work climates: A socioeconomic perspective. *The Journal of Socio-Economics 24*(2), 317–343.

Walzer, M. (1992). Moral minimalism. In W. R. Shea & G. A. Spadafora (Eds.), *The twilight of probability: Ethics and politics.* Canton, MA: Science History Publications, 3–14.

Author Index

Subject Index

CONTENTS

WITHDRAWN

INTRODUCTION

S tephen Lopez was eighteen years old and a recent
high school graduate. He had moved from Mexico to
Las Vegas, Nevada, when he was just a child and had
done well in school. His family wasn't rich, but things were
going well for them; Stephen's father had a good, steady job
at his brother's body shop.

But one night, everything changed. Stephen was
driving home and was hit by a driver who had run a red
light. Even though the accident wasn't Stephen's fault, the
police asked him to show his driver's license and registra-
tion. There was just one problem: Stephen was not a legal
resident of the United States. This lack of citizenship meant
that he could not get a driver's license in Nevada, which in
turn meant that he couldn't get car insurance.

Stephen was taken to jail. Unfortunately, this particular night was one when the Department of Homeland
Security did one of its frequent checks of the jail, making
sure that everyone held there was either a U.S. citizen or
legally allowed to be in the country. Stephen, of course,
could not prove either of these things. When his parents
came to bail him out, they couldn't show that they were
residents either, because they weren't. All three of them
were classified as illegal aliens. Only Stephen's younger
sister, Maria, who had been born in the United States,
was a U.S. citizen.

The Lopez family was given a notice to appear in
court for the proceedings that would send them back to
Mexico. Mr. Lopez had actually started the process to
become a legal citizen—with sponsorship by his brother—
but because this procedure took a long time (as long as ten
to twenty years in some cases, depending on the

4

Many immigrants who try to enter the United States illegally from Mexico are caught and detained before being escorted back to their own country.

immigrant's country of origin), it hadn't been completed by the time of Stephen's accident.

The Lopez family's immigration attorney could do very little for them other than offer up the possibility that the family might be able to stay because of the hardship it would cause Maria to be left alone in the United States. But as her uncle did live nearby, this possible outcome would be difficult to prove. It looked as though the family might have to split up, with Stephen and his parents going back to Mexico and Maria staying in Las Vegas.

All of Maria's schooling had been in Las Vegas, her friends were there, and it is where her culture and much of her social background came from. Although Stephen had not been born in the United States, he felt more American than Mexican. However, there existed no basis for him to be able to stay in the country of his choice, unless things changed drastically.

This scenario, which comes from a play on immigration entitled *Home Is Where the Heart Is...Or Is It?* illustrates just one of the situations that teens encounter when they are living illegally in the United States. For teens who have lived in the United States for much of their lives, and who feel thoroughly American as a result, just a small incident such as a traffic accident can snowball into being deported from the only homes they have ever known.

How exactly does a teen find himself or herself in the situation of being an undocumented or illegal immigrant in the United States? And what exactly does such a status mean in terms of rights under the law? Read on to learn about the problem and some possible courses of action to take.

CHAPTER 1

UNDOCUMENTED

Most teens in the United States never think twice about their right to be here. They were born in the United States, have the birth certificates and Social Security numbers to prove it, and enjoy all the rights and privileges that go with citizenship. They also know that they have certain rights under the law simply because they are U.S. citizens.

However, there is a growing number of teens who exist outside of the protection of citizenship or permanent residency. (The latter designation carries the same strength as citizenship when someone is arrested or otherwise involved with the law.) Such teenagers may have lived in the United

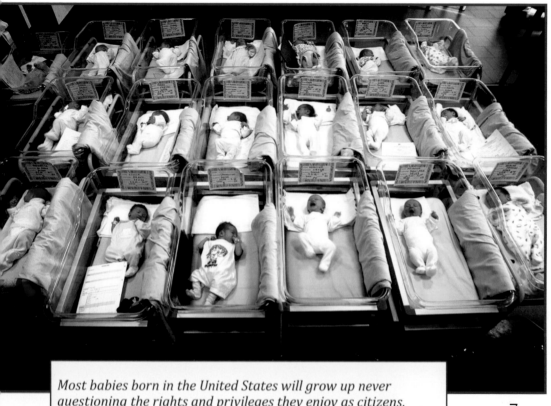

Most babies born in the United States will grow up never questioning the rights and privileges they enjoy as citizens.

States for as long as they can remember. They are often indistinguishable from American teens in the music they listen to, the foods they like, the clothes they wear, and the things they like to do for fun. However, they are not U.S. citizens because (1) they were not born here or (2) they were not born to parents who are U.S. citizens. They may have come to the United States illegally from another country; come here legally as tourists or students and stayed beyond the limits of their visas; or come here to work at a specific company with work visas, which are applicable only for a certain period of time and under certain specific circumstances. No matter what their reason is for being in the country, they are classified as illegal or undocumented aliens.

WHAT'S IN A NAME?

Is there a difference between being undocumented and being illegal? And why are people referred to as "aliens" and not simply as "immigrants"? Essentially, it depends on who is doing the naming.

According to the Worker's Defense Project, an organization that supports low-income workers such as immigrants, the difference in language is more about judgment than accuracy:

> Most immigrant rights organizations consider the term "illegal alien" to be derogatory and legally inaccurate. The word "illegal" carries a series of negative implications. For example, it is often assumed that "illegal" people have no civil or workplace rights, when in fact, all people have

rights regardless of immigration status. Additionally, some people falsely think that entering the country without a visa is a felony crime, when in fact it is a civil violation (such as not paying your taxes accurately). "Undocumented" is a more accurate and dignified term because it simply means an immigrant's status is not documented by immigration authorities.

Generally, people use the term *immigrant* when describing someone who migrates to the United States from another country, usually to settle here permanently. This term usually implies that they have come here legally according to U.S. laws and procedures, feel some allegiance to this country, and will respect U.S. laws and the Constitution. On the other hand, the term *alien* is often used for someone who comes from a foreign country but does not seem to owe the United States any allegiance. According to the LegalZoom website, "The Immigration and Nationality Act of 1952 defines an alien as a person who is not a citizen or national of the United States. In other words, an alien is anyone born in a country other than the United States to parents who are not United States citizens." Illegal alien is used to label someone who has entered the country without following the proper procedures. Basically, "illegal alien" sounds more sinister and derogatory than "undocumented immigrant." Generally, the way people refer to men, women, and children who are in the United States but aren't American citizens depends on what side of the immigration argument they are on.

CONTROVERSY AND IMMIGRATION

Many states are becoming less tolerant of illegal immigration. They feel that illegal immigrants take away jobs from U.S. citizens or unfairly receive public assistance benefits paid for by American taxpayers. They also feel that the U.S. government isn't doing enough to slow down the number of illegal immigrants entering the country. Several states have enacted strict anti-immigration legislation. In 2011, Georgia made it legal for law enforcement officers to ask immigration questions when arresting people in certain criminal investigations. The state also set heavy fines and jail sentences for people who use false identification to get jobs. Arizona passed legislation that required law enforcement officers to help apprehend and deport illegal immigrants. In 2010 alone, 1,400 bills were introduced in different states to allow those states to play a bigger role in immigration enforcement.

These pro-immigration demonstrators hold a vigil on November 24, 2014, in Lafayette Park near the White House to support children in Central America who want to immigrate to the United States in order to escape violence in their own countries.

THE USCIS IS WATCHING YOU

In the United States, the federal government agency that oversees lawful immigration is the U.S. Citizenship and Immigration Services (USCIS). Its mission, according to its website is as follows:

> *USCIS will secure America's promise as a nation of immigrants by providing accurate and useful information to our customers, granting immigration and citizenship benefits, promoting an awareness and understanding of citizenship, and ensuring the integrity of our immigration system.*

In late 2014, these immigrants from Central America surrender themselves to U.S. Border Patrol agents after crossing the Rio Grande from Mexico to McAllen, Texas.

However, the responsibility for enforcing immigration laws is handled by a different agency, U.S. Immigration and Customs Enforcement (ICE). Immigration is only a part of what this agency is involved in: its primary mission is "to promote homeland security and public safety through the criminal and civil enforcement of federal laws governing

11

A YEAR'S WORTH OF WORK

As the agency responsible for enforcing immigration laws, just what does ICE do in a single year? According to its website, here's what it accomplished in 2013:

› Conducted 133,551 removals of individuals apprehended in the interior of the U.S.

› Eighty-two percent of these individuals had been previously convicted of a crime.

› Conducted 235,093 removals of individuals apprehended along our borders while attempting to unlawfully enter the U.S.

› Fifty-nine percent of all ICE removals, a total of 216,810, had been previously convicted of a crime.

› Apprehended and removed 110,115 criminals from the interior of the U.S.

› Removed 106,695 criminals apprehended at the border while attempting to unlawfully enter the U.S.

border control, customs, trade and immigration." Both the USCIS and ICE are part of the U.S. Department of Homeland Security. Together they handle all issues of immigration and immigration law enforcement.

STATUSES, STATUSES . . .

For immigrants who come to the United States legally, there are many different types of statuses under which they might be classified. People from most other countries who travel to the United States are usually required to have a visa, which simply means that a U.S. official has reviewed the traveler's information and decided that he or she is eligible to enter the United States for a specific reason. Visas can be immigrant or nonimmigrant. Nonimmigrant visas are usually issued to people who are vacationing in the United States, are students, or are working in the country temporarily. Visas are issued according to the status of the person who wishes to come to the United States, and they are usually issued for a specific period of time.

For immigrants who intend to remain in the United States permanently, there is the Lawful Permanent Resident (LPR) and Conditional Permanent Resident (CPR) visas, which are usually issued to the spouses and children of U.S. citizens. People with LPR status are also called green-card holders (for the color of their identification card, which used to be green). Some immigrants come to the United States with refugee or asylee status because they have left their own country out of fear that they would face persecution there for their political or religious views. They come seeking safety in this country. Their children can also be admitted under this status, but only if they are accompanying the person(s) being persecuted or joining them at a later date. There is also the Temporary Protected Status (TPS) for people who do not have proper documentation for being in the United States, but because there are problems in their home country (such as a natural disaster or a war), they are allowed to stay until the danger is over. Immigrants must be from one of the officially designated TPS countries, which as of 2014 include El Salvador, Haiti, Honduras, Nicaragua, Somalia, Sudan, South Sudan, and Syria.

A green card is proof of legal residency in the United States.

Minor children, including teens, also have some special statuses of their own. They can apply for Special Immigrant Juvenile Status (SIJS) if they are under twenty-one and meet criteria such as being in the custody of a legal court or agency that is based in the United States, or because it would not be in their best interest to return to their own country. They can also apply for Deferred Action for Childhood Arrivals (DACA), which is a rela-tively new status that allows anyone who comes to the United States under the age of sixteen to have two years of protection from deportation.

Of course, all of these statuses are for immigrants who have come to the United States by following the U.S. government's procedures. Immigrants who have come ille-gally, usually by entering the country by crossing a border with Canada or Mexico, or who have remained beyond the expiration of their visas, don't have any legal status, which is why they are referred to as undocumented.

YOU'RE OUTTA HERE

The primary punishment for undocumented immigrants who are caught and detained by the ICE is deportation, also referred to as "removal." In such a case, the immigrant is forced to leave the United States and return to his or her own country. People who are not actual U.S. citizens—even people with LPR green-card status—can be deported, even if they've lived in the United States for nearly their entire lives, don't know the language of their home country, and don't know anyone who lives there.

People get deported for many reasons. The biggest one is for being in the United States without any papers, meaning that they don't have official permission to be here. They can also be deported for lying about their citizenship in order to get a job or vote. In some states, crimes ranging from forgery to theft, murder, or rape can also result in deportation. That said, for whatever reason, some of the more serious offenses will not trigger the risk of deportation, so the bottom line is that anyone who is not a U.S. citizen and is accused of *any* crime.

However, even undocumented and illegal immigrants have rights if ICE comes to their homes. Such immigrants can still ask to see a search warrant, do not have to sign anything (such as an Order of Voluntary Departure) without seeing a lawyer first, and do not have to answer questions without a lawyer. If they are arrested, they can still refuse to answer questions or sign papers without a lawyer's counsel, do not have to show any documents, and can request that their immigration hearing take place in the city closest to where they live so that they won't be transferred to a distant location.

Documented immigrants living in the United States according to a government-assigned status and obeying U.S. laws and regulations have their rights protected. But for teens who (for whatever reason) don't meet these categories and are living in the United States illegally and without documentation, it is vital to know exactly what rights they do have under the law—even though they are not citizens and don't have official permission to be here. And because teens are usually still part of a family unit, the family is the most important place to start when it comes to immigrant rights.

CHAPTER 2

IT'S ALL ABOUT FAMILY

Citizens of the United States take it for granted that families can always be together no matter what and that they all share the same citizenship status and enjoy the same rights. But when it comes to immigration, things can be much more complicated. Parents may be undocumented immigrants while their U.S.-born children are American citizens. Or the children may also be undocumented immigrants—even though they may have spent most of their lives in the United States. And if their parents are discovered and deported, then they are as well. Each situation creates its own hardships for families and children.

A MIXED FAMILY

In 2013, Cesia Soza, seventeen, and her brother Ronald Jr., fourteen, had been members of a mixed-status family for years; they were living in the United States legally but their parents were undocumented immigrants. Cesia was born in Nicaragua but came to the United States as a child and gained legal citizenship under the Deferred Action for Childhood Arrivals (DACA) program, which allows a two-year reprieve for undocumented youth who come to the United States as children. Her brother Ronald Jr. was born in the United States and was therefore a legal citizen. Their parents, however, were illegal immigrants. Their mother had been deported in

2008, their father remaining in the United States (feeling somewhat overwhelmed with the duties of being a single parent). Then, in September 2013, the teens came home from school to an empty house. As CNN reported the following month:

> *"Even though we knew my father might get deported, we never thought that it would actually happen, especially since ICE already took our mother away five years ago," Cesia said. But it did happen. Ronald Soza was deported to Nicaragua, joining his wife, Marisela. Suddenly, the teens' parents were gone and the Soza children faced a frightening future with foster families and unfamiliar schools. It's been weeks since that terrible day last September, and they still haven't seen either of their parents. The Soza kids "were devastated after their mother was deported," said Nora Sandigo, a family friend and immigrant rights activist. Now, they're "living a tragedy . . . they've lost everything, their parents, home . . . everything." Now they're living with Sandigo and her husband and two girls in Miami.*

This family—choosing to remain unidentified—eats lunch together at a taco restaurant in Tulsa, Oklahoma. While the restaurant used to serve a huge lunchtime crowd, business fell off when so many undocumented workers fled the state following Oklahoma's anti-illegal immigrant law.

WHERE THE VIOLENCE AGAINST WOMEN ACT FITS IN

Illegal immigrant women may face abuse from a husband, parent, or stepparent who is legally in the United States, but there is a special status available to women in this situation if they can document that they have suffered physical, sexual, or emotional abuse: the Violence Against Women Act (VAWA), a law that was enacted in 1994 and expired briefly in 2013. Women in abusive situations with legal residence can apply to become lawful permanent residents without having to have the sponsorship of the abuser. Girls must be under the age of twenty-one to be covered by this law.

Mixed-status families are common in immigration, and the number of children born in the United States to illegal immigrant parents is growing, making the problem of separating families by deportation even bigger. Many children of illegal immigrants who are themselves citizens may end up in foster care or, at best, living with family friends.

For children who were born in another country and who are—along with their entire families—in the United States illegally, deportation can rip them away from everything they've ever known. While they can apply for special statuses such as DACA or SIJS, doing so would mean being separated from their parents. Often these separations mean that children will not be able to see their parents again, since visiting them in their home country might jeopardize their own immigration status in the United States. Basically, in most scenarios that involve illegal immigrant families, the only options are separation or deportation.

BY THE BOOKS

But how exactly does immigration law work when it comes to family relationships? If one member of the family is a U.S. citizen, there are many options for family members to become citizens as well. The family member who is a citizen can petition for his or her relatives also to become citizens or legal permanent residents, but specific criteria have to be met:

- The relative of the citizen must be a husband or wife; an unmarried child under twenty-one; an unmarried son or daughter over twenty-one; a married son or daughter of any age; or a brother, sister, mother, or father (but only if the citizen is at least twenty-one).

- If the person is a permanent resident (green-card holder), he or she can petition for his or her spouse, unmarried child under twenty-one, or unmarried son or daughter over twenty-one. Legal permanent residents cannot petition for their parents, married sons or daughters, or brothers and sisters.

There are other family relationships where a U.S. citizen cannot petition for a family member's citizenship or residency, including children who were adopted after the age of sixteen, a stepparent or stepchild of a marriage that took place after the child's eighteenth birthday, or a husband or wife when the spouse was not physically present at the marriage ceremony. (Such a service is called a proxy wedding, and it takes places when conditions such as military service or imprisonment prevent one of the partners from attending his or her own wedding. Few U.S. states consider a proxy wedding to be legal.) Immigration law tends to look very carefully

Unaccompanied children who are undocumented immigrants are often placed in detention facilities while they wait for their cases to be processed in immigration courts. Here, a Honduran boy watches a movie at a U.S. Border Patrol holding center in McAllen, Texas, September 8, 2014.

at people who marry U.S. citizens in order to become legal residents of the country, since there are many cases of marriages that take place only to allow a husband or wife to gain residence in the United States.

There is also controversy about the myth that having a baby as an illegal immigrant in the United States—which means that the child is a U.S. citizen—will automatically let the parents become legal residents. This change of status is not necessarily true, according to a list called "10 Myths About Immigration" published in *Teaching Tolerance*, a magazine of the famously pro–civil rights law firm and organization the Southern Poverty Law Center (SPLC):

> *Many people also accuse immigrants of having "anchor babies"—children who allow the whole family to stay. According to the U.S. Constitution, a child born on U.S. soil is automatically an American citizen. That is true. But immigration judges will not keep immigrant parents in the United States just because their children are U.S. citizens. Between 1998 and 2007, the federal government deported about 108,000 foreign-born parents whose children had been born here. These children must wait until they are 21 before they can petition to allow their parents to join them in the United States. That process is long and difficult. In reality, there is no such thing as an "anchor baby."*

Of course, for children who are also illegal immigrants, there are few protections from being deported along with the rest of their families. Unless they apply for some of the special statuses available for minors, they, too,

THE VISA LOTTERY

One other option for gaining Lawful Permanent Resident/ green-card status is through the Diversity Immigrant Visa program, often referred to as the visa lottery. It makes 50,000 immigrant visas available every year, drawn randomly from immigration applications from countries with low rates of immigration to the United States. Lottery winners are given an LPR visa to live in the United States.

Argaw Oremo and his wife came to the United States from Ethiopia after Oremo won his visa in 2014 in the immigration lottery.

can be deported. And the threat of deportation can color many aspects of a family's life. Parents may not even tell their children that they are illegal, which creates a huge shock when the children try to get driver's licenses, or jobs, or apply for financial aid for college. Some families may not provide health care for their children or even send them to school for fear of having their illegal status discovered. Kids can also be face difficulties when they serve as translators for their parents, experience conflict with siblings who have a different immigration status, or even be sent for by their illegal-immigrant parents to join them in the U.S. illegally.

There is controversy about something known as "chain migration," where one family member who is a U.S. citizen can bring over family members more quickly than through any other type of immigration process. It is a confusing and often misused term because it can also refer to the tendency of people from certain places, nationalities, or ethnic groups to immigrate to places where other people from their group have settled and they are more likely to feel comfortable. As an issue concerning family immigration, it is frequently used as an argument against immigration by people who advocate tighter immigration limits overall, while supporters of immigrants to the United States call it a myth. It is becoming a bigger issue as the government considers immigration reforms, which opponents feel will open the floodgates for chain migrations for family reunification.

Some things have changed in recent years for children and teens who are illegal immigrants and living undocumented in the United States. It has to do with education, which has previously been something that has snagged immigrants in the past.

CHAPTER 3

SCHOOL DAYS

Many illegal immigrant students move through the American education system easily, often getting good grades and thinking about college and career options. But as they get older, they may also begin to realize that many of the things that American teens look forward to—such as getting a driver's license or a first job—are inaccessible to them because they are undocumented. But the biggest obstacle of all? College. Not necessarily in applying but in getting the needed scholarships and financial aid to attend.

A young woman from India who had been in the United States since she was five months old found this out the hard way (from her story posted at the site *How Did Diversity Affect Americans?*):

> *That fact hit me when I was applying for colleges. I was Valedictorian of my class, and I was receiving letters from Stanford, MIT, Yale, Princeton, and countless other elite schools that encouraged me to apply there. However, my only dream was to go to Northwestern University, and I was accepted early decision. I still remember to this day how excited I was because this school meant a lot to me. It was a door to my future, and I wanted to do great things in my life. Unfortunately when it came time to qualify for financial aid, I realized I had to prove that I was a citizen. Of course, I couldn't do that. When I read the notification saying that, my heart*

ASKING FOR HELP

A lack of financial resources isn't the only major problem for illegal immigrant students. From an early age, young undocumented immigrant kids attending public school may well face more problems than their American classmates. They are more prone to being bullied, often because they don't speak English well, they dress differently, or they don't understand American customs. They are also less likely to ask for help. According to the PBS Kids website It's My Life:

> Many immigrant kids, tweens, and teens often stay silent when they're having a hard time. They may feel that it's easier to stay "invisible," or be generally shy about living in a new place. They may even think that their particular immigration status means they don't have the right to ask for assistance. But here's the truth: everyone has the right to ask for—and get—help when they need it.

Any student, even an undocumented immigrant, has the right to ask a teacher, guidance counselor, or even a lawyer for help with anything from regular classroom problems to immigration issues.

Some immigrant students may have trouble fitting in with their American classmates.

*just sank because I knew right then and there that I
could never attend the school of my dreams. I can't
afford to pay such a large tuition.*

THE RIGHT TO EDUCATION . . . FOR A WHILE

In 1982, the United States Supreme Court, in *Plyler v. Doe*,
held that all children, regardless of their immigration
status, have a right to a free public education from
kindergarten through high school. The decision came out
of a Texas law that allowed school districts to withhold
funds for kids who were not "legally admitted" into the
United States and that the districts could decide not to
enroll those children. Some districts reacted to this 1975
law by kicking illegal immigrant children out of classrooms,
while others required them to pay tuition (in one case,
$1,000 a year). As a result, many poor immigrant children
could no longer go to school. Several organizations filed
suit and the case went to the Supreme Court. In its decision,
the Court said that "denying these children a basic
education" would "deny them the ability to live within the
structure of our civic institutions, and foreclose any
realistic possibility that they will contribute in even the
smallest way to the progress of our Nation."

As a result of *Plyler v. Doe*, immigrant children have the
right to attend public school in the United States. And every
year, approximately 65,000 of them graduate from high
school. But only 5–10% go on to college. It is not illegal for an
undocumented student to apply to college, and many schools

consider and accept students even if they can't provide a Social Security number or other standard proof of U.S. citizenship. It is also illegal to reject a student from a college simply due to his or her undocumented status. What stops teens from attending college is cost. While there is a growing number of states that will allow undocumented students to pay in-state tuition, including California, New York, Texas, and Nebraska, many other states require them to pay full out-of-state tuition, which is much higher. This fiscal fence, coupled with the fact that undocumented students cannot apply for federal financial aid—the biggest source of funding for college

Attending college and getting a good education can be an impossible dream for undocumented students. But schools such as the University of Texas at Austin, some students of which are seen here, allow undocumented students to pay in-state tuition.

educations—puts the cost of a college education beyond their reach. Undocumented students also cannot easily get jobs that might help them pay for their education, since they aren't legal citizens. And while there are special visas for college students who want to study in the United States, a student already living here cannot apply for one.

DREAM LEGISLATION

In 2001, a piece of legislation was introduced in Congress that would benefit these undocumented students. It was called the DREAM Act, also known as the Development, Relief, and Education for Alien Minors Act. According to the National Immigration Law Center (NILC), it would:

- " ...permit certain immigrant students who have grown up in the U.S. to apply for temporary legal status and to eventually obtain permanent legal status and become eligible for U.S. citizenship if they go to college or serve in the U.S. military; and
- " ...eliminate a federal provision that penalizes states that provide in-state tuition without regard to immigration status."

The benefit of the DREAM legislation would be to allow students to get college educations—a life-enhancing benefit in and of itself—so that they would get good jobs with good pay. Having such income would not only enable them to pay more taxes but also cut the costs of providing social services to unemployed or underemployed immigrants. The legislation would allow undocumented immigrants who serve in the military to earn their residency as well. At a time when recruitment is down, this would be an advantage to the U.S. military.

For students who want to go to college but can't get aid because they are undocumented, the DREAM Act would have made it possible not only to get an education but to become a legal U.S. resident as well.

Undocumented students may need help from lawyers and other volunteers to fill out the required paperwork to apply for DACA status.

However, over the many years since it was first proposed, and through several reintroductions to Congress, the DREAM Act has yet to pass. Several states have passed their own versions of the act, and President Barack Obama created the DACA status, which also gives young illegal immigrants a two-year extension on staying in the United States, thereby allowing them to obtain driver's licenses, work permits for jobs, and in some cases reduced college tuition. But it still does not address educational funding through *federal* aid.

AN ALPHABET OF VISAS

The legal path for students who wish to study in the United States and are still living in their home countries is to obtain a student visa. This visa cannot be applied for by someone already in the United States, even if they are here legally. An "F" category student visa is for students who wish to attend a U.S. college, university, conservatory, seminary, high school, private elementary school, or other academic training program (such as a language school). Students who wish to attend a vocational training school or other nonacademic institutions need to have an "M" visa. Students cannot apply for these visas until after they have applied to and been accepted by a U.S. school in one of these categories.

Some illegal immigrants will not even try to attend college. They are just as content to find good jobs and make money. But what happens to undocumented immigrants who are working in the United States?

CHAPTER 4

THE WORKING LIFE

When he was a teen, Jose Antonio Vargas already knew that he was an undocumented immigrant with a fake green card and passport, living in the United States with his grandparents. He had gotten used to the fact that he had to be careful not to be discovered. But in order to get a job and contribute to society, he was going to need a Social Security card. What he *didn't* know was that the Immigration and Naturalization Service (I.N.S.) would have a part to play in the process . . . or so it thought. As he told the *New York Times*:

> *"Using the fake passport, we went to the local Social Security Administration office and applied for a Social Security number and card. It was, I remember, a quick visit. When the card came in the mail, it had my full, real name, but it also clearly stated: "Valid for work only with I.N.S. authorization."*
>
> *When I began looking for work, my grandfather and I took the Social Security card to Kinko's, where he covered the "I.N.S. authorization" text with a sliver of white tape. We then made photocopies of the card. At a glance, at least, the copies would look like copies of a regular, unrestricted Social Security card.*

Using this card, Jose was able to get jobs at places such as Subway, the front desk of a local YMCA, and a tennis club.

Jose Antonio Vargas was able to use false documents in order to find work in the United States, despite being an undocumented immigrant.

Despite his lack of real documentation, he was still able to find work.

Other undocumented teens find employment at jobs that don't require documentation, such as babysitting, lawn care, or agriculture. Some employers don't question whether or not their employees are legal. They might care about whether the teen they employ is performing a job that meets the U.S. work law requirements for minors: nothing hazardous if you're sixteen or seventeen, and if you're fourteen or fifteen, only jobs with limited hours. But employers often turn a blind eye to documentation in jobs such as fast food and cleaning, where there are fewer Americans willing to do them. Undocumented immigrants often find themselves working in low-paying and even dangerous jobs, simply because it's all they can get without proper documentation.

FILLING OUT THE FORMS

For teens who may not even know they're undocumented immigrants, or who think they can get jobs without documentation, getting hired for a job where the employer isn't willing to overlook status can be a bucket of cold water. Their new employer will ask them to fill out a form called an I-9, issued by the Department of Homeland Security. To complete the form, they need to show proof of their identity and proof that they are eligible to work in the United States. If they do not have a driver's license, passport, Social Security card, birth certificate, green card, or government-issued work permit, their new job may end right then.

If a teen does manage to get a job with a high-enough wage needed to pay taxes, there is then another hurdle to overcome. Tax returns require the filer to provide a Social Security number or an Individual Taxpayer Identification Number (ITIN). However, getting an ITIN does not require immigration papers. The Internal Revenue Service, which handles United States taxes, will not give taxpayer information to the immigration agency. However, an ITIN does not give an undocumented immigrant permission to work in the United States—only a work permit can do that. It is important to pay taxes, however, because not only is not doing so illegal (and could result in imprisonment), non-payment of taxes can negatively impact immigration status and the chances of ever becoming a U.S. citizen or even just getting a green card.

There are ways for undocumented teens to work legally in the United States besides actually getting citizenship or residency. There is something called an

Employment-Based Application for residency, which means that the immigrant has a job offer from a U.S. employer in a field that has a shortage of workers because it requires unique skills. Immigrants can qualify if they can prove that there aren't enough workers in the United States who can do what they do and that they are not taking away a job from a U.S. worker. It is, however, a very long process, with the added difficulty of providing proof regarding any potential U.S. worker vying for the same position.

DACA AND THE EAD

The other option for teen immigrants who wish to work in the United States comes from the DACA program that President Barack Obama announced in 2012. It would no longer allow the deportation of certain young undocumented people. The first part of the policy allows young illegal immigrants temporary permission to remain in the United States, usually for a period of two years. But the second part of the policy deals with employment:

> PART 2: People who are granted deferred action through DACA will be eligible for an EAD [Employment Authorization Document] or "work permit," meaning they can work legally in the U.S. In other words, they can work "with papers."

While both the permission to remain in the United States and the EAD are good for only two years, they can both be renewed at the end of that time period.

It is generally advisable that teens who already have jobs (despite their illegal status) should not tell their employer that they have applied for DACA status:

WHOSE FAULT?

There is controversy about whether or not illegal immigrants—both teens and adults—are taking away jobs from American workers. There are many arguments on both sides of the issue, but overall, immigrants perform jobs that Americans simply don't do. And while American teens *are* having more difficulty getting part-time jobs than they used to, some of that situation isn't because of competition from illegal immigrant workers but rather from other American adults who have lost jobs during the economic downturn of the past years and are willing to do almost any job to make money.

Many undocumented immigrants work in jobs such as landscaping and lawn care, where employers are less likely to require proper documentation.

Under immigration law, employers have a responsibility to make sure that they do not employ unauthorized workers. If an employer learns that you are ineligible to work in the U.S., the employer has an obligation to fire you. If you tell your employer that you are applying for DACA, the employer will probably think that you are not eligible to work legally in the U.S. Even though you will be eligible to work legally once you receive deferred action and an EAD, you would be telling the employer that you are currently ineligible. Because of this, the employer might feel the need to fire you in order to avoid violating immigration law.

The EAD part of the DACA status is intended to help young people who want to go get jobs to pay for college, especially if they don't go to school in a state that has some version of the DREAM Act (which, as noted earlier, lets such teens apply for financial aid). Once a student has an EAD, he or she can apply for jobs and fill out the necessary I-9 to work legally.

Basically, undocumented immigrant teens may be able to find jobs, usually positions with employers who are willing to turn a blind eye toward proper documentation and may even pay their workers "under the table" (meaning that the money they pay these workers isn't reported to the government by the employer). Or they may get jobs using false documents. But unless they have prior authorization to work in the United States, working illegally may (1) get them fired if and when their employer does find out, (2) lead to imprisonment for nonpayment of taxes, or (3) result in deportation because they are discovered to be undocumented.

With so many hurdles in the way of getting a steady, paying, contributing job in the United States, some illegal immigrant teens may turn to the only other option they might think they have: crime.

EAD REQUIREMENTS

What are the requirements for getting DACA status and an EAD? According to the U.S. Citizenship and Immigration Services:

You may request consideration of deferred action for childhood arrivals if you:

1. Were under the age of 31 as of June 15, 2012;

2. Came to the United States before reaching your 16th birthday;

3. Have continuously resided in the United States since June 15, 2007, up to the present time;

4. Were physically present in the United States on June 15, 2012, and at the time of making your request for consideration of deferred action with USCIS;

5. Entered without inspection before June 15, 2012, or your lawful immigration status expired as of June 15, 2012;

6. Are currently in school, have graduated or obtained a certificate of completion from high school, have obtained a general education development (GED) certificate, or are an honorably discharged veteran of the Coast Guard or Armed Forces of the United States; and

7. Have not been convicted of a felony, significant misdemeanor, three or more other misdemeanors, and do not otherwise pose a threat to national security or public safety.

In 2012, the United States started accepting applications from undocumented students for DACA status. Here, Felipe Sousa Matos of Brazil holds his DACA papers during a 2012 news conference in Miami, Florida. Matos graduated summa cum laude from Miami's St. Thomas University.

CHAPTER 5

JUVENILE DELINQUENCY

Getting into trouble with the law is certainly not something that's limited to illegal immigrant teen-agers. American teens get into trouble as well, and while they, too, may have to deal with the consequences of breaking laws, because they are U.S. citizens, those consequences aren't quite as perilous as they can be for a non-citizen teen.

WHAT'S A JUVENILE DELINQUENT?

The definition of a juvenile delinquent—a term that is more likely to be used in a formal setting such as a court—is a minor who is considered to be lacking in responsibility because of his or her age, and as a result too young to be tried and sentenced in court as an adult. In addition, the term *juvenile delinquent* also implies that the minor in question is engaged in antisocial or illegal behavior that his or her parents can't control. Many teens who are habitual lawbreakers and frequently get into trouble will end up in the juvenile court system many times over the years, sometimes even being sentenced to a juvenile detention facility (a prison setting for minors) if their crimes are severe enough.

For illegal immigrant teens, however, criminal behavior that puts them in the juvenile delinquent category also means that they may, for the first time, be "on the radar" with the government. Just as Stephen Lopez was caught in a

Undocumented immigrant teens who get into trouble with the law are not only risking punishment but also deportation and any chance of becoming a legal resident of the United States.

jail check and exposed as being undocumented, the legal system will quickly determine whether or not a teen offender is a U.S. citizen.

One of the major reasons why illegal immigrant youth end up being discovered and often deported is becoming involved in the criminal or juvenile justice system. Not only are these teens getting into trouble with the law, they are also risking their futures. If they are actually in the country legally under some kind of visa, their visa may be revoked if they are arrested for certain crimes and have a criminal record that classifies them in the "removable" category. If they are *not* legal residents of the United States, even if they are not deported, having a criminal record classified in the "inadmissible" category may prevent them from ever obtaining legal status to stay in the United States, either as juveniles or later as adults, or could halt the process of any application for citizenship or residency that is already in progress. Accordingly, any non-citizen—whether treated as a juvenile or an adult under the law—should immediately consult with an immigration lawyer as well as a criminal lawyer after having any contact with law enforcement, making his or her immigration status known to each lawyer.

According to the National Juvenile Justice Network in its policy brief "Building Bridges to Benefit Youth":

> *What makes immigrant youth most vulnerable is that actions placing them in the "inadmissible" or "removable" classification do not have to be violent or especially serious. Actions that deem them inadmissible include engaging in prostitution, being a drug addict or abuser, making a false claim to U.S. citizenship, using false documents, and more significantly, providing the CIS with "reason to believe" that the youth ever has assisted or been a drug trafficker. An increasing list of more than 50 crimes can trigger deportation, including crimes that are considered misdemeanors under most state laws.*

In addition, violating protective or "no-contact" orders (also known as restraining orders, which are meant to prevent harassment as well as the threat of either violence or injury) can also trigger immigration restrictions. Indeed, even a mere "attempt" to commit a crime is considered a deportable offense. Behaving in a way that shows a mental disorder—including attempting suicide, alcoholism, sexual offenses against younger children, and even something known as "mayhem" (to maim someone intentionally or cause harm in an uncontrolled way)—can make a teen immigrant inadmissible for residency or citizenship.

PART OF THE GROUP

One of the most common ways that illegal immigrant teens get into trouble is through gangs. Existing gangs in larger cities may recruit new members from among recent immigrants. The immigrants have the chance to join a group that may speak their language. It's also a way to create a new circle of friends, especially for teens who feel alienated from mainstream American teenage life. They may even feel like outcasts among others who come from the same place they did but who have been in the United States for longer. Belonging to a gang is a way to overcome

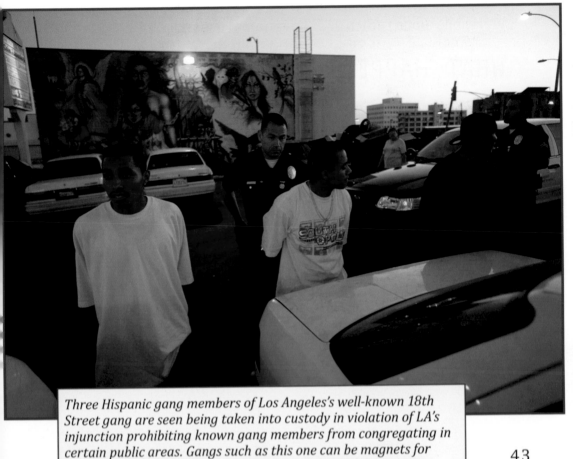

Three Hispanic gang members of Los Angeles's well-known 18th Street gang are seen being taken into custody in violation of LA's injunction prohibiting known gang members from congregating in certain public areas. Gangs such as this one can be magnets for undocumented teens, which can lead to arrest and deportation.

43

the alienation and exclusion from regular groups, and create a new identity with other gang members.

Belonging to a gang is not in itself illegal. In fact, one of the basic rights that Americans have is to gather together in groups. It's only when gangs perform illegal activities that members get into trouble. And unfortunately, when illegal immigrant teens are suspected of illegal gang activity, they are affected more than U.S. citizens because even if they have not committed a crime, they may find themselves involved in immigration proceedings. According to the National Juvenile Justice Network, "Seventy percent of foreign gang members who are apprehended are not ultimately charged with a crime and are then deported on immigration violations alone rather than on criminal grounds."

WHAT HAPPENS NEXT?

If any teen—American citizen or not—is apprehended for committing a crime, the first part of the process will be the same. The arresting police officer can issue a warning, refer him or her to a probation officer, or make an arrest, which lands the teen in a juvenile holding facility, separate from adults who have committed crimes. In some states, the law might require the teen's parents to be notified immediately or soon. There is also usually a limit on how long a juvenile can be held in custody.

If criminal charges are filed, they can be filed either under the juvenile status if the teen is under age eighteen (although in some states sixteen-year-olds are considered to be adults), or if the crime is especially severe, the teen might be charged as an adult. (In the latter case, teens are subject to the same process and sentencing that adults would go through.) If the case goes to juvenile court, then the teen has the right to have both an attorney and his or her parents present. Further, no other defendants or attorneys can be present in the courtroom when the case is discussed. Ultimately the court case will take place and the juvenile will be sentenced either to community service, probation, or a juvenile detention facility. To drive home a point made earlier, whenever criminal charges are involved, it is imperative for any non-citizen to consult both an immigration *and* a criminal attorney at the outset of any such case. An accused teen should immediately advise his or her lawyers regarding current immigration status, and the lawyers should then conduct independent research to verify whether the client has accurately assessed his or her status (many times people are not properly informed as to their precise status *and* it can change over time). The immigration consequences of each case should be a top priority. Also key is alerting one's attorney to any future goals in terms of residence, education, or employment, to ensure that the case does not impact any of these plans negatively, nor mitigate the impact that these aspects can take on a young person's life.

From here on, things can be more difficult for immigrant teens, even if the charges against them for the initial crime are dropped or they are found innocent in court. Illegal immigrant teens found innocent but whose illegal status is discovered can be put in an immigration detention facility to be held until their immigration case is processed. The Department of Homeland Securities and ICE can legally hold them for

THE HIGH COST OF CRIME

In 2013, the U.S. Senate passed the S.744 bill for immigration reform. Part of the bill specifically addresses gang-related crime. According to the Immigration Policy Center's *Guide to S.744*:

> *The bill makes immigrants inadmissible or deportable if they have been convicted of an offense that involves participating in a street gang and promoting the criminal activity of the gang. Undocumented immigrants involved in gangs will also be ineligible for Registered Provisional Immigrant status. The bill makes immigrants inadmissible if they have been convicted of a crime of domestic violence, stalking, child abuse, child neglect, or child abandonment for which they served at least one year in prison, or if they were convicted of more than one such crime.*

Even once someone has been convicted and faces deportation, an immigration lawyer can still petition the immigration court to keep that person from being deported, so there *are* possible avenues to remaining in the United States. Therefore, non-citizens should not simply give up and resign themselves to their fate. Rather, an immigrant in such a situation should engage an immigration attorney for advice of the best course of action (which sometimes could be simply waiving one's rights and agreeing to deportation . . . but it could also be initiating an action in immigration court).

President Barack Obama's pro-immigration policies made him popular with many U.S. immigrants but also created controversy among many American voters.

only twenty-four hours in a DHS facility, or up to seventy-two hours in an ICE facility. However, these guidelines aren't always strictly followed, and teens especially may find themselves being held much longer. Some juveniles who were arrested and held in DHS facilities remained there for anywhere from 6 to 225 days. Some of these facilities may not be very suitable for younger offenders, mixing them with adults.

Access to information may be limited for teen offenders, both about their cases and about their options. Many do not want to contact their parents for fear that if they too are undocumented, it might lead to the entire family being deported. It is also very difficult for teens to find legal representation if they have to go to court—especially a lawyer who handles both immigration law *and* criminal law. Teens may find that they are adrift in a confusing legal system, without legal help or family support, and with little chance to avoid being deported. Teens and children who have knowledgeable legal support are four times more likely to be granted asylum to stay in the United States by a judge and to avoid being held in a detention facility for too long or be deported.

Indeed, it is highly unlikely that a criminal lawyer will also be a qualified immigration attorney, and it constitutes ineffective assistance of counsel for a lawyer not to advise accurately his or her client as to the potential immigration consequences of his or her case. Accordingly, criminal lawyers should provide information on immigration consequences to the best of their abilities, and they should either consult with immigration lawyers themselves or suggest that clients retain such lawyers to handle the immigration side of the case. (A non-citizen should always ask an attorney whether he or she is qualified to deal with the immigration side of the case.) Happily, there are many organizations, such as the Immigrant Defense Project, that will provide free immigration advice to lawyers and to the public as to immigration consequences in a particular case. Such organizations can also help non-citizens obtain the assistance of immigration lawyers, even when they cannot afford the cost.

Luckily, there are many organizations that supply free legal counsel for immigrant teens. Community service organizations and nonprofit groups, especially in larger cities, often have these types of services. The Bar Association for the teen's state of residence will also have information about lawyers who practice teen

A LITTLE LIGHT AT THE END OF A DARK TUNNEL

There are few instances where the arrest and certainly the conviction of a non-citizen juvenile will not have immigration and other collateral consequences. Thus, as mentioned previously, both a criminal lawyer and an immigration lawyer should be consulted in these circumstances to mitigate any potential negative consequences. However, if such a teen comes from an abusive household, being placed in foster care and becoming eligible for a visa such as the VAWA or other protected status are possibilities.

immigration law pro bono, meaning that they don't expect to be paid.

A FINAL WORD

Many teen illegal immigrants are just as American as their U.S. citizen counterparts and hope to someday have permanent residency or citizenship themselves. While the consequences of illegal activities can be devastating to any teen's future (having a criminal record will often follow them for many years and deny them some opportunities), it is even more dire for undocumented immigrants as it can quite possibly result in deportation or the inability ever to become legal citizens. It might even affect their entire family's chances of becoming Americans. Although an undocumented teen presented with an illegal opportunity may sound like a great chance to make some money or fit in with a group, it is even more important to think carefully about the depth and breadth of the consequences.

GLOSSARY

activist Someone who campaigns or works for social change.

alien A foreigner, especially one who has not become a citizen of the country in which he or she lives.

asylee Someone who is seeking or has been given political asylum.

citizenship If a person has citizenship in a country (that is, being a citizen), he or she has the rights granted by that nation. Citizenship for adults may come with privileges such as voting, but also has requirements, such as paying taxes.

civic Relating to the administration of a city or town.

criteria A principle or standard used to make a judgment or decision.

defer To put off an action or event until a later time; to postpone.

deport To expel someone from a country, usually because the person is there illegally or has committed a crime.

derogatory Showing a critical or disrespectful attitude.

detain To keep someone in official custody.

eligible Having the right to do or obtain something; having satisfied the appropriate conditions.

green card In the United States, a green card is a document showing that its holder—someone born outside of the

50

U.S.—is to be considered a legal resident of America, and is thus allowed to work and reside in the U.S.

immigration The act of coming to live in a foreign country permanently.

indistinguishable Unable to be identified as different or distinct from another thing.

injunction A judicial order or ruling that restrains a person from beginning or continuing an action perceived as being threatening to or violating the rights of another/others.

passport An official identification document issued by a country to show that a person is a legal citizen and can travel under the protection of that country.

persecution Treating someone badly or with hostility, usually because of that person's race, religion, or political beliefs.

petition To make a formal request to an authority in a legal situation.

refugee Someone who left his or her own country due to such conditions as violence, political unrest, persecution, natural disasters, and/or other hardships

Social Security A U.S. federal program of benefits that include retirement income, disability, and medical insurance.

sponsorship The act of vouching for or being responsible for a person wishing to immigrate.

status The rank, position, or legal standing of someone.

tuition The money that a student is charged to attend a school, college, or university.

undocumented Not having the appropriate legal documents or licenses.

visa A document showing that a person is legally allowed to enter, stay in, or leave a country.

FOR MORE INFORMATION

American Immigration Council
1331 G Street NW
Suite 200
Washington, DC 20005
(202) 507-7500
Website: http://www.americanimmigrationcouncil.org
This organization supports immigrants, works for fairness
and equality in immigration policies, and educates
the public about the importance of immigration.

Immigrant Legal Resource Center (ILRC)
1663 Mission Street, Suite 602
San Francisco, CA 94103
(415) 255-9499
Website: http://www.ilrc.org
ILRC is a national nonprofit resource center that provides
legal training, educational materials, and advocacy
for immigrant rights.

Kids in Need of Defense (KIND)
1300 L Street, Suite 1100
Washington, DC 20005
(202) 824-8680
Website: http://www.supportkind.org
Founded by Angelina Jolie and the Microsoft Corporation,
KIND is a pro bono group of law firms, corporations,
nongovernmental organizations, universities, and
volunteers that provide legal counsel to unaccompanied refugee and immigrant children in the United
States.

National Immigration Law Project of the National
    Lawyers Guild
14 Beacon Street, Suite 602
Boston, MA 02108
(617) 227-9727
Website: http://www.nationalimmigrationproject.org
This is a national nonprofit organization that provides legal
    assistance and technical support to immigrant
    communities, legal professionals, and advocates
    working to advance the rights of noncitizens.

Public Counsel
610 South Ardmore Avenue
Los Angeles, CA 90005
(213) 385-2977
Website: http://www.publiccounsel.org
Public Counsel is a pro bono (free-service) law firm that
    represents immigrants who are seeking asylum or
    have been abused, as well as helping immigrant
    children.

U.S. Committee for Refugees and Immigrants (USCRI)
Immigrant Children's Legal Program
2231 Crystal Drive, Suite 350
Arlington, VA 22202-3711
(703) 310-1130
Website: http://www.refugees.org/our-work/child-migrants
This organization protects the needs of people who have
    been forced or have voluntarily migrated from other
    countries. Its child program supports unaccompanied
    children who have migrated to the United States.

U.S. Department of Health and Human Services
Office of Child Support Enforcement
370 L'Enfant Promenade SW
Washington, D.C. 20447
(202) 401-9373
Website: http://www.acf.hhs.gov/programs/css
This federal agency provides information (in English and
    in Spanish) regarding child support—be it financial,
    medical, or emotional.

WEBSITES

Because of the changing nature of Internet links, Rosen
Publishing has developed an online list of websites related
to the subject of this book. This site is updated regularly.
Please use this link to access the list:

http://www.rosenlinks.com/KYR/Immig

FOR FURTHER READING

Andreu, Maria E. *The Secret Side of Empty*. Philadelphia, PA: Running Press, 2014.

Barbour, Scott. *In Controversy: Does Illegal Immigration Harm Society?* San Diego, CA: Referencepoint Press, 2009.

Carleson, J. C. *The Tyrant's Daughter*. New York, NY: Knopf Books for Young Readers, 2014.

Cervantes, Angela. *Gaby, Lost and Found*. New York, NY: Scholastic Press, 2013.

Dipietro, Frank. *Latino Americans and Immigration Laws*. Broomall, PA: Mason Crest, 2012.

Gagne, Tammy. *My Guide to US Citizenship: Immigration in the US*. Hockessin, DE: Mitchell Lane Publishers, 2013.

Gagne, Tammy. *My Guide to US Citizenship: Your Guide to Becoming a US Citizen*. Hockessin, DE: Mitchell Lane Publishers, 2013.

Green, Robert. *Global Perspectives: Immigration*. North Mankato, MN: Cherry Lake Publishing, 2008.

Greenhaven Press editors. *At Issue: The Children of Undocumented Immigrants*. Farmington Hills, MI: Greenhaven Press, 2013.

Greenhaven Press editors. *At Issue: Should the US Close Its Borders?* Farmington Hills, MI: Greenhaven Press, 2014.

Haugen, David M. *Opposing Viewpoints: Illegal Immigration*. Farmington Hills, MI: Greenhaven Press, 2011.

Kenney, Karen. *Essential Viewpoints: Illegal Immigration*. Minneapolis, MN: ABDO Publishing, 2007.

Kleyn, Tatyana. *Immigration: The Ultimate Teen Guide*. Lanham, MD: Scarecrow Press, 2011.

Leavitt, Amie Jane. *My Guide to US Citizenship: US Immigration Services*. Hockessin, DE: Mitchell Lane Publishers, 2013.

Leavitt, Amie Jane. *My Guide to US Citizenship: US Laws of

Citizenship. Hockessin, DE: Mitchell Lane Publishers, 2013.

Marcovitz, Hal. *In Controversy: How Should American Respond to Illegal Immigration?* San Diego, CA: Referencepoint Press, 2011.

Miller, Debra A. *Current Controversies: Immigration.* Farmington Hills, MI: Greenhaven Press, 2010.

Morrow, Robert. *Immigration: Rich Diversity or Social Burden?* New York, NY: Twenty-First Century Books, 2009.

Senker, Cath. *Global Issues: Refugees.* New York, NY: Rosen Central, 2011.

Senker, Cath. *Immigrants and Refugees.* New York, NY: Franklin Watts, 2012.

BIBLIOGRAPHY

Adversity.net. "Definitions: Alien, Immigrant, Illegal Alien, Undocumented Immigrant." Retrieved March 8, 2014 (http://www.adversity.net/Terms_Definitions/ TERMS/Illegal-Undocumented.htm).

Classroom Law Project. "2007 Youth Summit–Immigration, Lesson 3: Immigration Stories." Retrieved March 2014 (http://www.classroomlaw.org/files/posts-pages/ resources/youth_summits/07-Lesson03.pdf).

Immigrant Legal Resource Center. "Living in the United States: A Guide for Immigrant Youth." Retrieved March 9, 2014

Immigration Policy Center. "A Guide to S.744: Understanding the 2013 Senate Immigration Bill." July 10, 2013. Retrieved March 2014 (http://www .immigrationpolicy.org/special-reports/guide -s744-understanding-2013-senate-immigration-bill).

Immihelp. "Categories for Family Based Green Card." 2014. Retrieved March 9, 2014 (http://www.immihelp.com/ greencard/familybasedimmigration/categories.html).

Legal Zoom. "Becoming American: Understanding Legal and Illegal Immigration." March 2006. Retrieved March 2014 (https://www.legalzoom.com/articles/becoming-american-understanding-legal-and-illegal-immigration).

Murphy, Katy. "The California Dream Act: By the Numbers." *Oakland Tribune*, March 7, 2013. Retrieved March 2014 (http://www.mercurynews.com/ci_22744531/ california-dream-act-by-numbers?source=pkg).

National Immigration Law Center. "DACA and Workplace Rights." November 2012. Retrieved March 2014 (http://www.nilc.org/dacaworkplacerights.html).

National Immigration Law Center. "DREAM Act: Summary."
    May 2011. Retrieved March 2014 (http://nilc.org/
    dreamsummary.html).

National Juvenile Justice Network. "Undocumented
    Immigrant Youth: Guide for Advocates and Service
    Providers." Building Bridges to Benefit Youth, Policy
    Brief No. 2, November 2006. Retrieved March 2014
    (http://www.refugees.org/resources/for-lawyers/
    special-immigrant-juvenile-status/undocumented
    -immigrant-youth.pdf).

News Know How. "Illegal Immigration." February 19, 2013.
    Retrieved March 2014 (http://www.newsknowhow
    .org/news-post/155).

PBS Kids Go! "Immigration: Finding Help, Giving Help." 2005.
    Retrieved March 2014 (http://pbskids.org/itsmylife/
    family/immigration/article7.html).

Public Counsel. "Immigration: What Teens Need to Know."
    2013. Retrieved March 2014 (http://www.
    publiccounsel.org/tools/publications/files/2013
    -Immagration.pdf).

Rodriguez, Cindy Y., and Adriana Hauser. "Deportations:
    Missing Parents, Scared Kids." CNN.com, October 27,
    2013. Retrieved March 2014 (http://www.cnn
    .com/2013/10/26/us/immigration-parents-deported-
    children-left-behind).

Romero, Anthony D. "School Is for Everyone: Celebrating
    Plyler v. Doe." American Civil Liberties Union, June 11,
    2012. Retrieved March 2014 (https://www.aclu.org/
    blog/immigrants-rights/school-everyone-celebrating
    -plyler-v-doe).

State Justice Institute. "Overview of Types of Immigration Status."
May 1, 2012. Retrieved March 2014 (http://sji.gov/PDF/
Immigration_Status.pdf).

Teaching Tolerance. "10 Myths About Immigration." Southern
Poverty Law Center, 2011. Retrieved March 2014 (http://
www.tolerance.org/immigration-myths).

U.S. Department of Homeland Security, U.S. Citizenship and
Immigration Services. "About Us." Retrieved March 8, 2014
(http://www.uscis.gov/aboutus).

U.S. Department of Homeland Security, U.S. Citizenship and
Immigration Services. "Consideration of Deferred Action for
Childhood Arrivals Process." January 18, 2013. Retrieved
March 2014 (http://www.uscis.gov/green-card/other-ways-
get-green-card/green-card-through
-diversity-immigration-visa-program/green-card-through-
diversity-immigrant-visa-program).

U.S. Department of Homeland Security, U.S. Citizenship and
Immigration Services. "Green Card Through the Diversity
Immigrant Visa Program." Retrieved March 9, 2014 (http://
www.ice.gov/removal-statistics).

U.S. Department of Homeland Security, U.S. Immigration and
Customs Enforcement. "FY 2013 ICE Immigration Removals."
Retrieved March 9, 2014 (http://www.uscis.gov/
humanitarian/consideration-deferred-action-childhood
-arrivals-process).

U.S. Department of Homeland Security, U.S. Immigration and
Customs Enforcement. "Overview." Retrieved March 8, 2014
(http://www.ice.gov/about/overview).

U.S. Department of Homeland Security, U.S. Immigration and
Customs Enforcement. "Temporary Protected Status:
Countries Currently Designated for TPS." Retrieved March 8,

2014 (http://www.uscis.gov/humanitarian/
temporary-protected-status-deferred-enforced
-departure/temporary-protected-status#Countries
Currently Designated for TPS).

U.S. Department of State, Bureau of Consular Affairs. "U.S.
Visas: Student Visas." Retrieved March 11, 2014
(http://travel.state.gov/content/visas/english/study
-exchange/student.html).

Valdes, Gustavo. "Georgia Governor Signs Controversial
Anti-Illegal Immigration Law." CNN.com, May 13,
2011. Retrieved March 2014 (http://www.cnn
.com/2011/US/05/13/georgia.immigration.law).

Vargas, Jose Antonio. "My Life as a Undocumented
Immigrant." *New York Times*, June 22, 2011. Retrieved
March 2014 (http://www.nytimes.com/2011/06/26/
magazine/my-life-as-an-undocumented-immigrant
.html?pagewanted=all&_r=0).

Workers Defense Project. "What's the Difference Between
'Illegal Alien' and 'Undocumented'?" Retrieved
March 8, 2014 (http://www.workersdefense.org/
programs-2/rap/immigration-2).

INDEX

Harris County Public Library
Houston, Texas

ABOUT THE AUTHOR

Marcia Amidon Lusted is the author of 100 books and over 450 magazine articles for young readers. She is also an editor for Cricket Media, producing magazines, books, and digital media for young readers. She lives in New Hampshire.

ABOUT THE EXPERT REVIEWER

Lindsay A. Lewis, Esq., is a practicing criminal defense attorney in New York City, where she handles a wide range of matters, from those discussed in this series to high-profile federal criminal cases. She believes that each and every defendant deserves a vigorous and informed defense. Lewis is a graduate of the Benjamin N. Cardozo School of Law and Vassar College.

PHOTO CREDITS

Cover © iStockphoto.com/PamelaJoeMcFarlane; cover (background), p. 1 Christophe Rolland/Shutterstock.com; pp. 5, 18–19 Chicago Tribune/McClatchy-Tribune/Getty Images; p. 7 Tips Images/SuperStock; p. 10 Saul Loeb/AFP/Getty Images; pp. 11, 22–23 John Moore/Getty Images; p. 14 fStop/SuperStock; pp. 24, 39, 46 © AP Images; p. 27 © Stefanie Felix/The Image Works; p. 29 © Bob Daemmrich/Alamy; pp. 30–31 © ZUMA Press, Inc./Alamy; p. 34 The Washington Post/Getty Images; p. 37 © Marmaduke St. John/Alamy; p. 41 © Bob Daemmrich/The Image Works; p. 43 Robert Nickelsberg/Getty Images.

Designer: Brian Garvey; Executive Editor: Hope Lourie Killcoyne